REINVENTING FATHERHOOD

To Ed + Ragna —

You are great
parents! Enjoy
parenthood.

Robert
4/24/94

REINVENTING FATHERHOOD

Jonathan W. Gould, Ph.D. and Robert E. Gunther

TAB Books
Division of McGraw-Hill, Inc.
Blue Ridge Summit, PA 17294-0850

Human Services Institute publishes books on human problems, especially those affecting families and relationships: addiction, stress, alienation, violence, parenting, gender, and health. Experts in psychology, medicine, and the social sciences have gained invaluable new knowledge about prevention and treatment, but there is a need to make this information available to the public. Human Services Institute books help bridge the information gap between experts and people with problems.

FIRST EDITION
FIRST PRINTING

Library of Congress Cataloging-in-Publication Data

Gould, Jonathan, 1953-
    Reinventing fatherhood / by Jonathan Gould and Robert Gunther
      p. cm.
    Includes bibliographical references.
    ISBN 0-8306-4219-6
    1. Fatherhood. 2. Fathers. I. Gunther, Robert, 1960-
II. Title.
HQ756.G59   1993
306.874′2—dc20   93-8026
                                                      CIP

Questions regarding the content of this book should be addressed to:

Human Services Institute, Inc.
P.O. Box 14610
Bradenton, FL 34280

Acquisitions Editor: Kimberly Tabor
Development Editor: Lee Marvin Joiner, Ph.D.
Copy Editor: Pat Holliday
Cover Design: Holberg Design, York, Pa.

Contents

The Journey

Chapter 1 Rude Awakenings   1
Chapter 2 I Don't Want To Be Like Dad   17
Chapter 3 Looking Back to Your Future   25

The Map

Chapter 4 Who Are We Supposed To Be?   36
Chapter 5 The Many Faces of Father   46
Chapter 6 Discovering the Child Within   58

Traveler's Tales

Chapter 7 Why Did You Do It?   66
Chapter 8 The First Trimester   74
Chapter 9 The Second Trimester   87
Chapter 10 The Third Trimester   97
Chapter 11 Honey, Get the Suitcase!   108
Chapter 12 Postpartum Novelties   124
Chapter 13 My Child and His Grandchild   136

Ambushes, Roadblocks and Potholes

Chapter 14 Responsibility   146
Chapter 15 Commitment   156
Chapter 16 Who Does What Around the House?   163
Chapter 17 Sex and Intimacy   169
Chapter 18 Work and Finances   179
Chapter 19 Not Enough Hours in the Day   184
Chapter 20 Stress   192
Chapter 21 Playing Favorites   203

Choosing New Directions

Chapter 22 Moral Direction   208
Chapter 23 Building Your Relationship with Your Child   218
Chapter 24 Understanding Your Belief Systems   233
Chapter 25 Healthy Couples   243
Chapter 26 A Teacher to Your Child   250
Chapter 27 Connecting with Your Child   257
Chapter 28 The Road Ahead   268

Notes   272
Bibliography   275

To Debra and Cindie
  for their gifts of love, humor and support.

To our children
  for whom we aspire to be the best fathers we can be.

Acknowledgments

This book could not have been written without the cooperation of the men and women who attended our fathering workshops. Their candor and honesty greatly contributed to the richness of this book. Their Lamaze leader, Joan Hipple, also deserves credit for recognizing the need for fatherhood education in pregnancy classes.

The doctors and nurses of *Doylestown Obstetrics and Gynecology Associates* also deserve our thanks. Drs. Choby, Sendzik and Fitzgerald recognized the importance of fatherhood education and supported our efforts to provide fatherhood information as a component of birthing classes. Nila Sendzik, office manager, was initially receptive to the idea of fatherhood education as part of birthing classes and maintained her support throughout.

Our editor, Lee Marvin Joiner, Ph.D., of Human Services Institute, Inc. showed an enthusiasm for the project from the moment he received the proposal. He has worked patiently and with skill in teaching us about writing and the often equally important area of the politics of publishing. We also wish to thank Ms. Pat Holliday, Associate Editor, who snipped and cut our original manuscript to a readable length.

We thank our families. We took many hours away from them to complete this book. We spent more time staring at our computer screens than chasing our kids around the house, and often imposed on our wives at all times of day and night to be surrogate editors. Thank you, Debra and Cindie for your love, patience and understanding. Thank you for your support and for recognizing the importance of this project.

Thank you Maddi, Robbie, Anders, Pelle and Stevi for letting us work long hours with only occasional interruptions. Now that the writing is over, it's time to play again!

Introduction

What does it mean to be a father? Men of our parents' generation gave this question little serious consideration. They believed that parenting was part of becoming an adult, as natural as walking or breathing, not something to be reflected upon or studied.

Then, along came these fancy professionals. People like me. We stuck our noses into this curiosity called parenting and noticed that parenting had rules, responsibilities, values and assumptions. But, we were paralyzed by a nagging inner voice. This voice of the 1960s told us that "everything is beautiful in its own way," that we must learn to accept and tolerate differences in lifestyles, in values and in beliefs. "To each his own and in his own way."

In the 1970s other voices talked about equality for women and minorities. These voices encouraged men to discard their *machismo* and learn to become more sensitive, more caring and more open. We took our definition of what it meant to be a man from the Women's Movement. We accepted a view of maleness, a view of fatherhood, as seen through feminine eyes. We lost our way.

Many of us heard this call to be a different, less controlling and less powerful man. We assumed that to be accepted we needed to become gentle, more "feminized." We gave up the strength and power of our maleness and became the "Sensitive Man" who would do anything for our wives. We learned how to communicate. We read *Cosmo* or *New Woman*. We cooked and helped with the housework. But, we had no idea about what it meant to be a man.

Recently, the Men's Movement has gained great momentum. Robert Bly, Sam Keen and others have provided a blueprint for how to reach into our male heritage and reveal to ourselves the meaning of maleness.

What their works have yet to discuss fully is integrating concepts from the men's movement into current thinking about what it means to be a father. This book is our humble attempt to bring maleness, the meaning of being a man, back into the legitimate arena of fatherhood.

Men are not masculine versions of women. Men are unique from women in their biology and psychology. We seek not to minimize these differences but to accent them, to channel them and to elaborate them into a finely woven mosaic of family membership and participation.

We want to rid ourselves of the absent father syndrome of generations past. We want to find ways to bring our male power, our male competition and the warrior in our soul *into* the family through cooperation and sharing, rather than relegating these "wilder" elements of maleness to outside the family unit. We want, first, to teach our new fathers not to be afraid of their "wildman" but to understand and respect him and his energies. Second, we want to teach our children, boys and girls alike, not to be afraid of the "wildman" who lurks within their fathers' souls, but introduce them to the meaning of being a man.

We want to teach a generation of new fathers not to be afraid of the strength, intensity and energy of their heritage as men. We aspire to guide a new generation of fathers to face squarely the challenge of their potency, through productive and interactive relationships with their children and wives.

Reinventing Fatherhood is about a philosophy of family, of parenting and of fatherhood. It is a composite of new ideas about fatherhood that challenge the old and the *status quo*. It also is a book of interviews with new fathers who participated in workshops and clinical interviews. These men attended Lamaze training classes and participated in a three-hour workshop emphasizing how to think about being a father. It is also a self-help book, with exercises to help you develop new fathering ideas and behaviors.

Reinventing Fatherhood will ask you to look back at your father. It will ask you to look forward to the father you want to be. And, it will give you guidance about how to get from how you were raised to how you want to raise your children.

Reinventing Fatherhood is not a scientific study. The men who participated in this book were not drawn from a scientifically designed random sample. They are men who attended birthing classes with their wives and who live life as you do. They struggle with their changing family situation and try to master their anxieties over becoming a father. They are typical fathers, married men who take responsibility for fathering their child, continue to live in a two-parent household and are committed to providing the highest level of health and welfare for their wife and child.

Finally, we have a word for you about our goals. Our goal is to challenge your ideas and beliefs. Our goal is to stimulate you to talk with the father inside you, the child inside you and the wife by your side. Our goal is to open you to the possibilities of being the best father you can be. And through that transformation, you will teach your children about love, caring, family and fatherhood.

PART ONE

THE JOURNEY

⟦ 1 ⟧

CHAPTER

Rude Awakenings

A man who . . . is not involved in the process of caring for and initiating the young remains a boy no matter what his achievements.

- Sam Keen[1]

I was sleeping soundly on a Wednesday night. We had turned off *The Tonight Show* about midnight and snuggled tightly under the covers. Lurking in the back of her mind was the thought that she might be pregnant. Lurking in the back of my mind was my pillow.

I didn't know what happened. I heard her first before I could get my eyes open. At three in the morning, I hear yelling, "It turned blue, it turned blue, it turned blue." I had no idea what she was talking about.

I opened my eyes to see a pair of halogen truck lights glaring in my face. (Well, it felt like truck lights.) Debra had brought in the light from my desk and was shining it in my face so I could see. Rude awakenings at 3 AM.

"What turned blue?" I asked.

"The stick, the stick. It turned blue."

"What stick?"

"The stick. The stick."

We were getting really far in this conversation. By now, my eyes had adjusted and I saw my wife beside the bed holding a popsicle stick. I thought she woke me to describe something from the freezer.

"Slow down," I said. "What are you holding and why did it turn blue?"

"It turned blue because you shot straight!"

I was still a bit confused. But, Debra usually woke me in the middle of the night for important concerns. She would wake me if there was a spider, a suspicion of a water bug somewhere in the house, when she fell out of bed, or when she was sure that there were monsters in the house. These are the thoughts of a grown woman in the middle of the night.

I put my hand on her thigh to calm her down.

"Not now," she said, thinking that I was getting amorous. "It turned blue. I'm pregnant. I'm pregnant. I'm pregnant."

CALLS TO FATHERHOOD

This is how I was jolted into fatherhood and, in many ways, this is the quintessential experience of fatherhood——being awakened from a peaceful sleep into the bright lights, with a woman shouting in your ear. Sometimes the voice at midnight whispers: "I really feel like a pint of Haagen Daaz honey-vanilla ice cream, and I know it's five degrees below zero and the store is ten miles down the road and our car is in the shop, but . . . well, I'd understand if you didn't go. It's not like I would consider it a sign that you didn't love me, but. . . . Oh, thanks, honey. Don't forget your coat."

Sometimes the voice is not a woman; sometimes it is the wail of a child that drags you across the cold floor in the middle of the night. But it is a voice that comes from the outside and moves you toward fatherhood. Sometimes, like the coos of a newborn, it is the sweetest sound in the world, and then again it is a siren's song, calling you toward the rocks.

For a mother, parenting is an experience that works from the inside out. Her body starts changing, the seed grows and blossoms into a child. This growing life changes her. She talks about it and it becomes a part of her.

But for the father, the experience runs in the opposite direction. It works its way in from the outside. During pregnancy, I had no physical attachment to my child save a slender genetic bond and my love for her mother. Sometimes during the night, snuggled under the covers, I received a solid kick——through my wife——into my ribs. But this is as close as it comes.

We know a lot about what women experience during pregnancy——the physical changes and shifts in emotions. Any bookstore is filled with volume after volume charting every hiccup from the first embrace of the sperm and egg to the last postpartum sobs.

We know how the baby experiences the pregnancy. We have color photos of every stage of its development from a little tailed creature, that by all appearances should grow up to be a chicken to make any barnyard hen proud, into a perfectly-formed human being floating in its tiny sea of tranquility.

The Still Point in the Storm

But men are the still point in this storm of change——the serving, hand-holding, coaching, pampering, solid-as-a-rock, shoulders to cry on. In this great drama of birth, we have a crucial, but supporting, role to play. The stars of the show are mother and child. How hard is it to be a fan cheering in the stands at the Super Bowl? The quarterback has to weave through the lines to a successful delivery. But there are no cheers for the figure up to his knees in new-fallen snow, cheering in the bleachers.

Yet men are not merely spectators or coaches. We actively undergo changes of our own. Think about how different you are from your own father and you have a glimpse of the depth of the transformation, the effects——some of which you may not consider altogether positive——of fatherhood. This is a transition as great as the change from childhood to adolescence. It is a transformation as prodigious as from individual to married couple. But there is no confirmation or *bar mitzvah*; there is no wedding ceremony. There is nothing to mark the change, no acknowledgement of the change. Work goes on. Life goes on. Somewhere in the confusion you become a father. Kids stop calling you by your first name and you become mister or sir or, even worse, the old man. You still feel eighteen, but the world sees your greying temples.

The Role of Father is Changing - But We're Not Sure How

As if this transformation isn't challenging enough, it occurs in an environment in which the roles of men are changing. You know, by virtue of having a child, that you are becoming a father, but what does it mean to *be* a father? Expectations for men are different and more varied than ever——we are supposed to be strong and soft, dedicated to work and family. We are supposed to be an effective mixture of everything that both our mothers and fathers were. Yet, there are no role models to show the way.

The combination of this individual transformation into fatherhood and changes in societal expectations for fathers is like the amusement ride called "The Zipper," in which cars rotate in a huge oval at the same time individual cars tumble end over end. It is a ride that shakes up your brains, leaves you a bit dazed, and makes all the loose change fall out of your pockets——an experience surprisingly similar to fatherhood.

What Does it Mean to Be a Father?

So there you stand, a new mother under one arm and a newborn under the other. You are now a father. It is not terribly difficult to father a child. It can happen in an instant. But to *be* a father——that is a lifetime project. How do we shape our definitions of fatherhood? How can we take advantage of this opportunity to create our own visions of fathering?

We could look to the past. But, for the most part, we are not supposed to be like our own fathers, nor do we wish it. These men saw the responsibilities and roles of fatherhood as a combination of disciplinarian, breadwinner and educator.

How would you describe the characteristics of a father? When we asked a group of expectant fathers to define a father, they responded with the following terms:

responsible	hard-working	role model
disciplinarian	entertainer	teacher
competent	trustworthy	dependable

Contrast these ideas with the words their wives used to describe mother:

nurturing	caring	balancing act
communicating	warm	loving
playful	tired	organizing
bonding	calm	happy

Expectant fathers described fathering in external terms, things that needed to be done *for* their family. Expectant mothers were more concerned about feelings and relationship concerns. In other words, men were focused *externally* on what they needed to *do* and the way they needed to *act*. Women, on the other hand, were focused internally, on the process, feelings and emotions of being a mother. The challenge for fathers is to go beyond this external focus to an internal transformation.

Fathers are not going to play the same role as mothers. But there has been a growing realization that they have a greater role to play in the emotional life of their families than in the past. They can do more than *do* things for the family. They have a larger role than the rock-solid center of the family. They can contribute in an important way to the emotional well-being of the family and the development of their children.

So where can we learn how to be fathers? Our fathers cannot help us because their roles centered on providing for and being responsible for the family. Their vision served them well in their world, but it does not prepare us, their adult children, for our world of equality in the workplace, the home and the heart.

We won't learn fatherhood from our wives. Our wives may know how to be nurturing, but they can't teach us to be fathers. In their impatience with our emotional ineptitude, clumsiness and confusion, they may rush in and artfully perform the emotionally necessary tasks with which we struggle. When they save us from our clumsiness and incompetence, we miss an opportunity to practice and improve on behaviors we desperately need to learn.

To whom do we turn for guidance? Men rarely turn to other men for guidance because men are reluctant to talk about their experiences of fatherhood. They exchange the latest football scores but do not discuss parenting styles and their children. When was the last time you heard two men talking about the experience of fatherhood?

This book explores the new roles of fathers and the ways expecting and new fathers have developed to deal with them. It draws on the stories of fathers, plus the latest research on the psychological changes of fatherhood, to provide a guide for men during their transition to fatherhood. While it won't tell you how to be a father——every man must come to terms with this question himself——it will raise the questions that you must answer in defining your role as a father.

OPENING UP: TEACHING EXPECTANT PARENTS

The idea for this book came to me years after my run-in with the blue-popsicle-stick-that-changed-my-life. That was a whirlwind. I really started thinking about this issue when I was asked to teach a Lamaze class to help expectant parents examine their ideas and beliefs about parenting *before* the birth of their child. I was concerned about the lack of educational options available to young parents to explore their ideas about parenting. As a clinical psychologist, I have seen many young families clash over different parenting styles and goals. These conflicts often came from poorly understood and communicated ideas about what it means to be a parent. Other struggles were the result of different expectations about how a father or a mother *should* act. I had hoped to inform these expectant parents about the value of thinking through, and talking about, the *meaning* of being a parent. I didn't want to teach them parenting skills because there are many resources already available to them. I wanted to help them examine how their respective upbringing and early learning experiences, in combination with their unexamined expectations about the role of mother and father, would guide them toward a unique definition of being a parent.

In preparing for that class, I was surprised to discover that there were few sources describing the changes a father experiences during pregnancy and early child rearing *as told from the father's perspective*. I found that the men who participated in my class were eager to share their experiences. Most needed a little encouragement to talk publicly, but all had insightful stories about their experiences during pregnancy and after delivery.

At first these expectant fathers were unsure if it was okay to talk about their experiences. Conventional wisdom is that pregnancy fears and anxieties are the province of wives. These men believed that to focus attention on their concerns would be selfish and wrong. But they saw changes in their wives, their marriage and its stability. They felt their futures were being dramatically altered in ways that thrilled, frightened and confused them. But they didn't feel they had a right to talk about these issues.

It turned out that their reluctance to draw attention to themselves went deeper than a concern for their wives. As each couple moved closer to their delivery date, we noticed a change in the frequency and types of jokes and teasing by fathers:

> I know that I won't be alone while Sherry is busy with our new child. I'll always have the dog to take for long, romantic walks in the moonlight.

> At what age will I need to get my kid a MAC card?

> I can't wait for Anne to be able to stay home with our child while I go to work everyday, every week, month after month, with no break, no vacation, no rest and no relaxation. But, this is what being a parent is all about, right?

> She tells me not to ask her to return to work until our children are in junior high school. Or did she say a junior in high school?

These men were expressing important feelings, but often were unaware of their relevance or meaning. I began to suspect that these men were content to keep attention on their wives *precisely because it was not on them.*

Often, I would begin a workshop with two questions: *What does it mean to be a father?* and *What is the purpose of fatherhood?* Usually, these expectant fathers would respond with "I don't know; I never thought about it." Even when pushed for an answer, they came up empty.

These men were less than four weeks away from their wives giving birth but had given no thought to the meaning or purpose of fatherhood. "What's the big deal about knowing what it means to be a father, anyway?" asked thirty-one-year-old Bill. "Why get on our case about being a father? This isn't something to think about. I'm gonna be a father soon. What else do I have to know?"

Although each of these men was experiencing a radical transition in his life, he had little, if any, idea about how or what to discuss regarding his feelings and thoughts. They had no common language, not a clue about how to initiate a conversation on this topic. This "pregnancy stuff" was definitely foreign territory and they avoided talking, shuffled their feet and stared at the ceiling, like boys at a school dance.

As one new father commented:

> Looking back, it was a whirlwind, a roller coaster, one of the greatest challenges that I have faced in my life. At the time, however, it was the day-to-day adjustments—like my wife leaving her job, spending more time at home rather than going out with friends, me putting more time in at work to compensate for her staying at home, lack of sex, and realizing that I have to paint the baby's room—that seemed like minor irritants. I really believed that these changes would quickly disappear once the baby came and things would gradually get back to normal—you know, the way they were before the pregnancy.

But the return to normal never comes. Parenting an infant becomes parenting a toddler, then a preschooler, then a school child, then an adolescent. The dream that things will go back to the way they were only delays the realization of the changes. As this father commented later:

> We never got back to the way things used to be. I never thought that getting pregnant and then caring for a newborn would change my life so radically. Suddenly, I had to rethink my relationship with my wife, my own parents and my role in the family. Now, with a nine month old crawling all over the house, I think that I have figured out that *change* is the only constant thing in our lives.

I asked him if talking about these changes with other men would have helped.

Looking back at the pregnancy, it was hard even to understand what was going on. I felt alone, confused and bewildered. I assumed that I was the only one feeling this. I thought all the other guys had figured out how to balance the changes and I just couldn't get it together to be a father. I had no idea that every guy in our class felt the same way. We never talked about these things—I don't know why. I guess I was afraid to appear weak and incompetent.

ROLE MODELS: WARRIORS, WIMPS, AND EXPLORERS

The most important question is not whether a "real man" eats quiche, but what role he plays at the family table while eating. Is he a warm and accessible parent, a strict disciplinarian, or a distant relative visiting for dinner? Defining what it means to be a "real man" is more than a matter of dietary preference. It is a lifetime exploration.

There is a growing realization among new fathers that they want to take a greater role in shaping their families. They forge ahead with enthusiasm, but without the advantages of proper role models. Our fathers were cut from a different cloth. Their mission and responsibility centered on work outside the home, not on emotional support within the home.

Some would have all of us become mild, cardigan-toting Mr. Rogers and shun the aggressive, gun-toting Rambo. But the role of fatherhood for most of us probably lies somewhere between the extremes and we discover this point only after struggling with our own past, personality and family.

Men are engaging in this struggle. We have seen the rise of the men's movement, with retreats into the wilderness, howling at the moon and rediscovering the primal essence of maleness. There is a struggle to come to terms with what it means to be a man— and understanding fatherhood is an essential part of that struggle.

Now the trouble is finding that role model for fatherhood. No problem, right? Our conscientious, involved father picks up a book on pregnancy and looks through it to try to figure out what his role should be. Not much help here. This is a woman's game.

Although he has become more of an active participant in birth, the father is left out in an emotional waiting room. Even the most progressive books usually mention the father only when discussing the role of the coach or of sex during pregnancy. A 1970 study found that only two of fifty-three popular parenting books even discussed the issue of whom should take responsibility for rearing the children. A 1980 study found that few fathers read parenting literature——perhaps because of its traditional focus on women. Today, however, new and expectant fathers have a great thirst for information about fatherhood, parenting and family life.[2]

Wait a second, you say. Do men really want to be up to their elbows in parenting? Weren't we better off leaving diaper changing and emotions to women? Is the "involved father" just a plot by women to take some parenting pressures off *them*?

Most men, whatever their actions, are very involved in their roles as fathers. The common belief was that men's traditionally low level of involvement in pregnancy and child care was a sign of disinterest in emotional and psychological involvement with their families. But recent research suggests that most men see their family responsibilities as more important than their paid work.[3] They are increasingly concerned with how to become more emotionally and psychologically involved with their families. The desire is there. How to act on that desire is baffling.

Plenty of advice is available, plenty of people telling fathers what they are *supposed* to be and do. But much of this advice just adds up to more pressure on the new father and less involvement in shaping his role in the family. It presents a lofty goal without providing the path to reach it. It fills the father's saddlebags without giving him a horse to get him where he wants to go. Psychologists and educators have been so busy telling men how to become enlightened, positive role models for the next generation that they have not stopped to listen to the stories about these relationship transitions.

The stories of men who have made this journey, on the other hand, offer insights into how they found their way. Moreover, they show that the journey into fatherhood is not only possible but rewarding.

Modifying Our Shape

Mark Twain once said, "A round man cannot be expected to fit in a square hole right away. He must have time to modify his shape." For all the talk about a new generation of fathers and for all the changes in working patterns and family structures, the role of men in the family hasn't changed much.

Despite the popular belief that men and women share more of the outside-the-home responsibilities in marriage, recent research suggests that today's men, compared to their fathers, have changed very little in the amount of time they allot to child care.

Research suggests that women who stay home with their children still take on the emotional responsibilities of meeting their children's needs, the social isolation that comes with child care, the lack of emotional support from their husbands, the absence of overt power within the family, the lower status of "only" raising children compared with working *and* raising children, and a lack of intellectual stimulation.[4]

Women with jobs outside the home and careers in the workplace take on the new responsibilities of their outside jobs while retaining most of their previous responsibilities inside the home. For many, their burden has become even more unfair and time consuming.

Men, on the other hand, are becoming more vocal about their desire for greater family involvement. Yet, it is frequently their emotional absence from the inner circles of the family that causes them to feel like outsiders. Rather than reflect on the discomfort of this emotional distance, these men direct their energies toward their jobs, putting in longer hours, or toward home-based tasks, like building a playhouse. Keeping busy deflects awareness of their emotional emptiness and gives the appearance that they, too, are working toward the general cohesiveness of the family unit.

The all-too-common result is that fathers become observers of their children's development, taking an active part in their growth only when mother feels too tired, too overwhelmed or too sick. Fathers can help to build a model plane, fix a broken dollhouse, teach how to ride a bike and drive us on trips. But the emotional realities of who father is remains unfamiliar to his children. Father remains an enigma. His children reach out to know the man they idolize and find that they cannot reach him. They learn what little they know about him through the filter of their mother's descriptions. They develop a view of their father distilled through the eyes of their mother, a view filled with distortion, partial information and flaws. Yet, this is all they have to go on.

In part, father remains unreachable because he has been taught to remain distant; emotional availability is the province of the mother. He also remains emotionally distant because he does not know how to reach within himself. *His* father, too, was an observer in his own family. One comment frequently heard in men's gatherings is that their idea of father is vague, poorly understood or unreachable. Our fathers were outsiders to the emotional lives of their families.

Some scholars suggest that children spend their entire lives trying to decipher the mystery of their father's physical and emotional absence. The result is that these people develop relationships in adult life with emotionally unavailable lovers and try desperately to transform them into the emotionally available parent they never had.

One way to solve the mystery of "Who is dad?" is to become him. Often, we see men who model their behavior on that of their fathers, trying to discover what dad was like on the inside. This ability to identify with the lost object promises that if you do what your father did, act the way your father acted, then you will know how he felt on the inside. The ultimate folly, of course, is that these adult children develop parenting styles which repeat, reflect and reinforce their fathers' behaviors and relationships. So the cycle continues: Emotional distance begetting emotional distance with their children's children being as alienated from the emotional core of their family as their fathers were from theirs.

NEW HEROES: BREAKING THE CYCLE

There is a whisper of hope that this cycle of detached fathering can be broken, that roles can change. Thirty years ago, "being a man" was defined through external feats of heroism epitomized by

John Wayne and James Bond. They were the new adventurers and frontiersman. Such heroism still fills our motion picture screens with the likes of Indiana Jones, Chuck Norris and Arnold Schwarzenegger.

Once the arrows stopped flying on the frontiers, being a father was defined through activities such as advice giving, problem solving, and going to work. Such were the heroes to Beaver Cleaver and Ricky Nelson. Typically, if the wife did not induce a crisis, the husband was content to remain on the emotional outskirts of his family system. Unless pushed into action, the traditional father would ride out the storm, often retreating to the security of the workplace to avoid the responsibilities of the father role.

Today, men are setting out on this journey on their own. Long after the Mississippi has been crossed and an astronaut's boot settled into the dust of the moon, this inner frontier stretches out before us. This new frontier is in our hearts. The late Joseph Campbell spoke of the modern hero's journey as an internal one. Today's men are called upon to redirect their heroic energies away from climbing Mt. Everest to sharing how they feel and becoming involved with those they love.

This journey is every bit as difficult and dangerous as the journeys of old; the discoveries along the way, every bit as rewarding as gazing on the Pacific Ocean or watching the Earth rise from the moon. Just as men in covered wagons generations ago sought a better life for their families and themselves, so we travel toward the same goal. By transforming ourselves, we transform our families.

THE JOURNEY OF THIS BOOK

As fathers, our "call to adventure" turns the quest inward and backward. We are asked to look into ourselves, into our fathers and our families. We are asked to evaluate critically which values, beliefs and behaviors were given to us (consciously and unconsciously) by our parents and which of these we *choose* to pass on to our children.

Reinventing Fatherhood draws on the experiences of modern-day fathers who have taken the leap from their own backgrounds into the future. These heroes, young fathers all, have shared their feelings, thoughts, confusion and joy about becoming fathers. They have shared transitions——in their marriages and their family life——with other men and, with guidance, have explored and discovered new avenues, wider vistas and greener fields.

You, like they, will examine this transition and your responsibility, commitment, changing roles, careers, sex, marriage and family. We will examine how attitudes about these issues evolve throughout the pregnancy.

Fatherhood begins long before sperm meets egg. The story begins in the primordial mists of the relationships with our own fathers, takes shape in courtship and comes to a focus in the decision to have children. We will be looking at this whole panorama. It is a broad view of fatherhood, but at the same time we will hear the stories of individual fathers as they go through each of these stages.

Like all travelers' tales, your own experiences may be very different from those of the fathers who speak from these pages. All the guidebooks on China won't prepare you for the restaurant with the dirt floor and pigs running through the kitchen. You have to experience that for yourself.

Your journey will be your own. On this journey into fatherhood, you will fill scrapbooks with your own memories and send your own letters back from the frontier. We hope our stories from new and expectant fathers point to the excitement and adventure that come from exploring your role in the family. We hope that this excitement will be an inspiration for you to pack your bags (or unpack your bags) and set out on your own journey into fatherhood.

This inner journey is a strangely liberating and threatening experience. We will discover that our strengths are our weaknesses. A new father ventures within to discover the expectations planted long ago in his consciousness by his own parents. We will discover that our view of parenting, our understanding of how to join with our wife to create a functioning, healthy family is rooted deeply in the soil of our family history.

If we decide to change, we will look for role models and find that good role models for nurturing, caring and emotional involvement are provided by women. We don't want to become women. We are men, but our definition of a man is derived from an archaic model that may have worked well in years past, but poorly serves our current needs.

Where do we find a new model? There is no single recipe for fatherhood. We must ask how we became who we are. We must wonder what motivates us to act, feel and think as we do. We must come to understand that our future is tied to the history of our past. *The primary responsibility of our modern father is to evaluate and choose the course of his actions based upon independent, critical exploration of the events that molded him.*

We stand at a crossroad in our family. With a new child entering the world, we have a chance to change course and leave a new legacy to the next generation or to carry on along the same path. By looking back through generations of our family, we can choose a path that integrates the best of our history, our traditions, our legacies and our strengths.

Although we may not be able to look to our wife or our father for assistance, help is available. The old heroes never asked for help because real men relied on smarts, a horse and a gun. Today, our new heroes seek assistance. Men who have discovered such paths nurture other men. Men turn to men to discover aspects of intimate friendships that for years have been the lifeblood of their wives existence.

Men who overcome the fear of reaching out to other men learn they need not fear revealing themselves to their family. Strength and commitment can come from our newfound family position. We discover that the power and elegance of male heroism lies not with our conquests, ribbons and medals.

Our power and courage lie in our awareness of how we feel. The new hero inside us no longer needs to hide, for to see us vulnerable and gentle is to see us at our best. Our courage and power come from belonging to the sanctuary of our family's emotional inner circle.

We are discovering and creating a new generation of fathers. It is part of the important work of men today. We new fathers are pioneers. We are breaking new ground and reaching uncharted territory. We know that we are expected to learn a new role that radically departs from that of our fathers. This role involves emotional honesty and expressiveness, sensitivity to our wives and children, and the family management skills of communication, problem solving and time management.

This is the most incredible opportunity for growth that you will have in your entire life. If marriage was a chance for a gentle education in the art of adulthood, parenting is an advanced degree. We have the opportunity to remake ourselves and build our families. This is vital work. If we can learn to be nurturing, involved fathers committed to the emotional well-being of our children and wives, we can change the structure and direction of the American family.

[[2]]
CHAPTER

I Don't Want To Be Like Dad

Growing up during the post-World War II baby boom, you could find two or three million children in every neighborhood. Mine was no different. There were kids everywhere.

One of my closest friends lived four houses away. His name was Barry and he was one of my baseball buddies. We played baseball at his house, at my house, at the local park, in our bedrooms, in the street and at our school.

One day during our tenth year, Barry and I were playing baseball in his backyard with a group of kids from an adjacent neighborhood. Barry's father was watching from the back porch. Barry hit a long fly ball into deep left field. The ball hit the fence (our home run wall), and bounced right into the left fielder's glove. He turned and threw to second base where Barry, sliding with his P.F. Flyers high in the air, was tagged out before he got to the bag.

Barry thought he was safe. Everyone else thought he was out. Barry began to argue the call with the second baseman, a good friend of his from school. Suddenly, Barry's dad appeared at second base. He called Barry "out" at second base and walked him back to the sidelines. Just before they sat down, his father smacked Barry in the face, shaking him and yelling, "Don't you ever embarrass me like that again!"

Barry fought back tears, but the intense red glow from his cheek and nose showed us just how hard he was hit. We wanted to help our friend, but we were frightened by his father. "What would he do to us," we thought, "if we try to help Barry?"

Barry didn't cry. He glared. He glared at his father with hate and anger that you could taste. He glared at us to stay away, trying through his pain to protect us from his father, too.

The game ended because we were too scared to be near Barry's dad. I picked up my mitt and bat and began to head home. I looked up from the ground, toward my house. I was crying for my friend. Then, I heard a familiar, safe voice. My dad had come over to get me for dinner:

"Jonathan," he said, "I saw how Barry's dad hit him. I don't want you playing at his house anymore."

Barry and I spoke later on the phone and I told him what my dad said. "I understand," he said. "Most of my friends can't play with me anymore because my dad frightens them. Don't ever tell him what your dad said because he'll blame it on me and I'll just get hit again."

I could not save my friend from a dreadful childhood of beatings and punishments. But, I can remember the fear, horror and mistrust that I felt whenever I was around Barry's dad. I decided I would never be like Barry's dad.

So many of us have been raised by fathers who wanted to love us but didn't know how to express it. They wanted to help us but didn't know how to teach. Instead, some fathers used their undisciplined power to show us "proper behavior." They missed opportunities for bonding and teaching. Instead, they taught us to fear them, to be untrusting of them. They taught us to hide our feelings, to protect our souls from the unpredictable actions of our fathers.

These fathers taught their children that being a man meant using force to assure compliance. The result is a generation of adult children who are emotionally learning disabled within their love relationships, men who desperately want to reach out to their own children, but find themselves unprepared, almost inept, in their understanding of how to be an emotionally available father.

I DON'T WANT TO BE LIKE DAD

My father had office hours every Saturday. He left the house at seven in the morning and worked until one in the afternoon. He would drive from his office to the country club. During the warmer months, he would play golf. During the winter, he would *schmooze* with his friends, take a steam bath and play cards. By the time he got home it was time for dinner. Saturday nights, of course, was time for dad to take mom out for dinner. So, we usually saw him for about an hour on Saturdays, between five and six. I never stopped to think about why he didn't spend time with me and my sister. I guess I believed mom's view that dad needed time to unwind from the week.

Sundays were a little different. Dad did rounds at the hospital and usually arrived home around eleven. The rest of the day was spent working with mom on the office billings. Finally, around four or five in the afternoon, dad stopped working and would sit with us and watch television.

I can't remember having breakfast with my father during my childhood, seldom dinners. I never questioned his involvement because I was told how important dad's work was. Now, as I prepare for a child of my own, I realize that I want to share meals with my little one. I want to give my child the attention I never got. I want to be there for my kid.

- Rob, twenty-six, medical resident

Dad Was Never Home

No matter what their background, it seems that fathers of the fifties and sixties were away for so many hours during the day that their presence around the house was experienced as a treat, more like a favorite uncle coming to visit than an ongoing participation.

We never thought twice about whether dad was home in time for dinner because mom made it clear that he was working long hours to enable us to live better than his parents *ever* lived. Parenting was the unique domain of women. When we were hurt, we turned to mom. When we were scared, we turned to mom. When we needed to talk about school, friends or life, we turned to mom.

Dad was away at work too often for us to be able to talk with him about everyday life. Besides, mom kept telling us not to bother dad with our "little details." He had more important things on his mind, like work.

Most of our fathers were raised with the belief that their contributions to parenting were limited to specific roles such as disciplinarian and activities consultant. Hence, many of our fathers missed opportunities to develop intimate relationships with their children.

> When I look back at my childhood, I see my mom hovering over us. She would drive us to Little League and out on dates. Dad took almost no part in our lives until I was in tenth grade. I remember that suddenly he began to drive us, to play with us and to talk with us. At the time, I never gave it a second thought. When he got sick a few years back, he and I began to get much closer. We talked about our relationship as father and son, then and now. He asked if I remembered him playing ball with me during high school. I said that I did, but that I didn't remember many playtimes during my earlier years.
>
> I remember that he turned away and a big smile crossed his face. 'Your mother and I had many fights over my unwillingness to play with you and Paul when you were younger. Fact is, you didn't become interesting or fun until you were fourteen or fifteen.'
>
> - Nicky, twenty-three, video store manager

AN ERA OF SCARCITY

Many of our fathers have carried with them the ghost of the Depression. They were raised during a time of unprecedented poverty. The scars from these years of deprivation and sacrifice resulted in many deciding early in their lives that they would never allow such desperation to touch their children. They became hardworking, self-sacrificing men who were driven to protect their families from the ghosts of their past.

One expectant father told the story of his father growing up in the Depression. The Dawson family was among the most popular on the block. When there was food in his house, it was cake, cookies and pies. The local kids lined up like dogs in heat to savor and indulge themselves in a dessert feeding frenzy. What they did not know was that the only food in the house was desserts. His grandfather was friendly with the owners of the local bakery. They would give him their day-old cakes, cookies and pies, which served as the staple of his dad's existence for many years.

Our emerging view of father is of a man who spent little time at home with his children. Although these men felt their family roles were more important than their paid work roles, few of our expectant fathers believed that their fathers wanted to be more involved in family life than they were.

> My dad loved his work. He built his business from the ground floor up. He loved being everyone's plumber. He would rush out on an emergency call at a moments notice. Dad loved to hear that he was the plumber everyone could depend on. Sometimes he went on an emergency call during Christmas day. When I was eight, dad and mom bought me a train set. Dad promised to put it together for me before bedtime. When bedtime came, dad was out on a call. It sounds dumb now, but I remember that I cried myself to sleep that night because my dad wasn't home to build my trains. He wasn't there when he said he would be.
>
> - Doug, thirty-four, general contractor

Why were so many of these fathers absent from the day-to-day activities of family life?

An interesting idea about why our fathers tended to spend inordinate amounts of time at work is offered by Price-Bonham and Skeen[1]. They suggest that fathers spent excessive amounts of time at work to avoid the responsibilities of fatherhood. Men need to avoid their role as father because they lack the knowledge and skill necessary to feel comfortable in the role. Therefore, the more often they can avoid the role, the less they need to show how little they know.

Our fathers could have played more involved roles but rarely found opportunities to do so. Occasionally, family crises forced them to take a more active fathering role, directing their energies toward family responsibilities, but when there was no crisis, our fathers retreated into a more passive, distant role, directing their energies toward work or other nonfamily activities.

I remember when my sister was sick. No one was sure what was the matter with her. Mom and dad stayed away all night when they took my sister to the hospital. It was the first time I remember that my father took an entire week off from work. I must have been about six or seven, but I remember thinking that it was great having dad around, even if it meant going to the hospital every day to see Mary.

The joke around the house was that dad had never cooked dinner before. We all were scared that after eating his dinner we would wind up in the hospital next to my sister. He made such a mess when he burned our grilled cheese sandwiches. To this day, I find myself remembering those horrible dinners whenever I have a grilled cheese.

As frightened as we were that my sister was really sick, there was something very special about dad being around for that entire week. It wasn't until grandma died that dad took time off from work again.

- Jeff, twenty-five, engineer

Mom had pneumonia once. She was flat on her back for three or four weeks. Dad came home every night before five. He has never done that since, but he was there when mom needed him.

- Alan, thirty-eight, lawyer

There are no clear-cut answers about why our fathers focused more on work than on family. Part of the answer is that fathers had gender-specific roles to fulfill. Men were responsible for supporting their families while women were the guiding light in child rearing.

Our fathers look askance at the complexities of today's life, in contrast to the perceived simplicity of the fifties and sixties. You see confidence in their eyes when they recall the clarity of roles when men were men, a home was a man's castle and work was the focus of their lives. Theirs is a sense of longing for the old days of 42nd Street, when "dame" was a term of affection, when girls knew how to type and take dictation and being a man meant getting what you wanted.

My dad still has trouble understanding this equality thing. He tells me time and again that the Bible teaches that a man is in charge of his home; that women are the weaker sex and need to be cared for because they can't do it themselves. A woman's work is to raise the kids. She has no place in the workplace. Jobs, the few that are available, are for the guys. Any woman who wants a career probably has trouble accepting that she's a girl. Once she gets married, then she'll understand her true calling. My dad's ideas about women go over real big with my wife, Janice.

- George, twenty-seven, graduate student

Today, there are many young men who are influenced by a call to a different idea about family and fatherhood. These men know they do not want to be like their fathers.

Their fathers placed a premium on the workplace and had little energy left for their home life. Today's man wants time with his family, with his children. He wants to maintain the positive legacies of his own fatherhood, but rejects the role of father as emotionally distant from the rest of the family.

We know that our fathers played an important role in teaching sex-role socialization for both sons and daughters. Our fathers tended to encourage femininity in their daughters and masculinity in their sons.

Our fathers typically reinforced friendliness and interpersonal skills when they interacted with their daughters, while discouraging independence and task mastery. They encouraged task mastery and independence in their sons, while discouraging nurturance and emotional expressiveness.[2]

Most expectant fathers who participated in our interviews expressed their desire to teach their children a different way of knowing their world. These men understood that teaching their children traditional sex-role socialization skills had an important place, but their children needed to know more. Their children, they said, needed to understand how men and women can better cooperate in the workplace, in the home and in life.

I look at my friends' children and realize the awesome responsibility that comes with being a parent. I want my daughter to have choices that my sister never had. I want my son to know it is all right to cry when he is upset. No more of this 'be a man' philosophy that my father shoved on me.

- Stephen, thirty-six, teacher

My wife and I have worked hard at learning how to be more expressive than the families we came from. I never heard my father tell me that he loved me. My wife never heard that from her parents, either. We know that we want to teach our kids to talk about their feelings, but we don't want to teach them to sound like wimps. There is a way to talk about feelings, yet not sound like you're always whining. I'm not sure that I know how to do that.

- Eric, twenty-two, mechanic

Our expectant fathers worried about how to teach their children to be less sex-role rigid, more open and enlightened. They understood they would be teachers to their children and they were poorly prepared to fulfill this assignment.

Our new father for the 1990s needs to develop more effective and efficient skills in child management, communications, nurturance, sensitivity, intimacy and expressiveness. He needs to involve himself with how his children feel not just with what they do. He needs to talk about his world as well as theirs. And he needs to be committed to sharing his ideas, his feelings and his energies with his children.

[[3]]

CHAPTER

Looking Back to Your Future

*What has been said about cultural history is true of individuals:
If we do not know our familial history, we are most likely to repeat
it.*

- John Bradshaw[1]

Whether we rebel or try to please our fathers, their messages form an important part of the fabric of our existence. We find their influence woven into our lives, and it surfaces when we least expect it, or want it—in our words, our actions and our expectations. Understanding our fathers' expectations provides insights into our own attitudes toward fatherhood. It helps us examine those expectations critically and see which ones to retain and which to discard.

During a recent workshop, Mike, a twenty-nine year-old store clerk, was asked his expectations about punishment. "I will talk to my child and explain to him how what he is doing is wrong. I will tell him what to do to make it right."

I asked Mike about the next step, if his child doesn't respond to his verbal prodding and directions, then what?

He hesitated, his eyes narrowed and said, "That's when a man has to set down the rules of the house. If he doesn't listen, then he'll get spanked."

His wife, Chris, jumped in and said, "You're not gonna hit *my* child! You told me how your daddy used to whip you and Teddy. You've hated him for those beatings. And, now, you tell me that you're going to hit our child. Not in my house, you won't."

Mike was dumbfounded by Chris's strong response. I stepped in and asked, "Mike, I want you to think about different ideas or strategies you might consider before you spank your child." Mike had no response. Mike had been raised in a house where the sequence of action was talk first, hit second. He had never considered alternative ways to discipline. He was not uncaring or unconcerned. He simply never considered an alternative because he was unaware that he carried in his head a sequence of actions that guided his behavior. This sequence programmed him to warn his child verbally first. If that failed, he was programmed to spank his child. This programming was automatic and preset. He had no idea it even existed until we began to talk about it during the workshop. Once he became aware of his expectations——to talk first and hit second——he and Chris were able to talk about developing alternative responses that did not include spanking.

Each of us has a vision of how to be the ideal father. Most of us want a relationship with our children that promotes harmony and encourages individual growth. We want to give love and have it returned. We want our children to achieve more, to enjoy life more and to succeed more.

A tragedy in many father-child relationships is that we don't think about *how* to develop this relationship. We spend hours upon hours learning to improve our golf game, our tennis swing or our jump shot. Yet, we spend very little time learning about how to be a better father.

I have always found it ironic that our society requires us to pass written and practical driving tests before we are awarded our driver's license. Find a job as a waiter and training will be required by the management to learn fundamental serving skills. Parenting, however, requires no course curriculum, no competency-based education and no previous experience. Parenting our children, the most precious and important experience of our adult life, requires no preparation. We wing it. Some of us succeed while others fail. And when we fail as parents, our children are irreparably hurt and may pass on that hurt and failure for generations to come.

The vision of the perfect father dancing through our fantasies is a combination of our wants and needs, what we have been exposed to through our family background and our expectations of how we want to be.

Before we ever have a child, the expectations we have inherited from our family of origin are rattling around inside our heads. These expectations are seldom clear and almost never discussed. As I write this chapter, my wife and I discovered we are going to have our third child. So, last evening, I arranged for us to go out for dinner both to celebrate and review. Between the linguini and the salad, I asked my wife to review with me how we have fared as parents. We talked about our ideas about parenting, about being a father and being a mother. We described where our roles overlap and where they are different. We looked to change our parenting to better reflect how we want our new child to be raised. And we planned ways for our other children to feel involved, without confusing the newborn about who is mom and dad.

Most of the expectant fathers who attended our workshops steadfastly maintained they held few expectations about fatherhood. They anticipated they would give more to their children than had been given to them.

> I know I want my child to love me and for me to love him. I want to give him everything I didn't get from my father. I want to be there for my child.
>
> - Elliott, twenty-seven, salesman

Elliott genuinely expected to be more physically and emotionally available to his child than his father had been to him. Elliott's father was a minor league baseball player, which required him to be on the road for much of the year. Elliott didn't realize that as a salesman whose territory included the northeastern United States, he, too, was continually away from his family. Traveling during the workweek, Elliott was home on weekends and saw himself as giving more to his family than his father had given him. The question posed during our workshop was whether his schedule would allow him the time he needed to be seen by his children as more available, physically and emotionally.

If someone were to ask you your expectations about fatherhood, you might deny having any. If someone were to ask you to define what your partner expects from you as a father, you might stare as blankly as most of our workshop participants. Don't believe me? Try it. Take a few minutes to think about what you expect from yourself and what your partner expects from you in your role as father. Then put pen to paper. Most people have a hard time putting words to their expectations about fatherhood—beyond the typical generalizations of happiness, caring, security, nurturance, protection, and safety.

KNOWING FATHER

Think about who your father was and the relationships he had with people, especially you. Then, answer the questions below. (To examine your mother's influence on your ideas about fatherhood, insert the word "mother" for "father" and complete the same exercise.)

1. How has your relationship with you father affected your ideas about being a man? A father?
2. How have your feelings about your father affected your feelings about yourself?
3. Describe four of your father's positive and negative qualities.
4. How have your feelings about your father changed during your lifetime?
5. Describe four positive characteristics of yourself that remind you of your father, and four negative reminders.
6. Describe how you and your father typically communicate and how you would like to change that? How you would like to communicate differently with your child than you did with your father?
7. Recall two positive experiences you have had with your father and describe what made them special.
8. Recall two negative experiences you have had with your father and describe what made them uncomfortable.
9. Describe four positive experiences you would like to share with your child.
10. Describe four negative experiences you would like to avoid with your child.

We all carry a long list of expectations about fatherhood that involves who we are, who we want to be, how we want our partner to accept us and how we want our relationship with our child to look. These are pretty big areas for conversation. However, it is only the tip of the iceberg. Don't forget that your spouse also holds expectations about your role as a father, plus her role as mother and your combined role as parents.

You know you have reached beneath the tip of the iceberg when you and your spouse have discussed each of your expectations in these three areas: (1) your expectations about fatherhood; (2) her expectations about fatherhood; and (3) your ideas about how fatherhood fits into your general picture of parenthood. Through such discussions with your spouse, you will bring your separate expectations about fatherhood into a cohesive, comfortable set of commonly held expectations and behaviors.

We develop expectations about fatherhood based upon how our fathers and mothers related to and treated us and by their comments or their relationships with other children. Sometimes we receive mixed messages from them. Harry's dad talked about treating all his children equally. But, Harry, as the eldest, was held to a higher standard of performance and responsibility than his siblings. Harry grew to dislike the pressure and decided that he would raise his children without pressure to achieve. Such an opposite reaction to fathering may lead to troubling parenting patterns.

It is important to identify these expectations about fatherhood developed when we were kids. These expectations fuel our behavior, direct our thinking and lead us to choices that may have dramatic effects on our happiness, our children and our spouses.

The Investigation Begins

A good place to start learning how your family background has helped to mold your thinking about fatherhood is to investigate your family of origin. Get pen and paper and write down your father's and mother's views about parenting. Do the same thing about their views of fathering. You might draw a line down the middle and put your mother's responses on one side and your father's on the other.

Write a paragraph about how your father viewed fatherhood. Do the same for your mother's views about fatherhood. Then, write down the ideas each parent viewed as important to successful fathering. For example, what did your father *say* about showing love? Then describe how he *showed* it. Ask yourself whether he was consistent in showing you the type of love he said was important. Evaluate each important expectation similarly.

Family History Questions

The next set of questions will help you understand the different influences on your parenting that come from your family background. It is most important to identify both the expectations and the behaviors you observed in your folks' parenting. Finally, the more you can focus on what they said versus what they did, the easier it will be to identify such discrepancies in your own fathering style.

Similar to the exercise above, your next step is to do the same exercise on *your* expectations about fatherhood. Ask the same questions and look at how similar or different your answers are from your parents. Are you happy with your responses? If not, how will you and your spouse change these ideas about fatherhood?

1. What are the spoken and unspoken messages in your family regarding the meaning and purpose of marriage?
2. What are the spoken and unspoken messages in your family regarding the meaning and purpose of fatherhood?
3. What are the spoken and unspoken messages in your family regarding the meaning and purpose of motherhood?
4. How or in what degree did fathering follow specific sex role expectations?   mothering?
5. Who took which family responsibilities? How was this done or displayed?
    a. Disciplinarian?
    b. Nurturance?

     c. Talker?
     d. Playful?
     e. Breaking bad news?
     f. Making/enforcing rules?
     g. Teacher?
     h. Who handled conflict? How?
     i. Who yelled? Who reasoned? What was said?
     Add other dimensions as you think of them . . .
6. What values did your father want to teach you about being a member of the family? A man/woman? A father?
7. How did your father feel about the responsibilities of being a father?
8. Was fathering different for different children? If so, how?
9. How does your partner perceive your family's fathering history? How do you perceive hers?
10. List the changes you would make in how *you* were fathered that will help you be more like the father you want to be.

Our expectant fathers were asked to complete the Family History Questions during our workshops. Mike and Susan shared their answers. Mike's answers are discussed below.

What are the spoken and unspoken messages in your family regarding the meaning and purpose of marriage?

When you ask about unspoken messages, I thought that you meant messages that were not spoken - what I call a hidden message. The hidden messages in my family about marriage were that dad and mom talked about working together to raise the kids, but mom did all the work. Dad either worked at the office or was out. He spent all his free time volunteering at the Red Cross or the Civil Defense program. He loved his military background and wanted to give his time and expertise to disaster relief planning, something he did during the war. Mom agreed to ignore his absence by focusing on how much dad was giving back to the country he loved. I could never figure out why she didn't feel furious with him for leaving her with the six of us.

The idea of marriage seemed to be that mothers are involved with their children and fathers are involved with people outside the house.

What are the spoken and unspoken messages in your family regarding the meaning and purpose of fatherhood?

My father used to tell me that nothing was more important than being a good father. He told me about treating everyone fairly. He talked about taking time to listen to each of us. Yet, when it came time to play with us or to see a school play or a baseball game, he was never there. He reminded me of Robin William's character in the movie *Hook*. Williams kept telling his son that he would come to this really important baseball game. He told his child, "My word is my bond." But, his son quickly learned that his word meant nothing, that he couldn't trust his father to be there for him. That was my dad. He talked a great game, but gave his time to everyone else but us, not his family.

How did your father discipline?

Discipline was not my dad's strong suit. He threatened to spank us when we were young, but I can't remember him ever hitting us. When we misbehaved, he would yell and holler. If that didn't work, he would leave the house. He'd go to the store or for a walk. He would simply leave. His version of discipline was that if he couldn't control us, then he would escape somehow.

What I learned was that I could do whatever I wanted to do. When things got too hot for dad, he'd leave. He never taught us how to respect him or the rules he was trying to teach us. It has taken me years to understand how he copped out on us. He simply didn't teach us any really important ideas about rule following and respecting others. This has haunted me since high school.

What values did your father want to teach you about being a member of the family?

Family values. That's a tough one because what he wanted us to do and what he showed us were two different things. I know that education was important to him because he never finished high school. But he never taught us how to study or how important reading was to success in school. So, I guess that the idea of education was an important value to him but not its practice.

Honesty and trust. Friendship. Cooperation. These were important to him, and I know that he was heartbroken whenever he found out that one of us lied to him. Trust was important, too. But, he was a lousy role model for that. He would tell us that he'd be there for us and then just not show up. How can you ever learn to trust a dad who does that all the time?

Was fathering different for different children?

There were six kids in our house. I guess that my dad treated us as fairly as he could. There were times, especially since I was the youngest, when my brothers got all over my case because I was being treated special. I was the baby of the family and I guess I milked it for as much as I could. But, overall, I'd say he treated all us boys the same way.

Mike's responses are the kind of answers that will help you to explore your family background. You need to take time to look at what was happening around you during your childhood. You need to look at your brothers and sisters, too. Often, it is helpful to talk with family members when completing the questions. Their reactions may help you to see your family background in a fuller, more open way. And, don't forget! It is imperative to include your wife in conversations about your background.

PART TWO

THE MAP

Who Are We Supposed To Be?

*There are two questions a man must ask himself: The first is
'Where am I going?' and the second is 'Who will go with me?' If
you ever get these questions in the wrong order you are in trouble.*
                                                    - Sam Keen[1]

When I spoke with my father about the ideas for this book, his
reaction was typical for his generation. "You think about and
analyze things like fatherhood. We never gave it a second thought.
We did what we did and focused on getting on with our lives.
Who thought about being a good father or a bad father? You did
what you thought was right at the time."

But what is right today? Today's father faces many competing
views of fatherhood. On the one hand we have Clifford Huxtable,
the affable, competent, involved father on the *Cosby Show*. He is
a communicator, a sensitive and intelligent husband and father,
and also a major participant in the intricate details of his children's lives. This father is strong through his openness, trust in his
children and belief in the power of family participation.

On the other hand, we have Al Bundy of *Married with
Children*. Al is a bumbling, evasive, intimacy-phobic dunce who
has risen to the highest levels of mediocrity through laziness,
cheating and manipulation. Sure, the show is funny, but it also
sends a strangely compelling message about today's father. This
father is weak, ineffective, often wrong and useless around the
house. His view of family participation is to watch television, to be
outside his family's emotional life.

The message is confusing. Are we weak, ineffective and
manipulative men waiting to find the next way out of respon-

sibilities? Or, are we striding toward openness, communication and sensitivity to others?

HOW DID WE GET HERE?

Men have traditionally defined themselves in relation to women. A generation or two ago, we pictured ourselves as the complement of women, joining to create a perfectly balanced whole. Men became the lesser part of their "better half." They spent their energies accumulating power and left emotions to the women.

Then came the shock waves. The man's role as breadwinner and warrior suffered major challenges. War was never the same after Vietnam. And feminism forever changed the relationships of men and women in society.

The father of the 1950s was hardworking, responsible, fairly well disciplined. In the words of Robert Bly, "He didn't see women's souls very well, though he looked at their bodies a lot."[2] He was easily swayed by what he thought he "should" be. Men were supposed to like football, be aggressive, stick up for their rights, never cry and always be good providers, no matter how much they sacrificed family time. The image of man lacked feminine space. It was without compassion, without awareness. It produced an unbalanced man who had a clear vision of who he was and his mission, but the vision contained massive mistakes and failings.

According to Bly, the horror and pain of the Vietnam War forced men to question what it meant to be a man. Fathers sent their children off to war and 55,000 never came home. In years gone by, giving one's life for the military seemed an honorable, just sacrifice. But these fathers had been through the destruction of World War II. They were tired of war. They wanted to pursue the American dream and feel safe and secure within the borders of their country, their home and their family. Sending children to war was not part of what fatherhood was about. That is what they fought for in the forties: the right and privilege to live in peace. Vietnam was too much, too soon.

Simultaneous with Vietnam, the women's movement asked men to question their beliefs and views of women. Some men began to see not only greater value in women, but also discovered a feminine side of themselves. The message from the women's movement reached many men, but in a distorted form. The message was that these women, strong women who were actively changing our world, wanted soft men. In response, we gave up that which makes us unique from women. We surrendered our maleness to a funny kind of feminized man. Women no longer feared us, for we were tame. We rolled over on our backs, bared our throats and gave away our power.

Some, of course, continued treating women as objects of desire, objects of control, objects to avoid. They were not touched by the women's movement. They continued to define their strength in relation to women's weaknesses and, to this day, develop families that follow fixed sex-role patterns. They do not concern themselves with the trivialities of emotional availability, intimacy or communication.

Man no longer define themselves only in relation to women. They need to find their own direction. They need to discover their own strengths and weaknesses that exist *because* they are men, not because they are *not* women.

The deterioration of the breadwinner role has created confusion among men. We were thrown off balance with the rise of the women's movement. Suddenly our definition of ourselves in relation to women became confused. Women showed that they could gain increasing power in society and greater equality in relationships.

We are shackled by the expectations of the past, with few clear visions for the future. Women have moved like the cavalry into the happy hunting grounds of men, and men have retreated to emotional reservations. There they bide their time on desolate land, cut off from society, worshipping ancestors and waiting for some vision to reignite them.

If the supermoms of feminism are worried about burnout, the modern father is worried about obsolescence. This fear is summed up by the popular feminist bumper sticker, "A woman needs a man like a fish needs a bicycle."

NOTHING ABOUT FATHERHOOD IS OBVIOUS

Research has shown us that men can be as nurturing as women. They can be loving and affectionate toward their children and those whom they love. Men do not nurture in the same way as women, but their style is nonetheless nurturing.

But, there is a problem. Nothing about the function of being a father is obvious. Lowell Streiker suggests that the role of fatherhood is psychologically foreign to men. "It may be necessary for the survival of the race, but it is hardly natural."[3]

We all know that mothering is tied directly to a woman's biology. It seems to come naturally to her, surging forth from deep inside——wanting to nurture, wanting to care for, wanting to give love and wanting to communicate.

But fathering? Where does that come from? It does not seem biological. Therefore, it must be a learned behavior. Where then do we learn to be fathers?

When we compare how little girls and little boys play, we discover important differences that eventually are reflected in parenting styles. Little girls are encouraged to talk more about their feelings. They are encouraged to play with dolls, to play house and to dress up. My own little girl has more than thirty Barbie dolls, some forty-five stuffed animals and drives her parents nuts by changing her dress three to four times each day.

From the moment we hold our little child, we tend to hold little girls differently than little boys. We speak to them using different intonations, gestures and words. We buy them different games and encourage them to play with different toys and behave in ways that reinforce their social and biological destiny.

In the words of Streiker, "Girls are constantly taught to be mothers by society, by the media, by their families, by their fathers, and, above all, by their moms. Girls are simply counted on to be mothers——to cook, wash, dress, and otherwise care for children . . . It is as though they have no choice."[4]

Boys are rewarded for different activities than girls. Little boys are infinitely more active, more physical. They play with guns, jump off furniture, destroy fantasy bad guys and spend hours playing with trucks, *Legos* and building blocks. While they are building and destroying their imaginary world with their *GI Joe's* and *Ninja Turtle* figurines, their sisters are playing house, serving imaginary tea and playing with *Polly Pocket*.

Boys are not encouraged to play father opposite their sister's mother. When my children play together, my daughter plays the role of the helpless, distressed princess who needs to be saved by her brother, the powerful, protective prince. We encourage them to switch roles, but neither one wants to play the other's part. "It's not what big boys do," as my son would say.

Boys receive almost no information or training about how to be a father. There are times when boys learn about nurturing, as when a new baby enters the home. Often boys will enjoy feeding the new baby and performing caretaking behaviors. But these are modeled on what mommy does, not on daddy's behavior.

Little boys don't have male role models who teach them about male nurturing, homemaking, emotional availability and communications! When was the last time you saw a little boy playing out the robust role played by father in and around the house?

When such role models are available to young children, they are portrayed as fools, idiots or, in some way, strange. Television series showing fathers taking care of children often portray the men as inept, clumsy and generally incompetent. Big screen movies, such as *Three Men and A Baby*, reveal to us that three men cannot care for one little girl but that one mother can care for nine children. Even when Hollywood tried to show how a man can stay at home and perform household chores, they show him being emasculated, ineffective in the performance of his duties and they name it *Mr. Mom* not *Mr. Dad*.

Little boys are poorly prepared by society to be fathers. They are not given encouragement from their own fathers to learn behaviors that will be needed later with their children. They probably will not learn it from their friends because they, too, have inadequate or clumsy role models themselves. They don't learn it at school, at college or through any accepted educational vehicle. They are totally ignorant about how to be part of their family, to give emotionally, to nurture and to participate, and there is no place to learn.

No More Mr. Nice Boy!

One type of man is more thoughtful, more gentle than those who came before him. "He's a nice boy who now not only pleases his mother but also the young woman he is living with."[5] Here is a man who is more conscious than his father of the need to be available to his family, to be aware of his environment and to be reasonable to those with whom he lives.

He is a feminized man. A gentle, soft soul who has sold his power, his aggression, his unique maleness to the church of complacency. He has surrendered what made men different from women because he now believes that feminism can tell him how to be a better lover, a better husband and a better father. He has given away his power because he doesn't know how to use it and because male power has been linked to pain, abuse and exploitation.

Male power does not have to be frightening. Our natural aggressiveness, our natural comfort with power and control makes us unique. We need to learn how to channel these energies toward a healthy, secure and productive end. Our new father can use his natural tendencies and bring them into the center of the family. The result will be to empower all whom he touches. But, his first goal is to learn not to fear the wondrous passion and energies that reside within him.

To begin the change toward a more involved, caring father whose roots lie within what it means to be a man, the new father must first take back the power he gave to his wife to be mother *and* father to his child. He must direct his energies away from his office, away from pleasing his mother, his father or his wife. He must concentrate on developing a sense of fatherhood that teaches his children that being a father is not being a mother. Our new father needs to search for his identity as a father within himself. He needs to turn to other men who have made the journey and taken the risk to find the emotional center of their family while maintaining their integrity and wholeness. Our exploring father can learn from them the unique style of nurturing, caring and sensitivity that is fathering.

All Things to All People

The problem is that men are killing themselves to be everything to all people. We are asked to be aggressive, soft, sensitive, macho, powerful, protective, sexual, respectful, fair, successful, providers, listeners, innovators, sensuous, handy, domestic, approachable, hard working, family oriented, diligent at work while relaxed and approachable at home.

Sam Keen writes that the central source of men's confusion over who they are is the absence of a sense about what it means to be a man.[6] This confusion, this wound that lies at the soul of who we are as men and as fathers, results from the absence of our fathers during both our childhood and adulthood. Having not been parented into the meaning of being a man, we are searching for a guide, a rule book or some inkling of hope, to tell us that we can be different from our fathers. We want to know what it means to be a father who can teach our children about the unique contribution that a man can make to their lives and their development.

New Fatherhood is Not Androgyny

Some see the new father as androgynous. Lowell Streiker suggests that we stride toward a vision of humanness in which masculine and feminine traits are balanced and harmonized.[7] He seeks to distribute maleness and femaleness evenly between men and women. Flatten the playing field so that differences do not exist.

No! Our new father is not being asked to give up what is unique about maleness and become androgynous. We seek a way to use what is special to us as men and bring that into the family. We do not seek to smooth out the curves and serve only white bread, white milk and white potatoes. We want to provide variety to our family; a variety that includes our male energies for power, loving, caring, sensitivity and emotional presence; a variety that complements our wife's female energies of connecting, nurturing, sensitivity and emotional presence. We want to be men who can teach our children about being a man and a man's perspective of life. We want to teach our sons and our daughters about maleness. We want our wives to teach our sons and daughters about femaleness. And we want to communicate this knowledge to foster cooperation and equality with our spouse while imparting to our children our distinctive view of life, of parenting, and of tomorrow and its possibilities.

The trouble with viewing father as androgynous is that it defines fatherhood using feminine traits. Fatherhood is not motherhood. It is a unique male experience.

Suzanne Fields warns us that the "New Sensitive Male" is a feminized father who is dangerous to himself as a man because he gives up what it means to be a man and in its places seeks to become a male version of a mother.[8] He is dangerous to his daughter and her emerging sense of self-esteem. She wants and needs to feel the security of knowing her father is there to protect her, complete with all his male force, courage and power. She does not need another mother. She needs a father.

He is dangerous to his son who learns to repress the maleness inside him—just like his daddy. He learns to fear his aggression, his power and his instincts. He continues the perilous fall away from his male roots and allows himself to be molded into some-one else's image of who he should be. The Sensitive Man as father teaches his son to be afraid of the natural energies and passions that live inside him. This father shows that to be a man means to deny and redirect what is innately special about being a man.

The feminized father is dangerous to his wife, too. The house is filled with two parents, both of whom are providing their children with much the same qualities, sensibilities and perspectives. If this man jettisons his maleness, jettisons his sense of fatherhood, in favor of more feminine concerns, he will have little to offer his daughters that their mother doesn't already give.

THE NEW FATHER REVEALED

The new father about whom we have been talking is really someone who must grasp strongly the roots of his basic maleness, while finding productive, responsive and caring ways to express it. The new father is being asked to be more fully human *without giving up the specialness that makes him a man.* He can choose to be a traditional father or a sensitive (small "s") man. He must never, however, give up the energies that make him different from his wife.

The new father is a more fully developed father. He has learned to feel comfortable with his problem solving and his passions. Yet, he has also learned that such characteristics are welcome within the emotional center of the family.

Bring your passions to your children and share them wisely, gently, but with gusto. Bring your power to your family; share with them, empower them and teach them how to direct it. Corny as it may sound, this is "The Force" within you. Just like in the *Star Wars* movies, the force left undirected, undisciplined and unexamined is a weak force whose potency remains unactualized. The force that is directed, cultivated, understood and accepted as an integral part of each man can guide us toward achievements unbounded.

You have a male force within you. You can learn about it, accept it as part of you and use it productively. Or, you can ignore it, pretend it is not there and allow others to strip you of your potentials, leaving you with their directions, their passions and their tomorrows.

Your children deserve a father who is willing to take the risk of understanding how to channel his energies toward a better tomorrow. Your children deserve to learn how to harness their strengths and, responsibly, point them to their goals, their achievements and their potentials.

The problem with our fathers and their fathers before them was that they were afraid of their intense inner energies. They didn't know how to control them, to direct them or to use them within the family. They feared themselves. They didn't trust themselves because no one ever challenged them to look inside and understand the beast of maleness, this "wildman." Once you understand your inner beast, your children will find your participation thrilling, your power inviting and your joy for life infectious.

AN IMPORTANT JOURNEY

Confusion still is king among many men today. They are unclear about why marriage is important ("Why buy the cow if you can have the milk free?"). Some give no thought to their purpose in having a family. Others consider that family development is best left to the women while financial support is his unique domain.

Our new father needs to embrace a simple belief: *Nothing is more important than his family.* Family health and happiness, its direction and the quality of its accomplishments define a successful family.

Many fathers are unclear about how to balance their limited time and energies between their family and their work. We are often tempted to sell our family time for the promise of tomorrow's big payday.

Sam Keen makes an interesting point when he talks about strong families as the cornerstone of our freedom. He suggests that the more distant fathers are from the emotional inner circle of their families the weaker become our families and our society.[9]

Keen, as well as others of the Men's Movement, talks about a "revolution" that will heal the wounds of past family neglect. He talks of bringing men and women together in family, both dedicated to the creation of a fertile family that places family value and honor at its core.

We want to heal the wounds of our own absent fathers' neglect so that our children will better understand what it means to be an emotionally available man.

The movement to bring fathers into the inner emotional sanctuary of family life revolves around this idea: Men cannot heal the wounds of their own absent fathers until they become the father they never had to *their* child. When we become aware of our pain, our loneliness, our anger, our disappointment and the physical touching, caressing and play we never had, then we can develop a road map for how we will parent our own children. Our children will profit from our understanding of what we did not receive.

⟦ 5 ⟧

CHAPTER

The Many Faces of Father

When I was a boy of 14, my father was so ignorant, I could hardly stand to have the Old Man around. But when I got to be 21, I was astonished at how much he had learned in seven years.

- Mark Twain

Erma Bombeck once said, "When I was a little kid, a father was like the light in the refrigerator. Every house had one, but no one knew what either of them did once the door was shut."[1] A father left many words unspoken. He yelled when he wanted to give us guidance.

Sometimes we were not sure if he was there at all. Sometimes he wasn't. Father has been increasingly pushed away by work, physically separated by divorce and made obsolete by a rising tide of working women. He has become the brunt of jokes, a small and pitiful Willie Loman pursuing business success, a Prufrock wondering if he should "dare disturb the universe." He is the object of pity, anger, awe, ridicule. But, even at his lowest, he is an awe-inspiring enigma, a powerful vacuum filled with mystery.

We grope in the dark to find him. The father we carry inside ourselves is in the shadows. He is undefined. Like the love our fathers felt but seldom put into words, this father in our minds is voiceless.

Where do you look for this father? There are two people inside yourself who are important to know. The first is the image of your father, who lives in your memories. If you think that your father was cold and detached, then the image of a father you carry in your head is that way too. If you think that he was a hero on a pedestal, you probably never knew him very well——or he never let you get close enough to know him. These, then, are the images that shape your ideas about fatherhood.

The second person you need to get to know is the child within, the little boy who lives inside the man. We will consider this little boy in the next chapter. Here, we will begin our search for the father within.

THE MANY FACES OF FATHER

Research by family therapists and psychologists points to the increasing desire of new fathers to be part of the emotional inner sanctuary of their family. Historically they were banished to the outside where they were most useful through their projects, earning potential and activities. Today, however, men are voicing their desires to be part of their children's lives.

There are few role models for this transition from the outside to the inside of the family's emotional center. The question becomes, where do we learn how to be fathers?

Having completed the family history exercise in Chapter Three, you probably discovered that your father was a very busy man who was kept away from most emotional involvement with his children.

> After I finished the family history exercise, I looked at how my folks put their marriage together and I didn't like it too much. My father talked about being the disciplinarian, but only after he couldn't get mom to do it. Dad was always the one who was absent from the family during a crisis. In part, that was mom's fault. Whenever a family crisis arose, mom would tell us that dad had to go to work. Dad then was free to trot off wherever he wanted. I remember one time when grandma was taken to the hospital, mom told dad to get out of the way by going out to play golf. That's nuts to me!
> - Andrew, twenty-seven, policeman

> My dad was great. He played ball with me, helped me with my homework and taught me a lot about working with tools. I remember in tenth grade I got dumped by my first girlfriend and really needed to talk to my parents. Dad was the only one home, so I asked him to talk with me about girls and how they think. As if it was yesterday,

I remember how he froze in his chair, pushed his head forward like a chicken and asked me to sit next to him and watch the football game together. When mom came back home, dad told her that I was upset and wanted to talk with her.

- Doug, twenty-eight, stockbroker

Often the image we have of a father is an affable, friendly, helpful presence around the house who acts like a stranger in a strange land when it comes time to talk about the "F" word - feelings. Let us look at some different faces fathers have worn that concealed their real needs, wants and feelings from their families, or worse, from themselves. In doing so, consider which faces are yours.

A Strong Silent Father

The emotional messages we got from our fathers were few in number and they were hard to unravel. It was a rare father who told his son he loved him or was proud of him. Perhaps he felt there was no need to say these things. So the messages that passed across this Iron Curtain of our childhood were even more special.

Shortly after the birth of my son, I called my father to invite him to come over and see the new grandchild.

"Were you there for the birth?" he asked.

"Yes, I cut the cord."

"Did they put the baby into her arms when it was born?"

"Yes, they sure did."

I wasn't sure where this line of questioning was leading but I was willing to follow along. "It was a slimy mess all over the place, but it was the most incredible thing that I have ever seen."

"Did you notice a look of ecstasy on her face when she first held the baby?"

"She seemed very happy."

"Maybe it was because I was looking for it. But when they put you in your mother's arms, I saw this look of ecstasy. I had read about it. You were a textbook delivery; everything went smoothly."

"You mean you were there for my delivery?"

I had a strong sense that my mother was probably there when I was born, but I had no idea what my father's role was. I had been around for about thirty years and hadn't heard him describe this moment, how my birth affected him. Even now, he was telling me how it affected my mother, but something came through.

"That was pretty uncommon back then," I said, with a bit of awe in my voice, not just that he had been there, but that he had shared it with me, that he had watched this incredible miracle I had just experienced, that there was a day when he had started his journey into fatherhood. There was a feeling of connection.

- Robert, thirty-one, writer

I recall my father's repeated struggles to say he loves me. He can show it in many wonderful ways, but he chokes on the words. In times of great emotional upheaval he is able to express his love, but not when life travels its normal path.

When I received my doctorate in psychology, I received congratulatory calls from friends and mentors. My wife took me out for dinner. My colleagues bought me a funny plaque about my office hours. My mother-in-law had a lovely desk set made with my name and new title. But, nothing from my father.

Years later when I developed the courage to ask him why he didn't acknowledge this important transition in my life, he said: "I don't need to celebrate or tell anyone how proud I am of you. I know how important your doctorate is to you and take pride in that. I don't have a need to talk about it. In my heart I know how I feel."

Like so many other fathers who have contributed greatly to their children's development, my father's comment is typical of how fathers of previous generations have missed opportunities to bond with their children by celebrating emotionally important events.

Father as Disciplinarian

"Just wait until your father gets home!" It is a phrase that struck terror in the hearts of generations of children. Worse than the giants in fairy tales, the iron-fisted father was a figure who could cause children to quake. Even when most leather belts are hung up, the father continues to play an important role in discipline.

The old model of family discipline was a dichotomy between the nurturing of the mother and the law enforcement of the father: Good Cop/Bad Cop. The father, as a more distant and detached participant in the family, could play the "heavy."

We were often in fear of father and his belt or paddle. They kept us honest. Mom would never use such devices of torture. Usually, though, dad was responsible for talking with us about right and wrong. He would spell out the right way to do things and explain the consequences if the task was not completed according to specs.

In recent years, the clarity of roles has been blurred. In some families, father has given up the role of disciplinarian because he fears being called a child abuser. He has lost sight of the line between appropriate discipline and physical abuse. Rather than examine where that line exists and how he can use it in a healthy and useful manner, he has abdicated his family power and along with it the role of disciplinarian.

The role of disciplinarian is more negotiable than in years past. There may, in fact, be no need to have a "heavy" strike terror in the hearts of small children. Both father and mother have an important role to play in creating an environment with clear and consistent rewards and consequences. This is not a reflection of anger from the parent, but a clear and ordered world in which actions have logical consequences. This type of environment has an educational effect, helping children to learn proper behaviors without crushing their self-esteem. The goal of this discipline is to promote self-discipline within the child rather than by imposing it from the outside.

Father as Warrior

Every man, whether on active duty or not, faces something that no woman in our society has to face. He can be sent to war involuntarily; sent to die. The warrior is such a traditionally male role that women are not allowed to fight on the front line in the United States armed forces nor are they drafted. Although women serve in the armed forces, they are not allowed to carry rifles onto the field of battle. They are asked to play different roles, of support and ordnance.

Men do the fighting. From barroom brawls to boxing matches, it is men who fight. Turn on female kick-boxing tournaments, which are aired on some cable TV stations, and observe your reactions to women fighting, kicking and generally beating the hell out of each other. There is something uncomfortable in watching it, even in describing it. The idea of man as warrior is deeply ingrained in our psyche and it is not limited to Western cultures. It is a universal role whose roots go back to our beginnings as animals who need to survive and procreate.

Battle, real or symbolic, is part of the male psyche. But the modern warrior is much more likely to be a Walter Mitty, a henpecked husband dreaming of going down in a blaze of glory, rather than a real honest-to-goodness hero. There are few areas in which men can gain unfettered glory for acts of violence. It is no great loss, really, but there is still a hole there where something used to be.

There is still a need for warriors. While the battlefield has less to offer the modern warriors, there are still avenues for heroics. There are still places for bravery. There is still a need to fight for justice. There is poverty. There is greed. There is corruption. These are all battles that modern warriors can fight.

There is also, and most importantly, the battle in defense of the family. There is the internal struggle for emotional honesty with your wife and children. There are fights against the patterns of the past, against addictions, against temptations.

For men today, there is strength under fire when things are not going well. There is an economic downturn that calls on us to work longer hours to make ends meet while at the same time we need to spend *more* time with our families, not less. We are asked to share with our children and participate in their sports, their dance and their science fairs. We are asked to contribute the emotional energies we have been taught to conserve. We are challenged every day to be emotionally present for our families, to talk with them not only about their day at school but also about our day at the office. Our greatest battle in fatherhood is to avoid

retreating to the emotional distance that was the protective
bunkers of our fathers.

Father as Listener and Nurturer

One of the most important roles a father can play is simply to
pay attention to his children; to show them love, respect and
interest. In the movie *Camelot*, King Arthur is feeling frustrated
by his inability to understand his queen. He asks Merlin how to
handle a woman, for he had run out of ideas, all of which hadn't
worked anyway. The answer that he receives is: simply love her.
The same is true for your children. Love them——but in a way that
they understand and can feel nurtured.

Too often, parents only half listen to what their children say.
After a while, parents develop the reflex of being able to think
about something else while throwing in an occasional comment
like "That's great!" "That's nice, dear." But, it is a different thing
to listen fully. At the end of this book are chapters to guide you
toward better listening skills.

Most people are not great listeners. They prefer to do the
talking. But to listen to your children is to get to know them. It is
to find out what they like, what they dislike, how they are growing
and developing. It is to hear their dreams and accomplishments,
their failures and their defeats. It is to develop an appreciation of
them not just as children, but as people.

Sometimes children just need a listening ear. We can provide
an accepting mirror and also a place to test out new ideas and
receive feedback. Remember, our children will accept the ideas of
those around them to the extent their ideas are considered, too.

Father as Teacher

Providing feedback is part of the role of father as teacher. If the
mother is the child's first teacher, then the father is a close
second, at least, he should be. He teaches his child about the
world, not just book learning, but how men interact in society,
how men make friends, how men treat women, how men treat

themselves, how men express feelings, how men live, work, laugh and experience life.

By sharing your interests with your children, you will pass on your knowledge and enthusiasm about what it means to be alive. You will teach your child about the purpose of life.

Some of your interests will not be your child's. So, some of your education may fall by the wayside. But, it provides a valuable connection, a way to give concretely to your future, to prepare your child to deal with the world. It gives your child a gift that keeps giving——it gives your child a part of you and your spirit.

> A tradition I inherited from my father is bedtime reading. Every evening when we were younger, he would gather us on his bed and read chapters of books that were way beyond our own reading abilities. We traveled the globe with Phinneas Fogg in *Around the World in Eighty Days* and scaled the icy cliffs of Antarctica with Admunsen in stories of adventure at the South Pole.
>
> This is a tradition I will carry on with my own son. I plan to read a chapter from a book every evening before we go to bed. I will share a wide range of tales, sometimes making up adventure stories.
>
> - Robert, thirty-one, writer

Father as Confidence Builder

Recently my son turned four. Among his presents, he received a basketball game to be played indoors. We took the game into our playroom and Robbie immediately began to shoot the ball toward the basket. He missed the first five shots, and not just by a little bit. Think in terms of miles, here.

It was clear that without imposing a structured approach to the game Robbie would quickly gain a sense of failure and give up. So, I talked with him about a simple strategy. I marked the floor with masking tape and suggested that he begin shooting baskets from the first floor marker. When he felt that he was ready to move further back, he could shoot baskets from the second floor marker.

Before I left the room, Robbie had made two baskets. "I now a basketball man, daddy!" He practiced shooting baskets from three different floor markers, each time getting better and better. You could just see the pride and confidence in his eyes!

Both father and mother serve as mirrors to their children. The child's self-image is reflected in the view she holds of her parents and in the view of her held by them. Children need parents who believe their child is lovable, capable and valuable. Parents who believe in their children raise children who believe in themselves. Helping children build a secure and strong sense of self-worth is the key to successful parenting.

Father as Playmate

When I leave my professional role at the office, I turn into a very playful father and husband. More than once I have conspired with my children to surprise their mother by tackling her to the ground and then tickling her. I lead the charge, but they follow, giggling all the way. When I came home from work the other day, they couldn't wait to tell me that they had tackled and tickled mommy all by themselves. They have internalized the fun involved in playful interaction with their parents. I expect that they, too, will raise their children playfully.

Sometimes it goes a little too far. Like the time my son tried to move a wall with his shoulders and discovered that his nose got in the way. Or the time my daughter did her very best Mary Lou Retton impression and tumbled on to my stomach . . . while I was still sleeping! Yet, I encourage them to take risks. I want my children to learn to trust themselves as modest risk-takers. They need to learn how to channel their energies into constructive play rather than be afraid of their own power and their passions.

I always cringe when I hear a young child tell me that she is not allowed to get wild. I see many children who are taught that they must always be proper and polite, good little children all. How can such children ever learn about the passions that burn within them?

Recently, my sister's child began to cry when she spilled some soda on her dress. "My mommy will yell at me now! She told me always be neat. Now I'm a bad girl because I'm not neat." When we teach our children to control themselves so tightly that the child within them is not allowed to come out and play——teaching, in essence, that little children cannot be little children——then we are teaching our children to be afraid of the wonderfully spontaneous, inquisitive explorer who resides inside them.

Sure, my children and I like to wrestle and tickle. Robbie likes to be a Ninja Turtle, protecting everything that he surveys. Maddi likes to jump on top of me, all the while pretending that I am attacking her. My co-writer, Robert, plays "bucking bronco" with his son. Anders climbs on his back and holds on for dear life as Robert plays a wild, unbroken horse.

All the while, our wives are convinced that someday our children will be hurt by our roughhouseing. We say not to worry. This is part of learning about who daddy is and what daddy has to offer. And our wives give us that look——you know the one——with the head tilted a bit to the side, a smirk and eyes peeking around the corner of her cheek. It begs to say "I told you so!"

Studies have found that fathers tend to play more with their children than with their wives. They also play more active, physical games than mothers. It may be, in part, because the soft nestling relationship that is okay for mom is not acceptable for dad. So this wrestling is an acceptable physical channel through which men can express their love for their children.

It also may be part of introducing your child to the world. While the mother provides a safe haven, the father provides a wild ride, a heart-throbbing adventure. It is play that is safe at the same time it is terrifying. It teaches trust during play. It teaches risk taking. It teaches cooperation and taking turns. It teaches sharing. It teaches competition. It teaches limits, respect for physical effort and the phrase "that's enough." Father as playmate teaches children about the value of play within a structure of safety.

There are many aspects to being a father. There are many options from which to choose. You can build your model for fatherhood from these and other building blocks. You need to consider how much your role will be shaped by these different types of fathers.

LEARNING ABOUT FATHER

How do we learn about our fathers? Ask. My co-author describes how simply asking allowed him to learn about his father's past.

My father was a stranger. He was a nice stranger, but a stranger nonetheless. I knew him through what my mother told me about him. And while it wasn't lies, it was her view. It was a long time before I realized that my father must have had a childhood. If our fathers don't talk about themselves, most of what we learn about them is filtered through the eyes of our mothers. "Your dad is such a hard worker." "Your dad is so intelligent." "Your dad is a jerk." "Your father did this to us, never forget and never forgive him." Think about how much we have learned from our fathers, firsthand. We think we know our fathers, but mostly what we know is our mothers' views of our fathers. There is a big difference.

So we have these mothers who are trying to be helpful by telling us about this missing person we call our father. If the father is really missing, either physically or emotionally, we don't have much choice but to accept our mother's version of the story. At least until we can look into it for ourselves.

I knew my dad was always there if I needed him. If I ever was hard-pressed for money or the time the brakes went out on the car at the top of the Walt Whitman bridge, he knew how to fix things. But, I knew he was more than a banker or a mechanic.

It was at a meeting of a group of men in upstate New York that I heard one man's story about a trip to the airport with his dad during which he told his life story to his son. The son never forgot that experience. It planted the seed in my mind and I started asking my dad about his childhood. At first he couldn't see why I would be interested. He didn't realize that the greatest stories you can tell your kids are about your life. They beg to hear about them again and again. I don't think it matters how old you are. Hearing stories about your dad captures the little boy inside you. That little boy will be part spellbound and part interrogator.

Parents are among the only human beings who spring fully grown into your young life. Think about it. You grow up with your friends. You see them change from children wishing to be Superman, Batman or Barbie, to adults who wish to be President, CEO or retired. You have a real sense that they wore diapers in the past. It's different with your parents.

They always seem a few years ahead of you. And parents don't want to bore their kids with anecdotes from their past. Beside, it might erode some of their omnipotence. Sometimes you have to ask.

So, I asked my dad to take me for a tour of his old neighborhood. To my pleasure, he willingly agreed. We spent the better part of a day cruising the streets around the house where he grew up.

This was a different world. In the stone row homes, he had a childhood. They used to tear apart a couple of skates, mount them on the bottom of a board, attach a wooden crate for handles to make scooters that would make a deafening roar as they rumbled down the hills with metal wheels jostling over concrete.

We saw where he and a friend got into trouble for running a radio antenna across the rooftops, the graveyard where he worked cutting grass, the school he attended. I heard how he was coming out of the movie theater when war was declared. At first, he seemed amused that I was interested in family history, but he also was glad to take me on the tour. I even asked him about *his* father.

Robert Bly points out that "children visit the King, but adults make a place where the King can visit them."[2] He says every man should build two rooms in his head. One room is for the open and generous side of his father. The other room is for the father's secretive and distant side.

Bly suggests that we need to understand who would live in these rooms. We need to understand how our fathers would decorate and furnish them. If we are unable to furnish these rooms with our father's passions, interests, accomplishments, failures and other mementos of life, then we cannot expect to know him very well.

How would you furnish the rooms in which the two sides of your father would live? How can you find out enough about this man to know how to furnish them? You can ask your father, other family members, friends of the family or use your memories of the man you called father.

⟦ 6 ⟧
CHAPTER

Discovering the Child Within

When I was a child, I spake as a child, I thought as a child: but when I became a man, I put away childish things.

- I Corinthians

We were sitting around the porch talking about our childhoods. Peter spoke about the importance of being the best kid in the class. His parents made it clear that their sense of pride came from his excelling in school. No matter that he was alienated from his classmates because he was so bright, his parents wore his academic achievements like a banner to be waved and paraded about the city.

As an adult, Peter is a big man with great potential——often unrealized potential. He seldom misses an opportunity to miss an opportunity whether it be business, love or fatherhood. For a man with such great compassion and wisdom, he is forever haunted by the smart little fat boy he used to be.

I never understood the little fat boy inside Peter until today. In our ramblings about our respective life experiences, Peter fell into a memory. He was unprepared for its emotional power but was compelled to tell me about it.

When Peter was eleven years old he weighed 190 pounds. He was, literally, twice as big as any other child in his class. He was the class pet, the straight-A student and the object of great scorn and misunderstanding.

The cruelty of his classmates was evident in their total exclusion of Peter from their play groups. The boys from his elementary school would get together to play baseball or football after school and Peter was never invited. During those rare times when he forced himself to show up at the field, no one chose him to be on a team. Peter was left to watch, to dream, but never to play.

He turned to his best friends: books. He read books to escape the pain of being alone. He read books to escape the pain of feeling rejected. He read books to escape the pain of being Peter.

One day at the beginning of sixth grade, Peter's gym class held races. At first, each child was racing against the clock——the 50-yard dash, the 100-yard dash, how many sit-ups in a minute and a quarter-mile run. Peter completed each task with the grace of a beached whale. He hated to run because of his weight. He couldn't do sit-ups because of his weight. And, although he could jog a quarter mile, he found himself alone on the outside of the track while his classmates took the inside lanes.

Peter's teacher approached him that day with a giant compliment. The teacher noticed that Peter had completed each leg of the exercises. He told Peter how proud he was that Peter finished what he started. This was the sign of a young man who wouldn't give up. He said that type of guy on a team is invaluable. Then, the teacher asked Peter to be captain of the blue relay team. The blue team had to race the red team.

Peter had never been a leader like this before. He wasn't sure if he was happy, scared, angry or confused. He began to bark commands about how to organize his blue team——the directions fell out of his mouth with clarity and precision. His team was ready to begin its part of the race a full five minutes before the red team.

The race began. Peter's organization had helped the blue team to capitalize on its strengths better than the red team. Peter felt wonderful! Suddenly, he had a group of boys who wanted him to be their leader!

Peter placed himself at the end of the relay line. His group had a full lap lead in the race and the final lap was up to him. His teammate plunged the baton into Peter's hand and Peter's feet began to move quickly, briskly toward the finish line, seventy-five yards away. He pumped his arms and legs as hard as he could. Blood was flowing to parts of his body he didn't know existed. He was competing and winning. He heard the footsteps of the red team's anchor chugging along at warp speed. Peter could see the white chalk on the ground just a few yards away.

Fifteen yards from the finish line, the red team anchor passed Peter and won the race by less than a second. Peter finished the race, crestfallen. He fell to his knees crying that he had failed. "I'm a failure! I failed! I failed!"

Twenty-five years after the race, Peter found himself crying at the end of the story. He still felt the pain of losing the race. He never learned how to lose; he only learned how to fail. We talked about his belief that people either win or fail. He refused to admit that anything positive could come out of losing, either as an adult in a business deal or as a child in a relay.

This wonderful man who has so much to give finds himself unable to reach his greatest potential because of his fear that should he not win then he shall fail. He never learned that great lessons come from losing as well as winning.

I saw the tears streaming down my friend's cheek. I saw the pain of that fat little boy who failed at the race. And I thought shame on his parents for never teaching him the importance and value in knowing how to lose and how to profit from it.

THE CHILD WITHIN

John Bradshaw points out that the great paradox in parenting is that a child's beliefs about parents come from the parents.[1] We teach our children about the meaning of the world around them, about the meaning of being a child and of being a parent. If father is absent, if father surrenders his maleness to the mother, if father stays away from the emotional center of the family, then the child learns that fathering is characterized by absence, surrender and emotional distance. Paraphrasing Bradshaw, the more a child has been abandoned by his father, the more he tends to cling to and idealize his father and the way in which he was raised. Idealizing parents leads the child to idealize the way they raised you. As adults, they strive toward the fathering ideal from their childhood, hoping to understand how daddy felt, all the while turning into the distant, unavailable father to *his* child that his father was to him.

Thus, the adult-child parents his son the way his father parented him. The cycle continues and father remains an enigma.

Like Peter, we all have an inner child who lives with us throughout our adulthood. Some are happy and playful, keeping us connected with the joy of youth. Some are sad or injured, carrying a grudge, fat and unpopular, or tall and dorky. They continue to live within us and influence our decisions and our relationships with our children.

Every child deserves a warm, safe home. Every child deserves a loving, nurturing relationship with mother and father. Every child deserves the opportunities to take her unique potential and develop it through education, activities and interests. Every child deserves a chance at life, to be the best she can be and give the most she can offer. A child needs to be nurtured, embraced and accepted unconditionally. If these needs are not met, they are carried into adulthood.

The needs of this inner child can sometimes get in the way of our relationships with our children. My co-author recalls when he first realized the insistent demands of this child. His parents had divorced when he was ten years old. Years later, he stood on a riverbank watching his father and his son together. His father, an avid kayaker, had hauled his five-year-old grandson onto the back of his boat and was paddling him up and down the shoreline.

> I realized I was jealous. Part of me wanted to be riding on the back of that boat. But at the same time, I realized I was too old to do it. I no longer fit on the back of a kayak. I could never regain the time I lost with my father in my childhood. After my parents broke up, we saw my dad, but it was always an exciting weekend party, not the boring, slow and steady pace of growing up. But I realized I had to mourn that loss and let go. I had to grow up. I didn't want to let it get in the way of my relationship with my own child.

Men have an especially rough time of it. As boys, we are thrust aside sooner, pushed away earlier, than girls. There is even some evidence to suggest that mothers who breastfeed typically wean their male children sooner than their female children. We are taught to be tough.

Real men don't cry or show emotion. Real men don't need and don't show nurturing. We solve problems. We use our heads not our hearts. We follow orders and rules. We are taught to stay within accepted male boundaries. I remember seeing a three-year-old boy in the toy section of a department store. He picked up a doll and began to play with it, placing a bottle in the doll's mouth and singing it a song. His mother rushed over to him, pushed him away from the doll and hurled the toy toward another aisle.

"Don't play with a doll, Ben! That's for little girls. Boys don't play with dolls. No one will like you if you play with dolls," she said.

Boys are not supposed to be nurturing or caretakers. They are snails and puppy dogs' tails.

Like any small child, the child within you will not allow you to ignore him. If you don't know him, don't understand his vulnerabilities, needs and desires, you may find that the little boy inside you runs your life. He may turn you into an angry, brooding person. Or, you may find yourself buried in your work so as to avoid his insistent calls. You may find yourself drinking in a bar instead of going home or bed hopping from one to another looking for that missing piece of yourself, for that feeling of acceptance and love that needs to be fulfilled, but always is empty after the night is done.

Until you take care of the child within yourself, you won't have the resources to deal with another child, your own child. You might be able to go through the motions of parenting, but you won't be able to go through the *emotions* of parenting.

CHOOSING FOR TODAY

There comes a time when we need to choose between the child of our past and the child of our future.

For me, it was the day when there was a radio show on adult children of divorce at the same time my son's school was holding its annual harvest festival. I had been looking for a show on this topic for a long time and was looking forward to it. I had planned to stop home and listen to the show before coming back to the day-long festival. My son asked me to stay and make a scarecrow. I went home, just for a little while.

I turned on the program but quickly realized that I was living in the past. In trying to come to terms with my own childhood, I was missing out on my son's childhood. I was missing out on being a parent, just like my dad had done to me. I went back to the harvest festival and we made the wildest looking scarecrow ever created. I didn't abandon the little child within me. I still have a place in my heart for him. But, I am learning to enjoy him by having him participate in the joys and accomplishments of parenting my own son. My little child inside has found a way to be nourished and cared for while no longer needing to compete with my son or trying to run my adult life.

- Robert, thirty-one, writer

When you find out that the tooth fairy is not real, it is an awakening. But when you *become* the tooth fairy, it is growing up. In the early part of your life, there was always someone there to look after you. Suddenly, you are that someone. This is a challenging transition. You must take care of yourself and take care of a family. You are thrown into a life with no soft edges, with countless and difficult decisions, grey areas and trade-offs.

Like many transitions, this one comes with a new title: Dad. Congratulations on your promotion. Like a baptism, you gain a new name and new responsibilities. It is time, definitely time, to leave never-never land.

This is not to say that some people don't make the leap into adulthood before that; not that some people don't check out of adulthood after their children are born. But, if you have been putting it off, planning to do it next week or next month, children will often provide the added push you need to enter adulthood. So while you are making the transition to parenthood, you will be shifting to adulthood at the same time.

You cannot be a father to your own child until you are able to take care of the little child inside you. You need to understand what that little boy inside needs from you and from others. You need to find a way to take the little boy inside you by the hand and provide him with what he needs to be whole. You need to teach yourself that you cannot recapture your childhood, but you can understand how the wounds of your childhood can be healed through the understanding of your own adult guidance.

PART THREE

TRAVELER'S TALES

[[7]]

CHAPTER

Why Did You Do It?

Familiarity breeds contempt -- and children.

- Mark Twain

A healthy marriage forms the foundation of a healthy family. And a healthy family stays healthy, in part, when couples can plan and prepare for major transitions such as having children.

The decision to have a baby will have a tremendous effect on your marriage and future. It will change the way you think about yourself, your responsibilities and your commitments. It will affect you as no other experience in the world. Nothing, but nothing, prepares you for the unique and exhilarating experience of being a father.

However, there are many different ways to plan for a baby. Some are planned far in advance while others are conceived in the heat of the moment. Some arrive because of a mutual decision to get pregnant and some at the insistence of one partner. Some are the result of years of struggle with medical technology, others of a single accident.

Therefore, it seemed that we needed to understand what motivated our expectant fathers to have children in the first place. When we asked our expectant fathers about their decision to have children, we discovered that they did not all agree to the importance of being emotionally involved with their new family. Several held ideas about marriage that appeared immature. Typically, these were voiced by men who had gotten married shortly after high school or college.

I got married right out of college. My ideas about marriage, family and parenthood were vague, undefined and incredibly self-centered. Marriage was an extension of our college relationship, only now we would share expenses. The thought of having children was for more mature couples, not for me. I never thought of fatherhood. I never considered myself father material. Our first child wasn't planned, it just happened. So, my introduction into fatherhood had nothing to do with my being ready. It had to do with bad luck.

- Bobby, twenty-two, assistant manager

Brenda got pregnant at the end of our senior year of high school. I decided I would do the manly thing and marry her. Even now, my parents tell me that I'm wrong to bring a baby into this world. I don't have a steady job and Brenda is at a two-year college. But, we love each other. We know that being parents is gonna be tough. But, she has it figured out. She'll stay home with the baby and I'll work as much as I can to make sure that there is enough money for us.

- Joey, nineteen, store clerk

Bobby is typical of men who married in their early twenties. They reported that they gave little or no thought to the notion of fatherhood. As a group, these men viewed their career as the center of their lives. They were concerned about the health of their marriage, but figured that the relationship would take care of itself as time passed. As fatherhood approached, they continued to focus their energies away from their homelife, to outside activities. It was the birth of their child and the multitude of changes required of both mother and father that forced them to change their focus. Even several months after the birth, some of these men were hard-pressed to accept their family responsibilities and commitments as primary.

Joey was a minority in our workshops. Over the course of two years, only one expectant father was in high school when the pregnancy occurred. Joey, of course, was frightened by the prospect of fatherhood, though he put up a tough front during class. Underneath it all was a young man, struggling to come to terms with adult responsibilities and commitments thrust upon him by the need to behave "the right way." Joey's ideas about fatherhood revolved around the notion that a father brings in money. He did not believe he had to participate in his child's upbringing because that would take time away from working at odd jobs that would bring in more money.

FIRST COMES LOVE, THEN COMES MARRIAGE, THEN COMES . . .

Most of our expectant fathers told us that their decision to have children was not well planned nor considered. They put little effort into preparing for fatherhood. These men carried a loose-fitting plan in their heads that went roughly like this: First I meet a girl. When I fall in love, we will live together for a while. If that works out, then we will get engaged. After engagement, we will marry. Then, sometime within the next three-to-five years we will have children. Childbearing will be over before I reach thirty (or thirty-five).

> Patti and I had been married about two years when her parents began to give her static about not having children yet. We had always wanted to have kids, but felt pushed by her folks to have kids real quick. We had some pretty nasty fights between us. We fought about how her parents were sticking their noses into our marriage. In fact, Patti left me for a couple of days and lived at home because of the fights we were having. I wanted to decide to have children when I was ready. I thought that Patti was being pressured by her parents. In the end, we got pregnant in our third year. I guess that I felt it was time to have kids. We had been married a while and everyone expected it of us.
>
> - Ed, twenty-seven, computer programmer

> One day Sarah asked me if I was ready to have kids. I remember asking her how I knew if I was ready. She told me that other people know they are ready when they have been married for at least three years and felt that the marriage was going to last. That sounded like a good reason to me, so we decided to have a family.
>
> - Richard, twenty-three, assistant manager

Many of these men put no effort into thinking about the varied and complex issues related to having a family. They believed that if the marriage was stable and they loved their wife, having children was the next logical step. There was no consideration of *why* having a family is important. There was no consideration of *how* children would change their relationship. There was no consideration of *whether* they were ready financially, emotionally or psychologically. There simply was no consideration; period.

As I listened to these men describe their unexamined ideas about having children, I realized that I was listening to the reasons of *their* fathers, men who believed that having children was a logical, commonsense next step in the development of a marriage. Men who would not examine reasons for having children. Men who would not plan about family development. Men who left the decision and planning for having children up to their wives or to some poorly understood imaginary timetable.

The following exchange from a workshop was typical of such expectant fathers. JG is me; WP, the workshop participant.

JG: Tell me what being a father means to you.

WP: I don't know. Never thought of it. Guess I'll find out in a few weeks, huh?

JG: Then, tell me about your ideas about being a father.

WP: I don't know. (Prolonged silence) I just don't know. Ask me again after we have our kid.

JG: Do you think that being a father is important?

WP: Yeah, I guess so. Never thought about it much. Guess I should, but I don't.

JG: You're a manager, right? Let's say that you are interviewing a potential employee for a job. Every time you ask him a question about the job he is applying for, he says that he doesn't know what he thinks about the job. He says that he just needs to wait until the job begins before he can decide how he will approach its tasks and responsibilities. You offer to talk with him about what other people have learned from this position and you want the applicant to talk with others who have held the job so as to learn more about what is expected. Still, the applicant says that he'll wait until the job starts to decide how to approach it. Would you hire the guy?

WP: Of course not. The guy lets you know that the job isn't important to him. If he's not willing to put the time into learning about the job now, how do I know that he will show me anything different - effortwise - when he is on the job? Na, he's telling me that the job ain't important to him.

JG: That's exactly my point about fathering. You need to be prepared before the job starts.

WP: Why? We're talking about fathering here. Not someone's job.

In contrast to Bobby, Warren is typical of another subgroup of our expectant fathers, men in their second marriages.

When I married my second wife, I was in my early thirties. I not only wanted a committed, monogamous relationship but I also wanted children. I knew when I met my wife that I was prepared for a commitment, for a family and for self-sacrifice.
                                    - Warren, thirty-three, accountant

We found that most men who remarried during their early thirties had a distinctly different view of marriage, monogamy, commitment and responsibility toward their new marriage compared to their previous marriage. These expectant fathers talked about placing their families at the center of their lives. They felt ready to take on the thrill and excitement of fatherhood. They felt they were emotionally prepared to embrace the responsibility of supporting and participating in a strong family-focused marriage.

Other fathers wanted to have children as a celebration of their relationship with their wives. As a group, these men appeared more concerned about and focused upon the well-being of their spouse than upon the idea that they were soon to have a newcomer to the family. As exemplified below by Andy, these men felt that they would make great parents with their current spouse. The decision to have a child was based upon the "fit" between husband and wife as potential parents rather than any internal assessment about being ready to be a parent.

The notion that I carried in my head about marriage was based upon my parents: Open, honest, active, sharing and equal. I looked long and hard for a partner who could share in both the values and activities. So often disappointment came when I discovered a current love might share the values but be a couch potato. It worked the other way, too. I found many people with whom to play, but few who also shared the same values and intellectual pursuits.

Of course, it took me years to figure out that I wanted a family just like the one in which I was raised, not just any family. Without being aware of it, I developed an intolerance for people who did not nurture or play with me. I was rather rigid.

When I discovered my wife, I saw the same values, the same playfulness and the same curiosity about the world. I knew that she and I would fit together well. I intuitively knew that we would be dynamite as a couple and as parents.

> - Andy, thirty-four, English teacher

A fifth subgroup was composed of men who had remarried after forty-five years of age. All these men had been married previously and had children from a former marriage. Of the fifteen who fit this category, thirteen married a younger woman in her late twenties who was having her first child. These men described their interest in having children in terms of what they could give to their brides.

I've done my time bringing up kids. If I hadn't met Betsy, I never would have thought of another child. They take so much energy. Plus, I'm looking forward to easing back on my workload. A new child will put a lot of pressure on me, financially. On the other hand, Betsy has never had a child before. I promised her that we would have at least one child. I know the experience is important to her. And, she promised to be in charge of most of the child care. She understands that I've already paid my dues.

> - Eddie, forty-eight, attorney

Two men married women who were in their late thirties. Both men and women had children by a previous marriage, yet made a decision as a couple that their marriage would be better confirmed through their union as parents.

We screwed up the first time with our kids. My first marriage was so bad that my kids suffered terribly. I wanted to prove to myself that I am a good father. Meeting and marrying Leigh gave me that chance. I know that she feels the same way. This is our last chance to prove that we can be good parents. Our children will be given everything that I didn't give my daughters.

- Stan, fifty-one, businessman

A concern that we had about some fathers was their focus on fathering as a way to prove something to themselves. During our workshops we attempted to stress that good fathering means putting the welfare and development of the child first. Fathering is not to confirm to the father that he is the little engine that could. It is to provide a child who will carry on your family legacy with the tools, skills and nurturance that will prepare her for a successful, healthy and happy life.

OUR NEW FATHER: REFLECTION AND PARTICIPATION

Those fathers-to-be who talked about their anticipations of family life showed much uncertainty about their purpose for having a family. Some talked about family as an accident. Others talked about family as an expression of guilt, holding the promise that through their second marriage they could prove to themselves that they really are good parents who were led astray during their first go-round.

The decision to have children needs the firm conviction that we are committed to family life and values. We need to be clear that family requires sacrifice, responsibility and hard work. Fathers need to show their children how a man nurtures. They need to show how a man loves and gives physical, as well as emotional, support. Being a father means caring deeply about the everyday events that define and direct his family.

Fathers need to have their feet firmly planted inside their family unit. They may take day trips to the office, maybe even an occasional business trip. But, their focus is on bringing their energies, their passions and their loyalties to their children and wives.

The decision to have a child needs to reflect both a personal as well as a marital decision about your readiness. This decision needs to include a commitment to who you will be as a father and what your family will stand for as a living, growing, striving emotional organism.

We are asking more from you than participation in the emotional lifeblood of your family. We are asking you to take time to consider, to plan and to reflect on the awesome responsibilities upon which you are embarking during your journey toward fatherhood. We want you to think about your legacy, your purpose and your meaning as a man and as a father.

If your decision is made in haste, you may shortchange both yourself and your children. Remember the old saying, "fools rush in where wise men fear to tread." Deciding to have a child is among the most important decisions you will ever make. In my view, it is second only to the decisions you make about how to nurture and develop your family.

If your decision is made with considered reflection and discussion with your wife, then include in those discussions explorations about the meaning of being a father, a mother and a family. Develop a set of guidelines and expectations about how your family can become the very best example of healthy family functioning.

My graduate school mentors used to remind me that the mark of a great teacher is when the student is cultivated and encouraged to surpass the expertise and skill of his teacher. Families need to have such lofty goals: To encourage and support each family member to reach beyond today and touch their possibilities for tomorrow.

[[8]]

CHAPTER

The First Trimester

My daughter has made a monumental decision. After watching her mother suffer through the first trimester of our current pregnancy, Maddi made an announcement at dinner the other night. "Mommy has been sick a lot from the new baby that is growing inside her tummy. I know that I will have babies when I am older, like Nina." Her cousin, Nina, is 10-years old. Maddi has a little to learn about age-appropriate behaviors. "But, I don't want to be sick like mommy so I want my husband to have my babies, instead."

THE BELL RINGS TO START THE ROUND

Normal people just don't act like a woman pregnant for the first time, or at least my wife didn't. Debra began to eat lemons. I mean, she ate them straight; cut them in half and settled down in her chair and noshed. Five years later, I still have an automatic pucker when I think of those lemon orgies.

Weekends were different than before. First, her sleeping habits changed. She would wake up, get dressed, eat breakfast and announce that she was ready for a nap. Nap time lasted until 10:00 A.M. Then, she would wake up and feel sick. Sometimes she wouldn't feel sick. Those were the days that she was "the bitch from beyond." Everything hurt or bothered her. I knew that she didn't want to feel such discomfort. I understood that her intentions were not to simulate a tornado, but she was a bit difficult to live with. And she felt horrible.

Afternoons were often spent napping, reading and throwing up. She attempted to keep up her jogging, but often felt too exhausted to complete her course. This went hand-in-hand with a sudden surge in her appetite. Instead of salads, pasta and fruit, she wanted red meat. She didn't care if it was cooked or still on the cow. The redder the better; followed, of course, by the ever-present lemons.

Television was tuned to the *Discovery* or *Lifetime* cable channels. Every program on pregnancy was devoured. Every book, every article was read. She subscribed to four or five thousand pregnancy and parenting magazines (at least it seemed like that many). She began to worship a new god, T. Berry Brazelton.

I admit acting differently, too. When I came home from work I would hug and kiss my wife. Then, I would bend low, put my mouth on her stomach and say hello to the growing embryo. I did this in the grocery store, too, and got some pretty strange looks.

Bedtime was an interesting experience. She would get into bed, pull the covers over her just like before she was pregnant. Then, without notice, she would rip the covers off saying, "I'm so warm. Open the windows." Then about thirty minutes later she would complain that she was too cold. Thirty minutes after that she was warm again. And, well you get the idea. She was no happy camper.

Noises bothered her as they never did before. "Put the dogs outside tonight. No, keep them in. No, you better put them out because their snoring will bother me. But, they'll bark at every car, cat or rabbit that's within five miles of here. Besides, I feel more secure knowing they're in the house. Keep them in but don't let them sleep in our room. But, I really sleep better with them outside. All right, I feel guilty about keeping them outside . . . let them stay in. . . ." The beginning of her pregnancy brought confusion to my lovely wife's world and completely baffled mine.

First trimester brings with it several emotional changes that are experienced directly by your wife and have ripple effects on you and your marriage. Your wife may gravitate toward different behaviors than my wife, but there will be changes. You can count on it.

If you are unclear about what causes these changes, I suggest two things. First, talk with your wife about what you see and explain that you are eager to understand her experiences. For example, you may want to say something like the following:

> I know the past few weeks have been full of changes for you. For me, too. I want to understand and share this pregnancy with you. I want to know what the experience is like for you and I want to talk about my feelings, too. I want to know when you feel a bit off, when you feel energized, when you feel sluggish or when you feel moody. I want to let you know when I am feeling a bit dazed, bewildered or excited. I am committed to taking the journey through pregnancy with you, as someone you can always talk to and rely on.

This is only one of several different ways to approach your wife during her pregnancy. The clear message is that you want to be involved in the ups and downs of your wife's pregnancy.

Second, get your hands on some pregnancy books. I suggest Mike and Nancy Samuels' *The Well Pregnancy Book* and *The Well Baby Book*; Geraldine Lux Flanagan's *The First Nine Months of Life*; Arlene Eisenberg, Heidi Murkoff and Sandee Hathaway's *What to Expect When Your Expecting*; Dr. Sheldon H. Cherry's *Understanding Pregnancy & Childbirth*, Sherry Jimenez', *Pregnant Woman's Comfort Guide*, and Sheila Kitzinger's, *Pregnancy: The Psychological Experience*. My wife slept with the Eisenberg, *et. al.*, book under her pillow. It was her guide, security and soothsayer.

FINDING OUT

We asked our expectant fathers how they discovered that their twosome was soon to be a threesome. We found that there were many different reactions to the news. Some dads-to-be were surprised, they couldn't believe they were pregnant.

> We had talked about having children and decided we would begin to try to get pregnant some time next year. In preparation, Nancie went off the pill. Two months later, she was pregnant. She called me at

work to tell me. My office mate tells me that all the blood rushed from my face. I was white. I hung up and couldn't stop shaking. I was excited. I was scared. I was confused. I was going to have a baby.
                                                    - Ron, twenty-five, office manager

We had talked about having a baby. We knew that we were ready for it. We also wanted to have a baby before my dad died. He's been pretty sick for a while. I never expected that she would get pregnant so quickly. I was thrilled for us and also proud to be able to tell my dad about it. When I told my dad that his first grandchild was on the way, he broke down, got real emotional and thanked us . . . We were so moved. It really showed us how important it is to share with him.
                                                    - Mort, thirty-three, salesman

Others felt something was different in their marriage but couldn't figure it out until they were told there was a little one on the way.

Gail was acting a bit off. I couldn't put my finger on it, but I thought that she was getting sick or something. She was sick in the morning and always tired. Something was wrong. I figured she had a virus. She said she was pregnant. I told her she was crazy. She proved to me I was the one who was wrong. At least, I knew something was different, give me credit for that.
                                                    - Alan, twenty-four, carpenter

Some husbands knew their wives were pregnant. I fell into this category. My wife always has trouble breathing when she first conceives. She is usually diagnosed as having a slight asthmatic attack. She has never had asthma at any other time in her life except when two weeks pregnant. We have had three pregnancies and each time I noticed the change in breathing before she did and suggested that she was pregnant, to her skeptical reception.

I could just tell that she was pregnant. Her color was different. There was a different sense about her. I can't describe it but I felt it. There was no doubt in my mind.
                                                    - Rob, twenty-six, medical resident

MINOR DISCOMFORTS OF PREGNANCY

There is no dispute that the lion's share of the work during pregnancy is the woman's—no great insight here. But, there is little attention paid to, and even less advice given to, husbands who live through this unusually tumultuous experience. First-time fathers, in the first trimester, often feel like strangers in a stranger land.

Some men discovered, during the first trimester, that pregnancy changed the direction and character of the marriage.

> The day she discovered that she was pregnant was the last day that she thought of herself as a career woman. To her surprise and mine, Sally found that being pregnant helped her to get in touch with a strong need to nurture her future offspring at home rather than focus on work. She *wanted* to be a mother who stayed home with her children.
>
> This was not what we had talked about. When we got married, she was insistent upon balancing work and family. I expected that she would continue to work soon after delivering. Once pregnant, her entire view of her role as a worker, as a mother and as a woman changed. I was unprepared. I felt trapped and scared. Where were we going to get the money?
>
> - Marty, thirty-five, consultant

> I was threatened and torn. I wanted to provide her with what she needed to raise our child as she saw fit. If that meant staying at home with our child, then that's the way it'll be. However, if I had known that she would abandon her career and want to stay home, exclusively, for the first few years, I would have waited a few more years before conceiving. But, we had no crystal ball to show us how each of us would react when we actually got pregnant.
>
> - Greg, thirty-one, graduate student

My experience was similar. No one prepared us, and I did not anticipate that being pregnant would change fundamentally the way Debra wanted to live her life. We have always been one of those couples who talk about and plan our future. Our execution of those plans may be less than perfect, but sketching our path became a rewarding and intimacy-producing pastime. Her fork in the road, the choice between staying home with her baby or continuing her path as a career woman, was never discussed because she had been unyielding in her determination to maintain her career. Her career was her power, her identity, her passion. We never talked about finding a middle ground between career woman and mother because she appeared so sure that she would immediately return to work after the baby was six weeks old. Once she discovered she was pregnant all that changed overnight.

Sharing How You Feel

Couples will experience a complex mosaic of feelings, desires and conflicts during pregnancy and so you should talk continuously about how *you* both are coping with changes in the marriage. Discuss the changes you have noticed in yourselves and in each other. Describe how you feel about these changes.

Many men found themselves becoming scattered and disorganized during the pregnancy. It was almost as if the thought of new responsibilities resulted in these men acting more childish.

> I know I looked foolish during our first trimester. I committed myself to as many different outside activities as I could. I joined a basketball league and a bowling league and bought season tickets to the 76ers' games. When I look back, I realize I was out of the house more than in the two years before. I guess I was scared of losing my freedom and, during the first trimester, I acted all that out.
> - Carl, twenty-eight, school psychologist

> I'm ashamed to admit it, but the thought of having a child after so many years of freedom lead me astray. I had an affair. It was totally wrong, completely irresponsible. I think it was because being with another woman helped me to feel that I still had my freedom.
> - Eddie, forty-nine, attorney

Other expectant fathers became more organized and home-focused with the news of their pregnancy.

My first impulse was to organize everything financially. I consolidated our bank accounts. I checked with our health insurance coverage to make sure that pregnancy was covered. I took out a life insurance policy. I hired a cleaning service for the house. I even began to clean the bathtub and change the kitty litter. I was a man transformed.

- Bobby, thirty-three, writer

I spoke with my boss and told him that I needed to arrange for a more normal schedule. I know that I couldn't deal with a nine-to-five routine, but I needed to know that I could be home at a more reasonable hour than the past four years. Since he just had another child, he understood my concern. I've been coming home by 7:00 P.M. for almost four months now.

- Bobby, twenty-six, store manager

In my case, first trimester pregnancy resulted in Debra's redirecting her attention from our relationship to her bodily concerns. This makes perfect sense considering the physical changes that were happening. Meanwhile, I spent many mornings and evenings preparing our meals. I cleaned more. I ironed more. I washed more. I swept more. I shopped more. And, worst of all, I had to take care of the kitty litter.

But, no one had prepared me for the continuous loss of gratitude. No had one prepared me for her preoccupation with the changes happening inside her. No had one prepared me for changes in a marriage that grew more lonely for me, a partner who was moodier and a lifestyle that was increasingly constricted.

These may sound like small bitches compared with the wonder of having a baby, but my marriage was being affected. Social etiquette encouraged me to conform, to ignore my needs. Debra was the one undergoing all the changes, right?

Wrong! Our marriage was changing and we had little control over it. She was changing. She was different——moody, tired, less playful, sleeping more during the day and sleeping less during the night. She was preoccupied, somewhat scattered and definitely less interested in socializing with friends.

Our intimacy was different, too. Playful roughhousing tapered off because she was sore, swollen or tired. Sex was different. She was sensitive to her gradual weight gain and physical changes and increasingly uncomfortable with her body image, which lead her to be less revealing to me. This caused a decrease in the frequency of our sexual and physical intimacy. Hell, I felt the same. But, Debra was different. And that put a strain on our marriage. By the end of the first trimester, I missed our prepregnancy routine. I missed our playfulness, our lifestyle. I wanted a little assurance that after our pregnancy we would get back to being us. But, I didn't know how to talk about this without offending her or appearing insensitive. So, I kept quiet. It was a mistake.

Changes in Attention

Our expectant fathers, too, knew that important changes were happening in their relationship during the first trimester of pregnancy. Some became angry. Others withdrew. Many avoided or denied the changes and pretended that nothing was changing. Only a few brave men took the initiative to talk with their wives about their concerns.

> Marge and I have always built our relationship on openness and communication. This was no different. I was feeling neglected and I talked with her. She was wonderful, explaining that she wanted to talk with me, too. That's all it took -- an acknowledgement that we needed to talk more.
>
> - Andy, thirty-two, broker

> I was pissed off that Sandy was getting all the attention. I wanted to be part of all the excitement, but no one wanted to talk with me, only with her. This had never happened before. I told her I wanted more of her time and energy. I told her that her responsibility was to give me what I needed and to worry about the baby later.
>
> - Jerry, twenty-nine, media professional

Jerry's reaction is typical of a small, but loud, voice among our group. Jerry was the youngest of five children, a popular and successful media professional who was accustomed to being the star. He was a star in his profession, a star in his family of origin and, before pregnancy, the star in his marriage. Pregnancy directed peoples' attention to his wife and Jerry was unaccustomed to being in the background. He insisted that Sandy, and her friends and family, continue giving him "star" recognition despite her pregnancy. His outlook was characteristic of about fifteen percent of the men who participated in our interviews.

Changes in Commitment

First trimester of pregnancy witnessed several of our expectant fathers changing what they thought about commitment toward their marriage and commitment toward themselves.

Several expectant fathers felt a need to become more self-involved, fearing the expectations they thought would be placed on them during the first trimester. Usually, these dads-to-be were uncertain about wanting to have a child and played out that ambiguity by indulging themselves. These men were committed to an image of themselves as independent, carefree and unprepared for being a grown-up.

> Looking back, I know I wanted nothing to do with her or her pregnancy. I hated the idea of being a father and of any commitment to my marriage that would change my way of living. I was having a blast with my friends and had no intention of growing up just because a baby was coming along. I refused to give up my card games, my Friday nights out with the boys or my cycle racing. I figured I was gonna have to be grown-up for a lot of years. No baby would care if I was around during the first year or so. She don't know who the daddy is. She don't know nothin' better.
>
> - Nicky, twenty-three, video store manager

> I didn't want the baby at first. During the first trimester, everything I did was to get away from the pregnancy. I didn't want the baby. I didn't want to get married. I was embarrassed by her pregnancy and felt that she got pregnant on purpose.
>
> - Joey, nineteen, store clerk

> I really wanted a new chance at having a baby. But when Leigh actually got pregnant, well that scared me. I spent ungodly hours at the club, playing golf, cards or drinking. I was really confused.

I'd failed terribly before and felt torn between wanting to prove that I can be a good parent and feeling afraid that if I failed again I would prove that I was, in fact, a failure at being a parent. I guess it really is about facing the anger of my children from my first marriage. All along they said I screwed up. Failing here would prove them right and lay responsibility entirely on me. I wasn't prepared to face that. At least, I wasn't ready then, at the beginning of the pregnancy.

- Stan, fifty-one, businessman

Most men fell into a group that could be described as having redirected their energies toward their wives. These men were attentive, concerned, available and a bit clumsy, tripping over their good intentions to make life easier for their pregnant spouses.

I loved taking care of my wife during her pregnancy. The first trimester showed me I could really make a difference in the house. Sharon was so sick during the first six or eight weeks that I had every opportunity to help her out. I was sure this would show her how much I loved her.

- John, thirty-two, businessman

For years, I promised Carly I would pay her back for all the sacrifices she made during the early years of our marriage. When she got pregnant, I knew that this was the time to pay her back. I was there for her.

- Elliott, twenty-seven, salesman

There is another side to these men who recommitted themselves toward their wives because of the pregnancy. In general, these men talked about giving. They may have given attention, taken on more responsibilities around the house, spent more time staying at home and talking or caretaking or reorganizing. However, a few men talked about how it felt after their energies were redirected toward their partner and their wives did not give back equally.

Most wives were experiencing physical changes resulting from the pregnancy: morning sickness at different times during the day, unusual tiredness and moodiness and a general sense of loss of

energy. It was no surprise that some women did not respond to
their husbands' giving in a way that the husbands expected.

> I was really into our pregnancy. So, I wanted to cater to Susan. I
> brought her breakfast in bed on the weekends. I would wake up
> before her and quietly go down to the kitchen and make her
> breakfast. She always had talked about wanting the "Lifestyle of the
> Rich and Famous," so I made her breakfast all the time.
>   I would take the breakfast tray upstairs, sit at the end of the
> bed and wait for her to wake up. More times than not, she would
> open her eyes and complain. She'd talk about how she didn't sleep
> good, about how tired she was and that she wanted to be left alone.
>   I felt really pissed off by that because I was doing something
> really nice for her and she didn't even say thank you. After a few
> weeks of this, I stopped being nice to her in the morning.
>   We had some pretty heated arguments over her rejecting me.
> I was real disappointed that, after all the times she said that she
> wanted me to do things like this, she would push me away like that.
>   - Drew, twenty-seven, customer service rep.

I have an untested belief about men. Below our macho "I'm
a man" exterior lies in all of us a little boy. Some little boys want
to please while others want to play. Some want to be obedient
while others want to throw off responsibility and roll around in
the mud. Different little boys live inside each of us. Some are
freer to do what they want while others lie in chains tied to a ball
of rules and regulations about what "good boys do."

When opportunities to please their wives arose, most of our
fathers took advantage of them, tryhing to do something special.
An unspoken part of this implied contract was "if I do something
special for you, then you will notice my good deed and recognize
my good, hard work." When their hard work was not acknowledged, the little boys within these men became angry and ignored
subsequent opportunities. Drew, in my judgement, is similar to
many men who pick the right time to do something nice, but hold
inappropriate expectations about how their wives will respond to
these gestures of selflessness and helpfulness.

A small, but vocal group of men didn't understand why they
had to change anything in *their* lives because of their wives'

pregnancy. They knew that their wives were pregnant. They usually supported and encouraged their wives during their pregnancy. They even were excited about the upcoming transition from marriage to family. Yet, they hadn't a clue about how they needed to redirect their time and energy to increase their participation in the marriage.

> In the beginning, Cheryl didn't make any demands on me. I was teaching (at the local university) and kept up my usual schedule of research, reading, library time, professional meetings and the like. It wasn't until I came back from San Diego that Cheryl laid into me for being so uninvolved in her pregnancy.
>
> I mean I really had no idea that she needed me to help out. She looked like she was handling everything fine. And I told her so. She lashed back at me with something about how I need to notice her more than the covers of my journals.
>
> Until then, I really just didn't think that she needed me any more. Hell, it was only the first two or three months of pregnancy. How hard could that be?
>
> - George, thirty-two, college teacher

> There were a couple of times when Jeanie called me at the office. She asked if I could come home earlier to help her out. I told her I had a lot of work to do and her stuff could wait. I did that all the time during her pregnancy. It wasn't until she took herself to the hospital because she was bleeding that I realized I had to make changes at the office. I did it reluctantly, but at least I made those changes.
>
> - Art, twenty-six, lawyer

Our new father-to-be needs to get his head out of the sand. We need to remember that our wives are experiencing a physical, emotional, biological, chemical and occasionally spiritual change resulting from this life growing within her. She may find herself more self-absorbed than before. This is usually temporary.

We need to learn that giving to her may be all the reward that we get, at least for a while. As much as it sounds corny, we need to accept the joy of giving without always expecting resounding applause from our audience. We need to be a little bit less demanding, less selfish and less concerned about our egos. We need to become more giving for giving's sake, more accepting of our partner's shifting moods, and more expressive about our enthusiasm to be with her every step of the way.

Our energies should be directed toward the idea of a marriage that is going through the transition to a family. We need to direct our energies to the notion that all transitions take work. All transitions take effort. All transitions take cooperation. All transitions need coordination and communication. Her part is to care for the growing embryo tucked safely away inside her. The most important way to take care of that new life is for your wife to take care of herself, first. If she has the energy, then she takes care of you.

You, on the other hand, have to strike a balance between your need to look after yourself and the obligation you have to take care of your wife and her new charge. The more you redirect your attention toward your new family life, the greater will be the future rewards for you, your wife and your new child.

STRIKING A BALANCE

We have spoken about the marital changes some men experience during the beginning stages of pregnancy. Here are some open-ended statements to complete that will help you decide how you want to redirect your energies during this period.

- When I think of men who change because of a wife's pregnancy, I usually think of someone who is:
- The type of man who takes on responsibilities that should be a woman's job around the house is:
- When my friends see me spending more time around the house with my wife, they will think that I'm:
- This is my wife's "wish list" of activities, sharing or time that she would like to see me give to her during this pregnancy:
- These are four new directions my wife feels my energies should take during her pregnancy:

Second Trimester

You have waited for this ever since you decided to have a baby. Place your hands on your wife's belly and you can feel your prodigy——the center of your future life——kicking, tumbling and doing chin-ups. Four months into your wife's pregnancy, you are able to more fully participate in your baby's growth. It is during the second trimester that fathers finally are able to feel this new life, a life that has been growing inside your wife for months, yet hiding from you . . . until now.

Second trimester brings more change. Many men reported their wives felt less active and less social. Most of our dads-to-be talked about a decrease in their wives' morning sickness, although a few described almost no noticeable changes.

The most obvious changes are the maternity clothes and talk about plans for the baby. Then there are the cravings and an increase in appetite.

To Beth, the pregnancy was real from the third or fourth week on. She was sick. She read books about every possible change that was happening to her and to our baby. For me, I felt I became involved the first day I felt my baby move. I wanted to talk to Beth about how excited I was. I never thought I would react like such a kid. But, I wanted to talk to everyone. I was really bummed out when she acted so unaffected. She felt excited for me but reminded me that she has been just as excited for over four months! I understood her view, I guess, but I felt pretty annoyed that she couldn't come out of her own private world long enough to let me enjoy this!

- Mike, thirty-three, insurance executive

Your wife will always be one step ahead of you during pregnancy. She knows, before you, that she is pregnant. She feels, before you, the life growing within her. She bonds, before you, with the budding embryo. She will know, before you, when it is time to give birth.

During the first trimester, your wife was beginning a process of mother-child bonding based, in part, on her awareness of physical changes within her. Her bonding arose from the inescapable knowledge that she was sustaining a new life. For you, though, knowledge of your new baby was an abstraction. There was nothing tangible tying you to your growing baby.

The most you could do was to talk about the idea of having a baby. You could talk about your understanding of pregnancy, of fatherhood, of motherhood and of family. But, there was nothing inside to touch you emotionally. Sure, you could talk with your wife about how she felt, but she was focused on the internal changes brought on by the pregnancy and only marginally aware of bonding with her baby.

Second trimester brings an exciting, yet potentially problematic, challenge to most couples. Your partner has already spent three months pandering and loving this life within her. Second trimester brings an increasing awareness of the physical and emotional reality of her baby. She feels it kick. She feels it move. She knows she is symbiotic with a life that she is bringing into the world.

In contrast, the father is only beginning to become aware of the reality of this pregnancy. Like many fathers, you may be experiencing mixed emotions. Some men feel an emerging sense of fatherhood. Finally, the pregnancy feels personal. You want to share this revelation with your spouse. She wants to share, too. However, she has already moved beyond your stage of awareness. She felt that excitement during the first trimester. She is now preparing for a more substantial, emotionally meaningful relationship with her baby.

You are at Stage One of emotional awareness of this pregnancy; she is at Stage Two or Three. There is nothing wrong with you and your wife feeling different things about the pregnancy. However, there is a lack of coordination, of being on the same page. You and your wife are out of step. During the first trimester, when she needed increased emotional support, you were not involved enough in the pregnancy to be available to her *in the way she needed you*. Now, during the second trimester, when you are in need of emotional closeness resulting from your newfound awareness of impending fatherhood, she is more involved in bonding with her baby than with you.[1]

Nothing is more annoying, more draining of positive energy in a relationship, than communications difficulties during a time that is supposed to be joyful. Here are some questions you can ask *each other* about your different experiences of pregnancy.

What are your feelings about our pregnancy?

How did you react the first time you felt the baby move?

How do you see me as a mother (father)?

How do you see yourself as a mother (father)?

DEEPENING RECOGNITION

Second trimester brings with it a deepening recognition of the reality of the pregnancy. Your wife will begin to show that she is pregnant. She will begin to feel physically uncomfortable.

Because she is beginning to show that she is pregnant, other people also will take notice; the pregnancy becomes more public. I remember my wife feeling very self-conscious about her first pregnancy, starting in the fifth month. She found that acquaintances would approach her, place their hands on her stomach and ask about the baby. She was embarrassed by people she didn't know well assuming they could touch her because she was pregnant.

A few men in our workshops reacted with suspicion to such advances. They were unsure who these people were, and for some of these men, it started them wondering about whether their wives lead a secret life.

> I didn't know who the hell all these people were. She's always been somewhat secretive. If I knew, I wouldn't allow her to have so many friends who I didn't know. She's gotta be faithful to me.
>
> - Joey, nineteen, store clerk

Many couples give nicknames or pet names to their baby-in-waiting. When my daughter was tumbling and kicking around inside Debra, we started to call her our little baby blowfish, named after our boat, *Blowfish I*. Five years later, Maddi still takes great pride in knowing her first nickname.

Couples begin to read books of baby names. Relatives suggest names. Friends provide ideas. And you and your wife will spend hours choosing a name you both like, one that doesn't offend every member of your family for whom the baby is *not* named. If you want to see TV's version of this balancing act, there is a wonderful episode of the old *Dick Van Dyke Show* in which Rob and Laura explain to their son, Richie, how it came to be that his middle name is Rosebud.

In the episode, each grandparent had a preference for a name. Their best friends also had ideas, as did Rob's work colleagues. Frustrated that the act of choosing a name would result in most family members and friends feeling slighted, if not hurt, they decided to take the first letter of each suggested name, fiddle with their order and create a middle name representing everyone's suggestions. They ended up with Rosebud.

Older Couples

For older couples who are having a baby, second trimester may mean a temporary hold on some enthusiasm. Today, more older parents-to-be are opting for *amniocentesis* testing, which usually occurs between weeks fourteen and eighteen. These tests are usually given to women thirty-five and over to find out if certain types of birth defects are present in the fetus. Parents-to-be who use these tests often avoid emotional and psychological bonding with their baby until they are certain the pregnancy is viable.

> Heidi's a bit older and I always teased her about needing a wheel-chair before me. But when we began to read about possible birth defects we got real scared. Heidi told me not to worry. But, I just couldn't let myself relax or even get excited about the pregnancy until all the test results were in. As you know, everything turned out okay, thank God.
>
> - Andy, thirty-four, English teacher

The amnio process is straightforward. If you are unclear about the procedure, ask you doctor to explain it. Also, ask how you might lend support to your wife during the procedure.

The first step is to arrange your schedule so that you are with your wife during amniocentesis testing. Drive her to and from the doctor's office or hospital. Second, be sensitive to your wife's anxiety. Talk with her about her concerns and share any uneasiness that you have. Before the procedure, talk with your doctor about any last minute worries.

The procedure itself takes about twenty minutes. First, the doctor performs an *ultrasound*. Once the ultrasound has clearly identified where the baby is within the womb, the procedure begins. Usually, you can sit by her side, hold her hand and talk with her about the excitement of your new baby. In our case, Debra and I watched the procedure on the ultrasound monitor; our little baby slept through the whole thing.

Father as Guardian

Like many men, I found myself verging on obsession about the health and safety of my baby. Like many women, Debra was calm and confident that our little charge would be born with all of her fingers, toes, ears, legs and arms.

Some researchers suggest that men's traditional protectiveness toward a wife and baby results from the cultural expectations of man as provider of security and protection. I think it's because we want to nurture our wives and babies but are told, by our culture, that men don't show such feelings. Therefore, we show the types of feelings we are allowed to show. We show concern, which is an extension of our expectations to protect. We need to worry about something related to the pregnancy and, since we already know how to protect and provide, we worry about what we have no control over.

We also begin to think about the kind of father we will be. Because the pregnancy feels real when we experience our baby's kicks and turns, we begin to consider how we will care for this soon-to-be infant. We begin to consider who we want to be as a father.

> I really got a kick out of feeling my kid move around in there. But I got scared, too. I mean, I'm gonna have to be this kid's dad. What the hell do I know about that?
>
> - Andrew, twenty-seven, policeman

OPTIONS AND DECISIONS

As mother grows bigger with her pregnancy, so does the realization that someone new will soon be living in your home. Our fathers began to talk about where junior will live, how her room will look, where it will be, and when to order furniture.

> I got serious about having a baby when my wife took me to Kiddie City and we began to look at cribs and dressers. I thought, 'Hey, this is really happening to me!' Can we afford this on my stipend?
>
> - George, twenty-seven, graduate student

> Without Shelly knowing, I began to save a little bit of money every week. I'd hide it from her because I knew she'd think I was being frivolous. When I'd see a toy sale, I'd take my stash and buy all these cute baby toys for our baby's room. Then, I'd hide all the stuff in the basement closet. When we finally had the baby's furniture delivered, I had all these toys to throw in, too. Shelly looked a bit frustrated with me, but I know she's a big kid too, just like me.
>
> - Jason, thirty-one, contractor

Cassie was raised in a real poor family. She never had much and never forgave her mom and dad for it. We spent a lot of time talking about how we would give our baby everything that Cassie never had as a child. Cassie asked me to help her find furniture and bedding and toys and stuffed animals. I knew she wanted to make our baby's room into her ideal baby's room. All I wanted to do was help her to do it.

- Bill, forty-two, store owner

Some of our fathers were unwilling to help their spouses design the room and purchase furniture. Most of these men were superstitious, believing that having baby's furniture delivered before the baby was born would jeopardize their baby's health.

I don't mind helping to buy the furniture. I don't even mind talking about how to set up the room. But nothing gets bought and brought into this house until after the baby's born.

- Lee, twenty-five, assistant manager

A few men had ghosts in their heads with whom they were continually fighting. One father had lost a baby during birth and, in his view, learned a painful lesson about how to prepare for his new child.

When our first child was stillborn, Beth and I had already set up the baby's room. We had bought the furniture and had it set up. We bought toys. We painted the room. We had a wooden plaque made with his name on it and put it on his door. We bought bottles and baby cups and baby shoes and baby pajamas and baby clothes.

It took us more than a year to be able to walk in his room. We have repainted everything and given away everything we bought. We will never let ourselves do that again. This time, we will wait until our baby is born and is healthy.

- Paul, twenty-nine, accountant

Generally, though, planning your baby's room can provide a wonderful opportunity to join with your wife and move together toward something you both anticipate with great excitement. There are pitfalls, to be sure. If you do not know how to negotiate

with your wife or need to be right and in control, then planning
for your baby's living space invites conflict. Some of our fathers
believed negotiation always meant saying "yes." Others interpreted
their role to be always letting their wives have their way. These
are not ideas we encourage. By negotiation, we mean to find a
way to cooperate; to discuss and evaluate ideas and judgments
about your baby and her life.

This is part of a new way to fatherhood, a new idea of what
it means to be a father and a man. It has little to do with how
strong you are, how adept you are at ordering people around, how
expensive your car is, how versatile you are with a set of tools or
how closely you identify with all the other male stereotype
attitudes and acts. Fatherhood has everything to do with the way
you manage your life: the way in which you conduct yourself as a
human being in terms of your wife, your child, your business
associates, your neighbors and your community. Fatherhood has
to do with how you cooperate and make decisions, and with your
courage to say no as well as to say yes. Fatherhood is about your
awareness and understanding of the consequences of your actions
and your decisions.

A little thing like participating in the development of your
child's living space places an everlasting imprint on your child.
Your participation——your choices——reflect a part of you and send
an important message to your child about your place in the family.

Birth Options

Second trimester brings another important decision to the table.
Parents begin to discuss birth options. Among the questions asked
are: Will you both participate in childbirth education classes?
What birth options will you choose? What part will you play in
your child's birth?[2]

Many fathers tried to answer these questions themselves,
rather than with their wives. By far most fathers followed their
wives' lead. They believed that because she was having the baby,
she had the right to set the pace and direction.

Donna was very clear with me from the start. It was her pregnancy and she was in charge. I was told she didn't want to hear any crap from me.

- Tony, twenty-four, store clerk

Shelly said she wanted my ideas. But, I never once gave her an idea that she didn't "yes, but" me on. I felt like a real outsider and got pretty angry at her.

- Jason, thirty-one, contractor

Although it is the mother who needs to feel comfortable, secure and in control of herself, she is nonetheless involved in a marriage requiring cooperation, participation and understanding. She needs to let you, her husband, join with her on all important decisions. You may feel uncertain about participating when your wife wants no participation at all. However, your responsibility is to let her know you want to be involved.

Being there, wanting to be there, committing oneself to being there, being proud of being there, putting up with the messes and disappointments and one's shortcomings, and still choosing to be there for (your wife and) this child; that is what fathering is all about. The more that dad is there - alert, aware, and responsive - the stronger the bonds that develop.[3]

At the same time, it is important for you to remember that your wife and your baby have a profoundly different relationship than the one between you and your baby. The life is growing within her. She feels the baby's every move. You are the observer to these wonderful events and, through sheer chance, happen to feel an occasional kick or movement. There is a trick to being able to respect your wife's unique attachment to your baby while at the same time reminding her that you need to participate fully, too.

Some researchers suggest that "it is probably best to let (your wife) take the lead and to help her by contributing your feelings as they occur. You will be in a position to advise, but she will be making the final decisions." [4]

This can be very frustrating, especially if you are accustomed to being in charge and making decisions. Your role in the Second Trimester is to support, to guide, to listen, to provide feedback and feelings, to advise and to question. Ultimately, your wife (and maybe your doctor) will make the final decision.

[[10]]

CHAPTER

The Third Trimester

My co-author likes to tell how he and his wife planned a trip from New Jersey to Maine during the third trimester of their first pregnancy. They tooled around in a little two-seater Volkswagen Kharman Ghia. His wife liked to drive and they planned to share the driving on the 500-mile trip. They were all packed and ready to go. Then she tried to slide in behind the wheel. They moved the seat all the way back. She still couldn't fit. He briefly considered trying some grease and a shoehorn, but then realized they would have to change their plans.

It was an unavoidable message: The life that had comfortably held them when they had no children would no longer fit. It had to be changed. The VW was eventually traded in for a family wagon. He realized that he would be in the driver's seat a lot more than in the past.

READY OR NOT, HERE I COME

Just as the mother's body has stretched out beyond its old borders, the physical presence of this child in the third trimester stretches out the father's life. By now, the baby is an inescapable presence in the family. It cannot be ignored. And its urgency brings with it the inescapable question: Am I ready?

Sometime in the next few weeks you will be awakened out of a sound sleep to feel, through your wife's stomach, your baby kicking and tumbling with delight. You gently put your hand on her movement, enraptured by her energy, her spunk and the knowledge that soon a new life will come into your world. SMACK! You feel the "Terminator" grip of your wife's hand. "Leave me alone, I'm trying to sleep!"

You role over to resume your *zzzzzzz*'s. Then, you get kicked again. This time you have learned. As active as your baby appears, you dare not disturb the one who is carrying her. She needs her sleep and doesn't feel the baby's kicking. You, of course, wanting to be close to your wife, cuddle close to her and continue to be kept up all night by the vibrant maneuvers of your soon-to-be-born child.

You move slightly away from bigfoot and fix your gaze toward the ceiling. You begin to think about your readiness. Is there enough money? Will I lose my job? Can I be effective at work while our newborn baby is at home? Will I forget my newborn while I am at work? Will I be a good father? Will she be a good mother? How quickly will I want another baby? Will the baby be born healthy? Will I know what to do with her when she gets ill? Where do I buy diapers? How will I know when she is sick? When she is tired? When she needs to be picked up? When she needs her mother? When she needs her father? When she wants to play? When she wants to sleep? How do I protect against SIDS? Should I stay up all night with her to be sure that she doesn't stop breathing? Do I know what to do in an emergency?

By the time you have thought about all the questions you have about your readiness, the sun has peeked through your shades, the coffee is beginning to drip, the dogs have to go outside and you need to get ready for another day at work. You dress, have breakfast, pack a lunch and take your briefcase and your worries with you to work. Thankfully, the train ride takes about forty-five minutes. There will be plenty of time to think about more things you are unsure about.

Our expectant fathers described the last trimester of pregnancy as similar to the end of a game. Some referred to it as the "fourth quarter." Others talked about their anticipation about the "final play of the game." All, however, carried some degree of apprehension and concern about the upcoming birth.

I guess I wanted to look the other way a lot during the early part of our pregnancy. I wasn't sure whether I wanted the baby because we weren't sure if we wanted the marriage to continue. But, as I look at Terry now, I see we have to make a commitment to each other *for the baby*. I guess I'm in this marriage to stay.

- Bud, thirty-one, security consultant

The closer we got to the birth, the more scared I got. I don't want to be like my father was to me, but I'm scared that I'll fail and be just like him.

- Elliott, twenty-seven, salesman

The last trimester brought ghosts to some of our fathers, like Elliott. These men were committed to being different fathers than their fathers were to them. They had participated in our fathering workshops and developed a plan for how to be different. Of course, they had no opportunity to practice these ideas until their baby was born. So, they sat and watched their pregnancy continue on schedule, each equipped with knowledge about how to be different, yet unsure of their ability to apply it appropriately. They were afraid of becoming the ghosts of fathers past.

I know that I don't want to hit my kid. I learned from my dad that hitting only gets kids mad as hell and they rebel, like I did. I want to be strong with my kid. I want to discipline him when he is wrong, but I hope I won't hit him. I've learned about different things to do instead of hitting, but I'm afraid of the feelings inside me. I've learned that the angry, hitting father who raised me is part of me, too. I'm afraid that I won't control it.

- Mike, twenty-nine, store clerk

I want to be there for my baby. But, I just hate staying at home and hanging around the house. I haven't been able to change that. I just don't know what to do when I feel that I want to bolt.

- Eddie, forty-nine, attorney

Other men were struggling with the increased workload around the house. They discovered that as the days of the third trimester moved closer to the actual birth their wives were less

able to do some routine chores around the house. The responsibilities rested on the fathers. They had not expected to take on
such household chores and most felt pretty annoyed.

These last three months have been really hard. I've worked longer
hours at the store because it's holiday time. Then, when I'm done,
there is all this crap to do at home. I know Debbie is tired and I'm
told the pregnancy really saps her energies. But, hey, I'm tired too.
I don't want to deal with this cleaning and cooking.

- Bobby, twenty-five, salesman

Summer break has always been a time for me to do my research. I
don't have to teach and there are few committee meetings. I just
didn't expect to have to play Mr. Mom while Cheryl was in her last
months. I hated doing the shopping! It's such a waste of time.

- George, thirty-two, college teacher

Some men opted for a less-clean home. They made a very
intentional, conscious decision that they would not be compulsive
about keeping their house clean. They were resigned to living in
a less orderly home. However, speaking out of both sides of their
mouths, many of these men felt angry that the house wasn't ship
shape. None came right out and blamed his wife for shirking her
responsibilities. They understood that the last stages of pregnancy
were tiring and difficult for her, too. Yet, they couldn't stop
feeling their wives let them down somehow.

I could never tell Jeanie that I feel she could have pushed herself to
clean up a little more. For God's sake, I'm at work all day and she's
been home for the past three weeks. She could do more if she paced
herself.

- Art, twenty-six, lawyer

I never realized how much of an easy trip the last stages of pregnancy are for women. They don't do anything. They sleep and eat and
watch TV. They do nothing around the house.

- Ron, twenty-five, office manager

Surprisingly, only a few men talked about their dissatisfaction with the quality and frequency of their sexual contact. Most said they understood the need to compromise their sexual needs during the last few months of pregnancy.

> Sex wasn't an issue for us. She felt uncomfortable in most positions and far less than passionate during most of the ninth month. So, we simply agreed to wait until after the birth. It was no big deal.
> — Paul, thirty-seven, counselor

Only a few of our interviewees acknowledged having an affair during the later stage of pregnancy. However, the literature suggests that late-stage pregnancy affairs occur among a few husbands. Usually, these men feel sexually rejected by their wives and do not talk with them about their feelings. Instead, they become involved with other women. Some researchers note that the late-stage pregnancy affair is associated with changes in their wife's appearance.

According to Shapiro, several factors were present in most late-stage pregnancy affairs[1].

- The affairs were with a close friend or relative of the wife.
- Most men saw their wives as attractive and were literally "turned on" by her pregnant shape.
- Many felt pushed away by the pregnancy and birth process.
- Most described a strong need to talk to someone.
- Most had no previous affairs.

Shapiro suggests that what motivates the late-stage pregnancy affair is a quest for affection. Many husbands felt emotionally abandoned as their wives turned their attention inward on the pregnancy and upcoming birth. He speculates that since many late-stage pregnancy affairs occurred with women who were, themselves, close to the wife, "this other person was also feeling pushed away by the wife and the pregnancy."[2]

Paralysis

> The closer we got to the birth, the more I was sure something was going to go wrong. At times, I felt paralyzed. At other times, I just felt overwhelmed.
>
> — George, twenty-seven, graduate student

Many men see the process of pregnancy and birthing as a mystery. Since it doesn't happen to us, we rarely spend time reading and preparing ourselves for the birth. As a result, we may become more anxious and unsure of ourselves during the late stages of pregnancy.

> No one prepared me for all these changes. What happens when Susan starts going into labor? What do I do?
>
> — Drew, twenty-seven, customer service rep.

Some men talked about feeling unsure about their ability to do what their wives needed when it needed to be done. They worried about being able to do their part during the delivery. They had heard horror stories about fathers passing out at the sight of their wife's blood. They had heard the stories about how fathers had more difficulty cutting the cord than their wives had in delivering the baby.

These men felt embarrassed by their possible incompetence. They were afraid they would fail and be seen as bumbling fools by their wives, the doctors and nurses.

> I've never been inside a delivery room before. I don't know what to do. I'm embarrassed to ask what is expected of me because, I guess, I think I should know already.
>
> — Bobby, thirty-one, writer

> What happens if I drop the baby? You may laugh, but I've never held a baby before. I don't want to hurt it. My wife would never forgive me.
>
> — Andrew, twenty-seven, policeman

I did chuckle during the interview and I apologized. But, the sheer terror on Andrew's face revealed a genuine insecurity about what to do when the baby arrives. I felt concern for Andrew because he was so worked up about his ability to perform well under pressure. I also felt annoyed that he had not been coached by the hospital or some other educational workshop about what to expect and how to act in the delivery room. Such experiences are not unusual for men. Health care professionals rarely have taken the time to prepare fathers adequately for their roles during delivery.

As the end of the pregnancy looms closer, some of our expectant fathers felt increasingly anxious about how well they could support their new family. Although most men from our groups experienced this financial anxiety during the second trimester, a few had trouble during the last trimester.

> I guess I never really accepted the idea that we were going to have a baby. But now, just look at her. She really is pregnant. Last week she stopped working. This is really happening and it's going to happen real soon. I don't know if we can make it on my salary alone.
> - Carl, twenty-eight, school psychologist

These men had tended to deny the pregnancy and upcoming birth until now. They talked more early in the pregnancy about whether to continue it. Apparently, one way to resolve their confusion about whether to have the baby was to make no decision and let biology make the decision for them.

> I knew that she was pregnant. I'm not that much of a fool. But, I guess, I just didn't think about how quickly nine months could go by. I wasn't prepared because I didn't think I'd have to prepare so quickly. I didn't save any money for the new baby. I guess that's a bit immature, huh?
> - Joey, nineteen, store clerk

As a group, most men were prepared and excited about the pregnancy. They had examined the best ways to organize their

finances. Some had contacted a financial planner while others
spoke with accountants or stock brokers about financial issues.

More than a few men realized that their obligation to take
care of their wife and new baby, financially, began before the birth
of their child. These men spoke with lawyers and arranged to have
wills drawn up. Some men also contacted insurance agents and
took out life insurance policies for themselves to cover their wife
and child adequately.

> A few weeks before Rebecca was born, I spoke with my broker about
> the best way to handle my finances. I asked him to do some research
> on what savings plan would be best for us in order to save for
> college for my kid. I guess he was surprised at my request because
> the baby hadn't even been born. But, I believe preparation is the
> best policy.
>
> - Jack, thirty-six, physician

> I had never thought about a will before. But, when I realized our
> child was going to be born within a few weeks, I realized I had a
> responsibility to my new family in case of an emergency. You know,
> I travel a lot and I wanted to be sure everything was set up for them
> . . . you know, just in case.
>
> - Bobby, twenty-five, salesman

Our expectant fathers talked about their increasing awareness
of being a parent. Most began to have frequent discussions with
their wives about parenting.

> During the last month, we talked about how we would be as parents.
> I know we talked about this stuff earlier in the pregnancy, but it felt
> real now. We agreed we wanted to be good parents, loving parents.
> And we felt ready to be parents.
>
> - Barry, thirty-two, dentist

Some fathers-to-be continued the time-honored male tradition
of thinking about issues of concern, but not talking with their
wives about them. Parenting readiness was no different.

I thought about being a parent. I guess she did, too. But, no, we didn't talk about what this means to be a parent. Why should we? We're the ones having a baby. We'll figure it out.

- Paul, twenty-four, factory worker

Most men in our groups became concerned about their wives' condition. They talked about calling home more often, needing to know how the last few weeks of the pregnancy were developing. It appeared their concerns were based on the genuine need to be available when their wives were ready to go to the hospital.

I found myself calling three-to-five times a day. I wanted to know how Mary was feeling and if she needed me at home.

- Jeff, twenty-six, engineer

I know I drove her crazy by working at home rather than the office, but I wanted to be close to her, just in case.

- Marty, thirty-five, consultant

Our expectant fathers were concerned, loving men who wanted to be available to their wives and to participate fully in the delivery and birth of their child. They thought the best way to communicate such involvement was to be a Hovercraft, lurking around her all the time, ready for the flight to the hospital.

Increased Conflict

Third trimester pregnancy led some of our interviewees to feel trapped in their marriages. These men did not reject the pregnancy nor did they feel they wanted to leave the marriage. Rather, they needed to get away from the perceived responsibilities that came with the approaching birth.

I took off and spent a week alone in the Poconos. I'd never taken a vacation without Sally, but I had to get away - from the house and my work. I wanted to hide and feel free to do whatever I wanted; to have someone pick up after me when I was done.

- Mitch, twenty-five, businessman

The most common stress resulted from lack of sleep or anxiety over the pending birth.

> The bigger she got, the less sleep I got. Margie couldn't sleep through the night. Either she was too uncomfortable or the baby was doing its Kurt Thomas impression. Either way, she would toss and turn and moan and bitch. I felt like I didn't sleep during the last month of her pregnancy. I was a bear at work, at home and with Margie. We argued about the silliest things and all because we were exhausted.
>
> - Andy, thirty-two, broker

> Shelly was driving me nuts with her questions about whether this kick or that twinge was normal. She was consumed in the anticipation of the birth. She turned into the biggest hypochondriac I know. I wanted her to shut up about all these worries. They were driving me nuts.
>
> - Jason, thirty-one, contractor

The upcoming birth of your child pushes you back a generation. For some men, the recognition that they were no longer the youngest generation led to feelings of discomfort about aging.

> When we had the final ultrasound, it dawned on me that I will not be the youngest generation anymore. Seeing my son through the ultrasound made me realize I'm getting older, my dad and mom are getting older, and I'm not as young as I think. I know getting older happens to everyone, but I didn't expect having a baby to make me look at this. I figured this would happen when they were teenagers, not babies.
>
> - George, thirty-two, college teacher

WORKING TOGETHER TOWARD YOUR BIRTH

This chapter has talked about different experiences men had during the last trimester of their wives' pregnancy. Nothing is as important as continuing to talk with her about how you feel, except maybe talking with her about how she feels.

During the last month of the pregnancy, you may be called on to do many more household chores than you ever imagined. You may find simple pleasures interrupted. For example, I remember during our second pregnancy that Deb and I went out to see a movie. About thirty minutes before the end, just as the movie was building up to a great climax, she said that she was too uncomfortable to sit in the theater seat any longer. She wanted to go home. I said I would do whatever she needed. She searched the theater floor for her shoes and discovered her feet had swollen too much to fit into them. So, with her arms draped around my back, I escorted her to our car. When we got home, she immediately went upstairs and fell asleep. I was still in a "go out and party mode" but there was no one to play with except my dogs. So, I grabbed a book, flipped on a *Star Trek* and settled down. Oh, by the way, it was 7:00 P.M. when we came back home.

The inescapable conclusion is that men need to talk with their wives about how they feel. Couples involved in late-stage pregnancy may need to take time to talk about how each person is feeling about the emotional and physical changes that are occurring within and between them. *You* need to be aware that your wife may want more time to herself or with her unborn child. *You* need to be aware that your responsibility is to talk with your wife about her gradual shift of attention away from you and toward the baby and the upcoming birth. *You* need to talk about your feelings. If you feel rejected, *you* need to take responsibility to talk about your feelings. If you feel abandoned, *you* need to take responsibility to talk about your feelings. If you feel left out, uninvolved, taken for granted, or unimportant, *you* need to take responsibility to talk about your feelings. Get the idea? *You need to talk about your feelings!*

⟦ 11 ⟧

CHAPTER

Honey, Get the Suitcase!

No matter how carefully you plan, when that fateful day arrives the emotions can overwhelm you. Witness my co-author's "Day of Reckoning."

I was running as fast as I could. The contractions were only a few minutes apart. Cindie was squatting in the living room. She couldn't get up. I was dashing in and out of the house like a madman packing the car, trying my hardest to think. And every few minutes I would race in to stand behind her to support her while she went into contortions. It was like trying to clean the house during television commercials without missing the show. I packed up our six-year-old, still sleeping, into the back of the car. I grabbed food from the refrigerator and cupboards. I packed clothes. We had everything we needed to survive for several years in the wilderness. There was just one thing missing. No wife.

Every time she got up to walk to the car, she doubled over with another contraction. She couldn't move. For a desperate moment, I thought we would have the baby right there in the living room, forty-five minutes from the nearest hospital. Right there, in the middle of nowhere. At midnight. On this chilly February night. By ourselves. Alone.

My mind was racing. Our neighbor had delivered a few calves on his farm. Maybe, he could help. After a calf, a little baby should be a piece of cake, right? But I couldn't imagine Cindie delivering with a feedbag strapped to her mouth. And the poor kid would be saddled with a name like Bossy for the rest of his life. Besides it would have taken forever to clean all that straw out of the living room after the birth. We had to get out of here. But how?

That panic was enough to propel us out the door. To this day, I don't know how my wife managed to get out of the house. I went out to pull the car up to the door—through the door if necessary—and I looked up to see her hobbling down the side steps.

Cindie kept her legs crossed and we made the forty-five minute drive to the birth center. I spent the entire drive scanning the side of the road for good spots to pull over, just in case. It was such a relief when we arrived. She was eight centimeters dilated. We had taken so long the midwife thought we had already had the baby along the way. Then I spent the rest of the night dashing out to the car between contractions to unload all the stuff I had packed into it. We parked our son in front of a television in the next room, because we hadn't been able to reach our babysitter. And he spent the night watching videos—dashing in once to tell us excitedly about the antics of a chimpanzee who fired a revolver in *Toby Tyler*—a drama he found much more interesting than what was going on next door.

Even before I got the car unpacked, our second son was born. We were exhausted and relieved. And when we looked into those tiny blue eyes for the first time, it was all worth it.

A ROLLER COASTER

Nothing can prepare you for that moment. Not the birthing classes nor Lamaze lessons. Not the book reading. Not the videos you rent from the library. Not nine months of watching your wife transform from the sexy fox you married to someone who swallowed a watermelon. Not even repeatedly watching *Poltergeist* or *The Exorcist* can prepare you. Nothing prepares you for the sheer adrenaline rush, the surreal experience of birth, the awesome miracle of your wife bringing a new life——one that you and she created together——into this world. Nothing prepares you for the sense of wonder and relief you feel when you finally hold that bluish, wet, slimy, beautiful little creature for the first time.

My stomach was all turned upsidedown when Jeanie finally gave birth to our baby. I couldn't believe a head was coming out of my wife! What a bizarre sight. My baby was coming out of my wife. I stood there speechless; and that ain't easy for a lawyer!

- Art, twenty-six, lawyer

There is no greater awe than to see your baby's head emerge from your wife. It would be absolutely comical if it weren't so intense. There is a lot of experience packed into a short span of time, channeled like a child through a small canal.

Most of our fathers-to-be made birth plans. They had planned who would do what during the critical time just before birth. But a birth plan is a bit like those hurricane evacuation plans that every shore community has. When the storm hits, you grab what you can and ride it out. The birth is something that happens *to* you. It happens when it wants to happen. And, it goes on as long as it wants to.

We had been at the hospital since seven in the morning. We had spent all day and all night walking the halls of the maternity ward, trying to induce labor. We watched *L.A. Law*. We watched Carson. We watched Letterman. We walked some more.

Then, about three in the morning, our doctor came in to tell us we couldn't wait any longer. He had to take the baby. It was C-section time. The sheer panic that crossed my mind when I heard those words left me unable to help my wife when she really needed help. We never expected a C-section. We only planned for a vaginal delivery. Great planning, huh?

- John, thirty-two, businessman

The anticipation leading up to the actual birth contains moments of terror and moments of stillness and reflection. There is the silence of driving to the hospital on a moonlit night with a carseat in the back, knowing that the seat will be filled on the return trip. There are ice chips, back rubs and sneaking restaurant food into her room and bringing the hospital food home for the dogs.

There are agonizing moments for her when she says she can't take it anymore. There are agonizing moments for you as you watch your wife in pain and frustration. There is your helplessness at not being able to do anything to get that baby from the inside out.

Your child's birth is moving. Suddenly you are face-to-face with your closest relative, meeting for the first time. Almost every other bond in this world can be broken. Husbands and wives can decide to separate. Business partnerships can dissolve. Jobs can be lost and gained. But, your children will be your children forever. You can run away from the responsibilities of fatherhood, but you can never resign from being a father. It is a lifetime commitment that your children will always want you to honor.

Most of our fathers discovered the true meaning of love at first sight.

> About fifteen minutes after my son was born, the nurse took my son out of the room to suction out some fluids. I didn't realize until my wife told me afterward that I followed the nurse out of the room. After all that work, I wasn't about to let that kid out of my sight. It was like I was drawn by magnetism. I watched as she uncovered him and he peed on her. That's my son! And I trailed her back into the room like a Secret Service agent on the presidential detail.
>
> - Robert, thirty-one, writer

> I admit that I wept. I saw my baby. I saw my wife. And I felt that our bond had finally been made in heaven. Our child; only we made this baby. It was ours. And we loved her from the moment she emerged.
>
> - Eddie, forty-eight, lawyer

Like John's story above, Debra and I have experienced three C-sections. When I realized that our daughter was stubbornly clinging to the warmth of her womb rather than greeting the cold January air, I spoke with Debra about the possibility of a C-section. We walked through how she would feel about hearing the doctor tell her about the need for a C-section. We practiced imaging her emotional reaction. We talked about as many possible variations on a theme as possible. When our wonderful doctor, Stewart First, came in to tell Debra about his decision to deliver the baby by C-section, she was prepared. Bravo for Debra!

EVERY BIRTH IS DIFFERENT

Every birth is unique. The birth is shaped by the mother and father. It is shaped by the setting and those who attend to your family's well being. And, it is shaped by the baby. Some births take place at home while others occur in a downtown hospital. Some take place in beds surrounded by pinks, blues, cotton and fresh linens while others occur on operating tables with their shiny, cold efficiency.

My favorite story comes from my close friend, a physician, who nearly fainted when his wife began to go into labor. And in the delivery room, the nurses brought him a chair because he was weak in the knees. I chuckled when he told me about this incident because I would have expected that a physician, of all people, would have negotiated the anxiety of labor and delivery better than your average bear. His response was, "When it's one of your own, it's a different experience!" All his medical training didn't prepare him for the excitement, anxiety and concerns about his wife and his baby.

There are fathers who cut the cord and fathers who wait for word outside the door. Even with the same two people, different births have their own character. As my co-author comments:

> With our first child, my wife was the iron woman. She didn't need anyone. She went into a trance and had the baby. I sat by her bedside and held her hand. Later, she told me she held *my* hand so I wouldn't feel left out. I caught my son with these two hands, cut his cord and welcomed him into the world.
>
> The second birth was completely different. It was shorter and much more intense. Cindie didn't want me to leave her side. I was behind her when she was standing on the bed screaming like a banshee. And I was holding her when our second son came into the world. It was one of the closest experiences of our ten years of marriage and we basked in the glow of it for weeks afterward.

WHAT IS THIS FATHER DOING HERE?

There is a good chance that your father wasn't there when you were born. Chances are you came into the world with your mother, a doctor and maybe a nurse or two.

Your father was an outsider. He may have been in the waiting room or at home. He may have been at work or at the local bar. He probably heard about your birth from a doctor, with a handshake and a word of encouragement. Or, he may have heard about your birth from the long end of a phonewire.

His first look at you may have been through a glass window in the hospital nursery. Certainly, he had little chance of holding you immediately after birth. Fathers could look but not touch. He could smoke a cigar in pride but not cuddle his prodigy next to his warm body.

As late as 1972, a survey of American hospitals found that fathers were permitted in the delivery room only 27 percent of the time. The tide began to turn in 1974 when the American College of Obstetricians and Gynecologists endorsed the father's presence during labor. By 1980, fathers were admitted to delivery rooms in almost 80 percent of American hospitals. Today, fathers are almost required to be present at the birth of their newborn. They are encouraged to support their wife, to participate in the experience and to bond with their newborn immediately after birth.

But is the renewed presence of fathers at the births of their children just so these poor guys don't feel left out? After all, the woman is doing all the work. Why does the father have to be in the delivery room?

The most obvious and frequently talked about reason why we are included in the delivery room is to provide support to our wives. We are also there to protect our wives during the delivery. She is focused on the birth and has little energy or time to devote to other issues such as dealing with hospital staff or relatives. We are there to divert the demons who wish to intrude upon our special birthing experience.

In some primitive cultures, fathers take action to remove the demons *from* their wives. These fathers go through their own mock labor and delivery while the mothers are undergoing theirs.

Ross D. Parke describes the practice of *couvade* found in primitive societies.[1] For example, in one tribe in southern India, when the mother goes into labor, the husband puts on some of this wife's clothes, goes to a dark room and lies down in bed. When the child is born, it is placed on a cot next to the father. This ritual is designed to decoy any evil spirits that might be in the area away from his wife.

That ritual is rather tame compared with a quaint custom of the Huichol Indians of Mexico. According to Mike and Nancy Samuels, the tradition in this tribe was to place the father in a squatting position in the rafters above the mother. Ropes were attached to his scrotum. When the mother felt contractions, she pulled on the ropes so that her husband, too, could share in the emotional experience of the event.[2] At least the mother couldn't tell the father that he didn't understand what she was going through. Of course, it also might have been a way to reduce the chances of a repeat performance. I know if it were me in those rafters, I'd limit myself to a one-child family!

The modern father, while we don't recommend going to the extremes of the Huichol Indians, can be a listening ear and a sympathetic supporter of this wife during the labor and delivery. Although he can't feel what she is feeling, he can listen to her, hold her hand, soothe her with his voice and empathize with her.

This brings us to the most important role for the father during childbirth: supporting the mother. Women whose husbands participated in both labor and delivery reported less pain, received less medication and felt more positive about the birth than women whose husbands were not present. The father's presence increased the mother's emotional experience of birth. Of the men who missed their children's birth, eighty-eight percent felt bad about it.[3]

Father as Relaxation Guru

Relaxation helps smooth the passage of the child into the world. A mother's state of mind during the pregnancy and delivery has an important impact on the experience. While not the only determinant of the progress of the labor, the degree of your wife's relaxation is important. Fear is the enemy of relaxation and fathers can play an important role in calming the anxieties of their wives from the first contraction to the child's first cry. The father who can set aside *his* fears and discomforts to create a safe place for his wife will be helping both the mother and child.

This is also good practice for the many times you as a father will have to substitute calmness for the sheer terror that you may feel in your heart to create a safe place for your children. You will have to put aside your own fear of lightning storms, snakes or car failures to give your child as safe a place as possible in a world that is far from safe.

Father as Father

When it's show time and your wife is involved in being a mother, you need to remember that you are not there *only* to serve her. You are there in your own right. You have an independent relationship with your child. And, delivery will be the first experience you will have as a father. First impressions count!

Your first encounter with your baby can help to set the tone and establish patterns of later involvement. Your participation at the birth of your child has an impact on the emotional bonding between you and this new bundle of life. And it is a reflection of your future involvement with fathering.

Researchers have reported that when you are interested in the details and progress of your wife's pregnancy, you are more likely to hold your baby more often during the first six weeks of life. The more you are interested in the pregnancy, the more you will pay attention to your child, particularly when she cries. Finally, the more positively you feel about the pregnancy and birth, the greater your wife's enjoyment of motherhood.[4]

The impact of this early relationship between father and child on later parenting can be seen in two different types of birthing experiences: fathers of children who are born by Cesarean section and fathers who have delivered their own babies.

With the mother engaged in a more lengthy recovery, the father plays a larger role in the early care of the child. Research has shown that this role continues well into the relationship between father and child. Fathers of C-section delivered babies were found to spend more time in routine care and feeding of their infants up to five months after the birth. There is also evidence that the more active fathering role just after birth persists.[5] Fathers who participate in the delivery of their child have been found to spend more time with their children during the first three months of life than fathers who do not participate in the birth.[6]

THE MORE YOU KNOW, THE BETTER

To be most helpful during delivery, you need to know what is going on. The more you know, the more you can participate with your wife and the delivery team. The more confident you are about what your role and responsibilities are, the more you can reassure your wife that what is happening is normal.

Most fathers today participate in childbirth classes during late-stage pregnancy. You will have panted with your wife—not just during conception but also throughout the pregnancy. Today, there are very few husbands who enter the delivery room expecting to shake hands with a stork. But, because there is so little material available about the father's role in the delivery, we will discuss a few of the important issues for you to consider when it is time to pack the suitcase.

The key decision here is: Is it real or is it just the kid playing with your mind? There is a fine line to walk here because you don't want to take unnecessary risks and underestimate the speed at which the labor will occur. On the other hand, you don't want to be calling your doctor after each contraction. "They're two days apart. Should we come in?"

The wisest approach is to talk with your doctor *months* before your due date and discuss guidelines about how and when to know your baby is really on her way. Always be conservative in your approach. Remember that nothing is more important than the health of your wife and your baby. So, err on the side of more physician involvement rather than less.

Once you learn, with your wife and her doctor, that your baby is really coming down the chute, then the next question is how to get to wherever your wife is.

> I was in rush hour traffic about forty-five minutes from home. Heidi was home and feeling that she needed to be on her way to the hospital. She was afraid to drive by herself. Every one of our neighbors was either stuck in traffic on their way home or picking up their kids from after school activities. Her mother was in Jersey. My dad was in New York. Her sisters were still at work and my sister was at a rehearsal. I panicked. She panicked. It was a mess!
>
> - Andy, thirty-four, English teacher

The final challenge is how to get all of you to where you are going to deliver the baby. The trick is to arrive at roughly the same time your baby arrives. If you show up too early, you may be sent home or over to your doctor's office for an examination. But you never want to time it so that you go from the car into final stage delivery. You and your wife need time to adjust to the hospital and the reality that your baby is coming. You also want your doctor to have time to get to the hospital, examine your wife and prepare for all possible contingencies. Again, we reemphasize, when you are unsure about when to get into your car and drive to the hospital or birthing center, consult with your medical professional.

Stage One

No matter how long it takes for your wife to move beyond the first stage of labor, she will be bent out of shape, literally. It is during this period that the tube-like cervix will flatten out and enlarge like a balloon to ten centimeters. This normally takes about twelve-to-fourteen hours, but it can go much longer. It is by far the longest stretch of labor and the one in which the husband can provide critical support.[7]

Dr. Emanuel Friedman divides this stage into a long and relatively calm latent phase and a shorter, more dramatic and active phase.[8] The latent phase is a type of predelivery calisthenics for the uterine muscles. Not much work on dilating the cervix happens during this period. Rest is important and whatever you can do to help your wife relax is very valuable. The attending doctor or nurse may recommend that the mother walk around; father can help ensure that she remains upright through contractions.

In the active phase, the mother is often quite uncomfortable. If labor has been long, the mother may feel frustrated, frazzled, tired and impatient. This is where fathers need to be exceptionally aware of what their wives need. Many books recommend that fathers provide support, encouragement and a boost of optimism. What these books don't tell you is that different women need different types of support, encouragement and optimism. Use your understanding of your wife to talk with her about *what she needs to talk about*. For example, we have heard many new fathers talk about their confusion:

> We had been in labor for eighteen hours. She was exhausted and wanted me to reassure her that this pain was all worth it. So, I told her to think about how pretty our baby would look and how wonderful it would feel to hold him in our arms and kiss him. I assured her that, no matter how long it took, we would have a healthy baby.
>
> My wife turned to me and yelled, 'Don't tell me how much longer I will have to deal with this! I want you to tell me that it will be over real soon, not that I will have something really special waiting for me ten hours from now!'
>
> - Doug, twenty-eight, broker

Talk to your wife about what she wants to hear *not* what she needs to know. Leave the facts to your doctor. You are there to provide comfort and guidance during the journey. Let someone else tell her how long the journey will take.

Stage Two

It's all downhill from here. In the second stage of labor, the baby finishes her descent and enters the world. This is much easier said than done. According to Samuels and Samuels, this stage is very intense and usually fairly short.9 Stage two averages about fifty minutes during a first delivery and twenty minutes in subsequent deliveries. For you and your wife, this may feel more like a lifetime.

Now that the door is open wide, it doesn't take long for the little tyke to wander out. She usually dives out headfirst, although her head has to be a bit mushy to get through that narrow opening. She turns her head to the side like a swimmer gasping for air. Then come the shoulders, one at a time. A wriggle and a squirm and the feet slide out.

And, you have yourself a bouncing baby. It will never cease to amaze me that, in all the many births in movies and sitcoms, the babies always emerge clean and pink.

Actually, babies are covered with slime, called *vernix*, and goop. These are the scientific terms. They are also covered with some blood. Even the healthiest baby may be a bit misshapen. Who can blame them after being flushed out of a hole the size of a drainpipe?

But even if they temporarily have a face that only a mother and father could love, they are in luck because *their* mother and father just happen to be at the birth.

Stage Three

This is a bit of an anticlimax. The baby is already here. You are oohing and aahing. The nurses are checking out the baby's sex, fingers, toes, breathing, heart rate and reflexes.

Meanwhile the last contractions deliver the placenta. After the placenta is removed, the uterus makes a sudden attempt to recapture its prepregnancy shape. It contracts and in the process helps to clamp down on blood vessels and begins to pull itself together.10

Who is This Woman?

Hell hath no fury like a woman in labor! Ah, the stories you hear about the call of the wild, about women who suddenly turn on their husbands or doctors. The furious rush of hormones, the bewildering events, the extraordinary task before them all make their reactions somewhat unpredictable. Some of these stories may be old husband's tales, but best be prepared for anything.

> Our doctor came into our room, looked at the monitor and decided it was time to go to the delivery room. Only my wife! Carla wouldn't move until she put on her make-up. Make-up at a time like this?
> - Joel, thirty-eight, businessman

> When Joanie went into the final stages of labor, I thought that she was reciting a comedy routine. She was screaming for drugs to kill the pain. "No woman should have to put up with this much pain," she yelled. "Pain and pregnancy are a conspiracy to keep woman humbled and thankful to their male doctors." I mean, she was on a roll! She was screaming at me for putting her into this mess. Screaming at the doctors for not more quickly inducing labor. Screaming at the nurses because they were there.
> - John, forty-one, businessman

Circum-Decision

If you have a son, you will have to make a critical decision about his future sometime within the first few days of his birth. You will have to decide about circumcision. This decision used to be routine, but it is coming under increasing question. It is also a decision that involves a complex mix of personal and religious issues that parents must weigh.

Sam Keen expresses some of these concerns about the circumcision procedure:[11]

> That so primitive and brutal a rite continues to be practiced nearly automatically in modern times when most medical evidence shows that it is unnecessary, painful, and dangerous suggests that circumcision remains a mythic act whose real significance is stubbornly buried in the unconscious. That men and women who supposedly love their sons refuse to examine and stop this barbaric practice strongly suggests that something powerfully strange is going on here that is obscured by a conspiracy of silence.

It might be a good idea to consider this and discuss with your wife the purpose, meaning and concerns about circumcision. The father often plays an important role in this decision, whether it is for religious reasons or because he doesn't want his son to be different from other men, different from himself.

Your Birth Plan

Our fathers had few choices in participating in the births of their children. Their role was dictated by hospital policy and traditions that relegated them to passive observer. Today, there are as many ways for you to participate in the birth of your child as there are options for birthing. How you choose to take part in the birth of your children will be shaped by your own feelings about the process, your wife's feelings and the environment in which you choose to give birth.

While you can't plan for everything, your role in the delivery of your child begins long before the first stage of labor. Your experience will be shaped by decisions you make about your role in the labor and delivery of your child.

As we saw above, fathers play many important roles in the births of their children. But your own role will depend on your relationship with your wife, her ideas about the birth, the relationships you have with the delivery team, particularly the physician or midwife who guides the birth, the relationship you envision with your child and your comfort with the process.

Some husbands defer to their wives on these decisions, at least in part because the mother's comfort with the setting and her ability to be relaxed during the delivery are vital.

We have provided a set of issues and concerns to discuss with your wife that should help guide you toward a better planned birthing.

QUESTIONS TO CONSIDER

- Do you want to go to the doctor's office with your wife for her prenatal visits? How does your wife feel about this?
- What role do you and your wife envision for *you* during labor and delivery?
- What can you do to help your wife during labor and delivery? How can you help her to relax at those times?

The key here is communication. You should be discussing these questions with your wife and with your doctor, too.

Also, you will want to ask yourself several other questions.

- What issues that are peripheral to the birth is she most likely to be concerned about?
- What can you do to take care of these issues?
- Do you want to help the doctor cut the cord?
- Have you spoken with your physician about wanting to participate in the birth of your child? If no, make an appointment to talk with your doctor.
- If a Cesarean or other intervention is necessary, what role will you feel comfortable playing?
- If your child is male, will he be circumcised? By whom? Which relatives would want to be present for the circumcision?
- Will your wife breastfeed or bottlefeed? How do you feel about these options? How does she feel?
- What do you need to bring with you to the hospital on the day that the baby is scheduled to be taken home?
- When do you plan on having relatives and friends over to see the baby for the first time?
- Who will help around the house while your wife is in the hospital?
- Do you plan to take time off from work when the baby is born? If yes, how long and is it arranged?
- What will your wife need during the first few days home from the hospital?

It is important to share your thoughts and feelings about these issues. You'll find it helpful, too, to begin immediately carrying out any plans and doing any chores that you have noted. You will not only ease introducing your new baby to your family but you will also enhance your anticipation.

[[12]]

CHAPTER

Postpartum Novelties

Clinical psychologists have weird hours. We provide our services when our clients are available, not the other way around. We begin early in the morning and work late into the evening. This results in many late nights during the week.

Two weeks after the birth of our son, my wife felt well enough for me to resume my normal work schedule. She had a Caesarian Section and discovered that recovering from major surgery played second fiddle to caring for our newborn.

It was about 10 P.M. when I opened the door of our home and was enraptured by the smell of dinner. I hadn't expected Debra to make me dinner because I understood how difficult it was for her to get around the house, particularly going up and down the stairs.

I gave her a big hug and expressed my joy and pleasure at her hard work. I ate quickly, cleaned up the kitchen and settled down in the living room to talk before she went to bed.

"How was the chicken?" she asked.

"It was really good. I love it when you cook. Next time, though, put on a little less red pepper. It was a bit spicy for me."

I was ready to move on and talk about how her day had gone but she put herself in overdrive. I could see it in her eyes. She was pissed!

"Too much red pepper, huh? How dare you try to control my life? You're just like all other men! You take what I give and then try to control me! You don't allow women the chance to be themselves! How dare you! Less red pepper, indeed! I will not be controlled by you or any other man. . . ."

This went on for about ten minutes. She was out-of-control with anger. If I had known red pepper was so important to her I would have said the chicken was fine. I also knew she was deep in the throes of postpartum reactions. My guess was that her reaction may be a little, iddy-bitty bit of an overreaction resulting from her hormonal rollercoaster. I had the sense, however, not to explain to her why I thought she was reacting as she was. Instead, I asked in my very best clinical voice, "Deb, I need you to help me with something here. I don't understand how you got from my comment about the chicken needing less red pepper to the point about how all men control all women. Would you help me to understand how you got from A to B?"

She looked at me with a look that said "You dare to question me?" Then, she reflected upon my question and tried to answer it. She could find no link. God knows, she tried. She wouldn't give up her position without a fight, but I didn't fight back. I simply asked her to help me understand how red pepper and controlling men are associated. When she tried to engage me in a fight, I simply asked for clarification. My mamma didn't raise no dummy. I knew a losing situation when I saw it.

After she calmed down and realized red pepper and control had little in common, she said, "I've had a rough day, today. I think I'm a bit depressed and thinking a little funny. Maybe it's postpartum stuff." Amen to that, I thought.

CHANGES FROM THE UNKNOWN

After the euphoria of the birth wears off, the mother and father are hit with the challenges of being a new family. Overnight, the family has been turned on its head by a wailing little infant.

In the first few days, most of the caretaking is the responsibility of the mother. The results of many of these changes add a special, often unanticipated, burden on the father. This chapter explores the challenges that our new fathers faced after delivery.

Not all women show clear signs of a postpartum reaction. However, I have never met a father who didn't have at least two or three million stories about life after delivery.

Dealing with postpartum experiences is an important part of early adjustment to family life. However, our interviewees reported many other experiences during the first few weeks of their journey into fatherhood. This chapter explores the challenges that faced our expectant fathers after delivery.

Rules and regulations governing hospital stays allow women to stay in the hospital about three days after delivery. Then, mother, infant and father drive home to begin their new life as a family. Some hospitals, like ours, provide new parents with a wonderful send-off. The night before mother and child are released from the hospital, we were ushered into a lovely room, with other new parents, and served a special dinner. Our choices were roast beef or lobster tail with champagne and cake. The nurses talk about this as their send-off dinner to new parents. After three children I realize this was their way of saying we would have no quiet meals again for a very long time.

Our new fathers talked about changes in their marriage in areas such as less sleep, more noise, greater joint responsibilities in caring for their baby, and less time to be a couple.

Sleep Deprivation

In our workshops, we ask our expectant fathers what they think will be the hardest part of early fatherhood. They respond with concerns about childrearing, being a good parent or balancing home and work. When we talk to our fathers *after* the birth of their child, they tell us that they have never been so tired in their lives.

Fatigue is the constant companion of new fatherhood. Your baby will feed when she is hungry. She doesn't care that it is 2:00 A.M. and you have an important meeting in the morning. So, your wife gets up to feed your baby and you are awakened. This may happen once during the night or it may happen four times. It depends on your child.

I felt pretty worn out for about the first month. I was tired when I got up, tired when I went to work, and tired when I came home. It felt like our little bundle of joy was robbing me of my sanity!
- George, thirty-two, college teacher

One father, Peter, described the morning after his son came home from the hospital:

When I woke up that first morning, I was excited to see Brian. I felt so proud that my son had slept through the whole night without waking up. I walked downstairs about 9:00 A.M. and there, sitting around the table, was my wife and her parents, playing with Brian.

Pretty bright kid, I said. Brian slept through the whole night. I told you that this was going to be easy.

Then Joanie raised her head. She looked exhausted. Come to think of it, so did my in-laws.

You slept through all of his crying, she said. Brian woke up four times during the night. We have been up since 3:00 A.M. caring for *your* son. You slept through everything.

Unless you can sleep as soundly as Peter, there is no quick solution to help you to feel better about your lack of sleep or the increased irritability that comes with fatigue. One father reported that he found placing his head between two pillows helped him to sleep through the night. Other fathers talked about sleeping in a different room for the first three months.

These solutions are not high on my priority list because they place most of the work on your wife. Instead, here are a few suggestions your may want to share with your wife.

- First, remember this won't last forever. No matter how much you may feel you will never sleep again, all babies grow up and learn to sleep through the night.

- Second, read about early infancy. Most of the time your baby will keep to her own sleep/wake cycle and her own feeding timetable. There are some instances, however, when the parent may be inadvertently teaching the baby to maintain inappropriate sleeping or feeding behaviors. The infancy books may help you to figure out how you may be contributing to your baby's habits.

- Third, if you are unsure how you may be influencing your baby's habits, talk to your pediatrician.

- A fourth idea is to rotate the nights when you are in charge of nighttime feedings. Most couples *rotate* feedings during the night. This allows each parent to take some responsibility for caretaking at some time during the night. However, other parents talk about *rotating nights* rather than feedings. In this way, one parent is able to sleep undisturbed for most of the night every other night. You need to experiment and find which method works best for you.

YOUR BABY NEEDS TO KNOW YOU

So you wander off to work, feeling not quite as rested as you would like. You put in a full workday and come home. Your wife has been with the baby all day and needs some relief. She asks you to take your baby for a while so she can shower, rest, walk, shop, exercise, read, watch TV, listen to music and so on. What she does is not important. What is important is that you have agreed to share childcare responsibility.

You come home exhausted, tense and ready to relax. You may want to unwind from the day by reading the paper, taking a drink or going to the gym. But, there is a new priority in the house. Your baby needs to know her daddy. Your responsibility is to let her get to know and trust you and for you to know and trust her. Nothing is more important during the early stages of your baby's development than having her get to know and explore her father as well as she does her mother. Some dads were able to adjust to this easily while others did not.

We had just finished a marathon negotiating session with a company we were trying to buy out. This had been a three-day trip and I wanted nothing more than to walk in the door, jump into a nice warm shower and have a home-cooked meal. Whenever I had gone on trips before, my wife prepared unbelievable feasts for me.

When I walked in the door, everything was quiet. Elaine was asleep. Taylor was just getting up. I could hear her beginning to cry, announcing to the world that she wanted attention.

There was virtually nothing in the house to eat. I couldn't use the shower because I would wake up my family. So, I made myself a tuna fish sandwich. I admit I was pretty annoyed that Elaine hadn't prepared anything for me. She knew I was coming home.

I got so angry that she was sleeping when Taylor awoke that I woke *her* up. She knew I had been away on a business trip. I was hungry and tired. I didn't want to hassle with taking care of Taylor right now. Hell, all Elaine had to do was watch the kid. I had to work these past few days!

- Alan, thirty-eight, lawyer

The first day I went back to work, I couldn't wait to get home and play with my son, Brian. On the way home I bought him a baseball glove, bat and ball. Of course I knew he was too young to use it. I was just so excited about having a little boy; my own little boy. When I got home, I told my wife she had time off from baby duty. I wanted to play with Brian. I wanted to hold him, kiss him and just look at him. I was a complete nut with our kid. Our son! What a kick!

- Barry, thirty-two, dentist

There were some pretty important changes that happened to fathers during the early days of fatherhood. A fairly common experience among these men was being unprepared for their role as father. They had wanted to be a father, but they were accustomed to being a father-to-be. This differed from being a father. Fathers-to-be were observers of a process that was happening inside their wives. Fathers, on the other hand, were called upon to be active participants. Many had no idea what to do. They were confused. They were fearful. They were perplexed. Among the most commonly observed reactions from our new fathers were the following, newly developed psychiatric categories:

- Diaperaphobia: the fear of not knowing how to diaper your own child.
- Touchaphobia: the fear of touching your child because she will break or you will hurt her.
- Playaphobia: closely related to touchaphobia but involves not knowing how to play with a new baby.

- Misdirectaphobia: holding your child away from your body with her facing away from you rather than toward you.
- Cryaphobia: panic sets in when your baby begins to cry, triggering father's reflex action to hand the baby back to mommy.
- Rigidaphobia: father unable to relax when holding new baby.
- Yurmuthraphobia: blaming every mess your baby makes on your wife's side of the family.

There are many more "father-phobias." Many are the result of the father's poor preparation. Most people think of fathering as a very natural human response. I suggest that fatherhood is a skill that needs to be learned. Most fathers were looking for OJT (on-the-job training), but felt intimidated by their lack of knowledge. They hadn't prepared for fatherhood. They hadn't given much thought to being a father. Although they had looked forward to fatherhood, they didn't take the time to learn about it.

> The first time I held Molly, I was sure that I would drop her. She was so little, only about five or six pounds. I was scared to hold her. What if she started crying, how would I stop her?
> - Gene, twenty-eight, insurance underwriter

> I kept handing Rachel back to my wife or to my mother-in-law. I didn't know what to do with her. Then the nurse came in and asked me to help her diaper Rachel. How? After the nurse showed me, I felt pretty good that I did it. It wasn't that hard!
> - Greg, twenty-four, electrician

Little babies won't break when you pick them up. They are light and weigh less than your average oven-stuffer roaster. Yet, many men (and some women) feel afraid to approach their new baby.

My first suggestion is "Just Do It!" You will eventually touch, diaper and hold your baby. It's pretty unreasonable to assume you can avoid physical contact with your child for any length of time.

The sooner you begin to bond physically with your baby, the better it is for you, your wife and your baby.

Second, find out whether your hospital offers parents courses that teach about breast-feeding, diapering and other infant care concerns. These classes may help you feel more comfortable working with your newborn. If your hospital doesn't offer such classes, the Red Cross often does.

Finally, you might want to consider taking a course in Infant CPR. Many parents feel more confident knowing the essentials of how to help their baby in an emergency.

GETTING IT BACK TOGETHER

Most of our fathers found that their marriages had changed. They wanted to feel close to their wives again. They wanted to be intimate and sexual again. They wanted to return to going out with friends and socializing. They wanted to play the way they did before. They found that although their wives shared the same feelings, her attention was focused primarily upon her little baby. This created tension and distress in many marriages.

> I was ready for us to go back to being a couple. We hadn't seen a movie in at least three months because Kathy was uncomfortable sitting for that long. Now that the baby was here, I figured that we could get a sitter and spend time together going out to dinners, movies and concerts. Kathy wouldn't leave the baby for the first six months. This caused us a few pretty intense arguments.
>
> - Edward, thirty-three, educator

> We had always had a pretty hot sex life. It stayed that way until the end of her pregnancy. But after Carla's birth, we didn't do anything sexual for months. I told her that she was putting off intercourse because of how she feels about me. We argue a lot about this, even to this day. I just can't believe that she lost interest in me.
>
> - Jay, thirty-three, chemist

> Nothing bothered me more than when she would tell me that we couldn't have sex because she couldn't hear the baby.
>
> - Joey, nineteen, store clerk

Some fathers felt rejected wives after the birth of their child. Many felt lonely but were unable to talk about it. They believed it was "unmanly." Others felt angry that the focus of their wives' attention had shifted to their baby. Again, most of these men did not talk with their wives about these feelings.

When I see such behavior among my patients, I feel as if I am witnessing the birth of a new and dangerous game about how to develop bizarre communications. Call it "guess right or lose." These men were telling their wives about their discomfort in indirect and opaque manners. Then they would get frustrated and angry when their messages were misunderstood or ignored.

The most frequently seen game strategy was to leave the house and stay away for hours. The belief was: "The longer I am away from home the more she will know I need her attention. If she gives me attention, I won't leave." Of course, all too often what the woman saw was a man running away from his responsibilities toward her and the baby.

When they finally did talk about what was wrong, they now had to deal with *his* anger toward her and *her* anger toward him. Both felt rejected and unwanted. Both felt abandoned. Both began to question who is this person to whom I am married? Like so many other things in relationships, the decision to avoid talking about their needs and concerns led to a solution that made the problem worse.

The best solution to these problems is to talk with your spouse about how the changes are affecting her. You need to talk about how you are experiencing these changes too. So often, men control the direction of a conversation about feelings like a conductor controls an orchestra: I will help her to talk about her feelings and direct attention away from my feelings. You need to be different. You need to participate by talking about your feelings and having your wife talk about her feelings.

Many of these obstacles arise because each member of the marriage is holding onto a set of concealed and unacknowledged expectations about the other person's behavior. These expectations have been implied. They have been wished for. They have been imagined. But, they have seldom been discussed. Here is a way to discuss them in a rational, adult and effective way:

1. How did we each expect our lives to change after we had our child?
2. The most surprising things, different than what we expected are:
3. The most difficult things, different than what we expected are:
4. The four most important things we need to discuss in finding new ways to deal with our changing family life are:
5. During the next week, we agree to find time to talk about solutions to these concerns on: (fill in day, time and place of conversation)

The purpose of this exercise is for you and your wife to commit to a day, time and place to discuss your concerns. Keep the discussions short, ranging from thirty to sixty minutes. The objective is to negotiate a solution to the changes caused by your baby's ability to turn your life upside down. This is *not* an opportunity to tell her how ineffective she is or how much better you are. This is an opportunity to come together as a couple, to share in the adventure and challenge of joint problem solving and to set a precedent that when problems arise you, as a couple, can cooperate and develop effective solutions.

ANYBODY HOME?

When you bring home your newborn, most couples want to spend time alone. They need to figure out who they are as this new family. They need time to adjust to new routines and new schedules. They need to begin the process of discovering themselves as husband and wife *with* a child.

This is a special time for every couple with a new baby. Some sit cuddled in front of a fire, new mother gently rocking her new charge to sleep while father gazes adoringly at both mother and child. Other couples sit on the living room floor watching every movement, every twitch for a sign of intelligence, playfulness or hunger. Still other couples put the newborn into her crib, place the crib in the master bedroom and catch up on the months of sleep lost during the pregnancy.

No matter how you decide to spend this exciting time with your spouse, every uncle, aunt, cousin, friend, acquaintance, colleague and passerby will stop by to see the newborn. No one tells you about these intrusions. It is socially uncomfortable to tell people to call first since they have already rung your doorbell, especially Aunt Agnes who drove from Saint Olaf, Minnesota. So, what do you do? Many couples fight.

> When we got home from the hospital, I wanted to spend time just the two of us. No one invited my parents, they just stopped by. Beth was furious with me. She was sure that I had invited my folks over without asking her first. Some first day that turned out to be.
>   - Mike, thirty-three insurance executive

Other couples grin and bear it.

> Joe had wanted to be called when we were on our way home from the hospital. He was my best friend and I knew that he was almost as excited as us. So, I called to tell him the good news. We walked into the house and discovered that he had arranged a surprise party for us. It was real nice of him, but we were so tired. We had to put on our 'party' face. We couldn't wait for them all to go home.
>   - Carl, twenty-eight, school psychologist

No matter how you deal with unexpected visitors, know this: They will come out of the woodwork when you least expect it.

Most of our fathers were pretty accepting of the fuss made by in-laws and friends. Their main concern was in overtaxing their wives and exposing their newborn to potential illnesses carried in by their guests. Grandparents were usually the biggest offenders, along with those who were generally excused from calling before visiting. Our fathers talked about how their mothers-in-law usually stepped right in to work with the newborn, allowing their wives to catch some much needed rest.

What can you do? You can set limits on the visits by arranging them at convenient times during the day. You can limit their duration to a few hours. Most, although not all, relatives understand the stress and fatigue associated with having a new child. They respect and appreciate the family's desire to spend time alone with the new arrival. But unless you talk about your concerns, your guests will not know what you need.

⟦ 13 ⟧

CHAPTER

My Child and His Grandchild

The birth of your child places you in a different position in your family of origin. You are no longer the adult-child. You are now the adult-child with a child, a real adult. Your father is a grandfather. Your mother becomes a grandmother. Recognition of these transitions often leads to increased awareness of one's aging, one's mortality.

For years into my twenties, my father used to kid me that he was still twenty-one and that I was the one getting older. Jack Benny will thirty-nine forever. Such games of denial reveal our sensitivity to getting older. We are acutely aware of our aging and we struggle to find clever, often funny, ways to deny our aging.

The birth of a grandchild places that march toward maturity squarely in one's view. For some grandfathers, it produces an uneasy tension. On the one hand, they want to celebrate the arrival of their legacy for a new generation. On the other hand, the birth is a reminder that their children are old enough to have children, which means that they (the grandparents) are beyond that stage.

> When Karen was born, I asked my father to join us at the hospital. Unannounced, he left for a business trip to Los Angeles. It was unplanned and very spontaneous. I was hurt that he placed this mysterious business trip ahead of seeing his first grandchild.
>
> - Barry, thirty-two, dentist

There are other grandfathers who want to recapture the spirit and excitement of young family life.

> When my father heard Matt was born, he hopped a plane from Boca, ready to stay for as long as we needed him. *He* wanted to help with the cooking. He wanted to watch the baby while we put our lives back in order. He wanted to be right in the thick of things. It was my wife who felt a bit intruded upon with his energy and willingness to stay and help.
>
> — George, thirty-two, college teacher

Another experience contributing to grandfather being reminded of his aging is the response of his friends. People who care for him respond with well wishes for the newborn. Grandpa is often reminded——ten, twenty, thirty times a day——by his friends that he is a grandfather. If your dad is unprepared to deal with his aging, then his friends' congratulations may be a painful reminder of his mortatlity.

NO LONGER JUST A SON

An important transition occurs between your father and you when you have your baby. You have a new horizon to explore and share. He has already raised at least one child. He has experience. He has knowledge along with his parenting battle scars. Your father can be a valuable source of information, guidance and support. Yet, very few of our expectant fathers wanted their fathers' assistance.

> I know what my dad would say because he said it to me so often when I was growing up. Anyway, if I did call him, all he would do is lecture. I don't want to hear that crap.
>
> — Andrew, twenty-seven, policeman

> I never considered my father as a resource for my child. I need to think about how much I want him to be involved. He tries to make everything his way. I would be scared he would bully me in directions he thought were good for me rather than what I needed from him.

But, maybe if I approach him in the right way, it might not be a bad idea.

- Art, twenty-six, lawyer

A recurring theme for many of our fathers was the fear that if they included their fathers as a source of guidance or support it would quickly turn into either a competition or a shouting match over who was right.

I love my dad. I would do anything for him. But, he treats me like a little kid who doesn't know his way. I hate when he does that. It's the only thing we fight over. I don't want that type of scene in my house.

- Greg, thirty-one, electrician

Daughters-in-Law

An interesting transition involved our expectant fathers feeling that their fathers, because of their grandchild, saw their daughters-in-law in a different light. Some saw the mother of the baby was now as a legitimate member of the family. Their logic was that since she contributed something of worth to the family history, she may enter the family as a bona fide member.

My dad changed toward Kathy, too. It was really strange. He was always kind to her. But now, he treats her the same way has he does my sisters. I know that she feels the difference. She feels welcomed and accepted. I think that my dad is unaware of it. Isn't that strange?

- Edward, thirty-three, educator

Lack of Involvement

Many of our fathers described feeling disappointed by the lack of involvement their fathers had with their new grandchild. Their expectations were that granddad would be intimately involved in the lives of his grandchild. Most of our dads imagined their fathers would take a more active role in grandparenting than they did as parents themselves. Almost to a man, they were disappointed.

I wanted my baby to know his grandfather. It took me years to know my dad and even then it was hard to feel he cared. Now, he talks about wanting to be involved, but he sees my kid only on birthdays, Christmas and Easter.

- Gene, twenty-eight, insurance underwriter

A small minority discovered their parents were not interested in seeing the newborn. For these fathers, concerns about their specialness in their family of origin were touched. One father talked about his anger and disgust over his parents' lack of enthusiasm about visiting the new baby.

All my life I wanted them to care about me. All their life they cared only about themselves. I thought I had put all that shit in the right place. But their refusal to see my baby has gotten me started all over again with these feelings of rejection. No one knows this pain. My child will never know this pain.

- Jay, thirty-three, chemist

Jay raised an interesting and painful question about the role of grandparents. He questioned whether his grandparents "owe" it to their grandchildren to spend time knowing them. He asked himself, and also me, how he could deal with the pain of his parents' rejection, while not revealing it to his children.

Rich asked similar questions. He was my client for several years and we lived through his marital ups and downs and the birth of his three children. During a series of intense therapy sessions, Rich and his wife, Megan, focused on the question of the role of grandparents in their lives.

Rich and Megan want their children to know their grandparents. They believe their children's lives will be enriched by frequent exposure to their grandparents. Grandparents bring to their grandchildren a quality of love and caring that is different from that of their parents. Grandparents provide children with a sense of continuity across generations. They provide an understanding of family history and meaning that elaborates and enhances their parents' understanding.

Megan's parents travel from Lancaster every other weekend to visit their grandchildren. Occasionally, grandma will surprise her granddaughter after school and take her out to go shopping or to the zoo. Megan's parents firmly believe in the importance of sharing in their grandchildrens' formative years. And the grandchildren——they could light up a small city with their smiles when they see their grandparents driving up for a visit.

Rich's parents, however, follow a different path. Living only four miles away, Rich's parents see the children five times a year, Christmas, every other Thanksgiving, Easter and each of their birthdays. They always talk about visiting more frequently, but they seldom make time in their busy schedule. In fact, Rich and Megan figured the last time his parents visited on a day other than a holiday or birthday was sometime in 1986. Rich and Megan often ask if they may bring their children to visit their grandparents. But, between the house in Palm Beach, the townhouse in the Poconos, and their travels to exotic places, his parents have no time to give.

Rich has repeatedly asked his parents to take a greater role in their grandchildren's lives. They say they will make time for their grandchildren, but never do. Rich feels disappointed and often rejected by his parents' refusal to take a more active role. Yet, if you were to ask them, his parents would talk about the excitement of their world travel, golf and vacation homes. In their eyes, retirement is a time to throw off the shackles of responsibility and punctuality and play, play, play.

Rich and Megan raised an intriguing question: Do grandparents have a responsibility to get to know their grandchildren? If they had asked "should" grandparents get to know their grandchildren, the answer would be an unequivocal yes. But, phrasing the question within the realm of responsibility begs the question of morality.

First, is grandparenting a moral responsibility? Rich and Megan clearly felt that it was. Then, I asked about the purpose of a grandparent's moral responsibility. It seemed to me that without understanding the purpose of this responsibility, the responsibility itself is meaningless.

They suggested the purpose of grandparenting is to enhance the quality of belonging to a family unit. Megan said grandparents can provide a rudder to the course of a family from generation-to-generation. She pointed to her own family system in which four generations of Walker's have lived within a four-square-mile-area. She talked about the interdependency among families, the closeness among cousins and the continuity from child to parent to grandparent.

I posed another question: If grandparenting is a moral responsibility, then how do you define the responsibilities of grandparenting? I wanted Megan and Rich to focus on the often conflicting pulls between family responsibilities and the freedom that may come with retirement. I wanted them to see from Rich's parent's perspective that retirement and freedom is an entitlement, a license to become a kid again and answer to nobody.

Intellectually, Megan and Rich understood his parents' desire to play and travel. However, they were tied into the emotional pull of their children, who want to know their grandparents. Rich and Megan, like so many other couples, will struggle with wanting more family focus while settling for less. There is no easy answer about how much involvement grandparents should have with their grandchildren.

In my life, my mother-in-law visits frequently and talks about the rights of grandparents. Yet, when asked to define those rights, she finds herself unable to cite anything beyond the right to see her grandchildren. Participation in my children's lives gives her a sense of being a mother again. She spends one weekend a month escaping into renewed motherhood. Grandparenting gives her life a purpose that enables her to pretend to be a better parent with her grandchildren than she was with her own children. The purpose of grandparenting, here, is to rewrite the grandparent's history of how she was as a parent. Is this right? Is this wrong? I don't know, but I believe it is necessary for her to right some wrong she feels she committed as a younger woman. At the same time, she is providing an enriched relationship to my children, one they would not have if she were not intimately involved in their lives.

So we end back at the original question: Do grandparents have a responsibility to get to know their grandchildren? If your answer is yes, then spend time talking about what the purpose of that responsibility is. Then sit down with the grandparents of your children and have the same discussion.

RESOLUTIONS AND APOLOGIES

A final area of transition revealed in our talks was the emerging new relationship between fathers and sons. Apparently the birth of a grandchild was a catalyst for change, providing a new link between them and their fathers.

> I remember before my dad died he spoke with me about his feelings at my birth. He told me about how excited he was that he had a boy and the name of his family would continue for another generation. That was real important to him. Then he began to give me advice about how a man should father his baby. He tried so hard to show me the right way to be a father and to be a husband, but his ideas were from the forties not the nineties. I couldn't tell him, though.
>
> - Nick, twenty-three, video store manager

> My father had been really into the pregnancy. He loved the idea that he was going to be a grandfather. Just before Jack's birth, my dad started telling me about his youth in Nazi Germany. The stories were so vivid to him, as if he was reliving them. He told me about his parents and how they treated him. He told me about the friends he lost during the war. He wanted me to understand that family is very important and in the blink of an eye you can lose it all. He told me always to treat my children with respect and they will give that respect back to me.
>
> - Andy, thirty-four, English teacher

Many new fathers expressed satisfaction at developing a fresh dimension to their relationship with their father. For some, this new connection was bittersweet. It raised issues about their own childhood and what they missed. But for most, finding a way to extend their relationship with their fathers appeared an unexpected and welcome by-product of the pregnancy.

I know I don't always tell my dad I love him, but now we can talk about having children, we can meet as adults. We've never done that before. It feels a bit odd but really good.

- Doug, twenty-eight, broker

When we began to talk about the values dad wanted to teach me, his whole demeanor changed. He looked very solemn and thoughtful. He said he would do things differently if he had a chance. He wanted to spend more time with me when I was growing up. He was concerned he failed in teaching me the value of being close to your family. He said he would not make that mistake with his grandchild.

- Wes, thirty-four, real estate agent

Some of our fathers described discussions with their fathers about what *their* fathers believed they had done wrong during their parenting. They talked about wanting to relive the excitement of their son's early youth, with particular emphasis on the years in junior and senior high school.

I was surprised to see dad cry. He never cries. He looked at me sitting next to the baseball mitt and bat that I bought for our son-to-be and got emotional. He told me he wanted to have pictures in his head about my Little League days and my high school football career. He really cried and said he was sorry he was working all the time. He never thought about what he was missing because he was too busy making a living.

- Art, twenty-six, lawyer

My dad laid a heavy load on me. We were talking about Terri's due date and my dad said something like: 'When you were a kid, I was a kid myself. I was a lousy husband and a poor father. I didn't want to grow up. I drank too much and played the field. Your mother never forgave me. I want to be the grandfather to your child I never was to you as my son. Don't keep me out of your life anymore. I want you to see I can be a good father. Even if it is twenty years too late for you and me.' How do you say no to that?

- Chris, thirty-three, architect

Lessons to Be Used

A conclusion we drew from our new fathers' experiences with their fathers is that having a new baby adds a new dimension to everyone's life. Yet, our new fathers felt uneasy about what to talk about with their fathers. So many of us carry baggage from our relationship with our fathers that the happiness of a new birth unleashes a flood of memories that cascades into our consciousness. Here are some ideas to talk about with your father when you are expecting a child.

- What was it like *for you* when mom first told you that she was pregnant?
- How did you know that you were ready to have a child?
- What did you look forward to when I was born?
- If you could do it all over, what would you do differently?
- What type of grandfather do you want to be?
- How involved with our children do you want to be?
- How has our pregnancy gotten you to think about our relationship, as father and son?
- What do you feel are important values about you and about our family you want to see passed on to our child?
- What do you see as the most important responsibilities of fatherhood?
- What did you learn about fatherhood that you think I should know?

PART FOUR

AMBUSHES
ROADBLOCKS
and
POTHOLES

[[14]]

CHAPTER

Responsibility

Everyone living in today's world of slow economic growth knows that we are working hard every day, making more money than our parents ever dreamed of making at our age. Yet, there is no money left to save; no discretionary income to play with. We have become almost obsessed with stretching our paycheck so that the month runs out before the money.

Similarly, time seems to shrink. When I was growing up, an hour used to be sixty-minutes long. Today, an hour passes in the blink of an eye. Yesterday was August and vacation in the warmth and beauty of the Jersey shore. When I woke up this morning, the forecast was for snow. Man or woman, married or single, with or without child, as we move closer to the turn of the century, it seems that time is moving faster. The result is that we feel unanticipated pressures. No one ever told us that becoming an adult and raising a family would be so stressful, so time consuming and so demanding of all our energies.

When today's couple makes the decision to have a child, they need to prepare themselves for radical changes in the practical, day-to-day routines of their lives. We will talk about some of these changes in the pages that follow.

If you are like me, you will find that the later stages of pregnancy through the first six-to-twelve months of your child's life will be among the most stressful you will encounter. Your wife's routine will have already changed greatly. Your sex life probably has changed, with less playtime or intimate time. Your finances may be shrinking due to expenses related either to the pregnancy, the baby's arrival or the multitude of baby toys and outfits that you may have bought surreptitiously for the new baby.

This is a wonderful opportunity for you to practice being in the emotional center of your family. You can be proactive. You can initiate discussions about how well your wife feels the house is running with the current arrangements. You can initiate discussions about how *you* feel about the changes that are going on around you. You can share your fears, your worries and your pride.

CHOICES

Men are seeing the vast responsibilities and choices about fatherhood facing them. Many are looking back at the nature and quality of their relationship with their fathers. Most are saying that they want to change the nature of the father-child relationship. No longer do fathers want to remain distant, wary and unavailable. They want to break the cycle. But they are uncertain how to change. A few, by refusing to father children, break the cycle by stopping it completely. Most, however, break the cycle by changing it.

Our technology has given us a gift with a double-edged blade. We have greater control over our decisions about when to have a family and how many children to have in that family. Professionals tell us about the importance of developing a secure marital environment before we bring a child into this world. They tell us that having a child means greater responsibility, greater financial commitments and more stress on the marriage. Experts teach that having a child means examining how child care responsibilities are divided between father and mother. We are told to consider when is the right time to have a child. We are supposed to talk about family planning issues, such as family size and how far apart in age the children should be.

The other side of increasing control over our reproductive destiny is knowing how to apply it wisely. In the words of Jerrold Lee Shapiro, "Having greater freedom of choice however, does not necessarily make things easier. Any freedom entails corresponding responsibility."1

Used wisely, our freedom to decide involves knowing what our choices are and taking responsibility for carrying them out. Too many of us approach fatherhood having given little serious thought to our readiness to have a family. We haven't been taught to think about who we will be as fathers, either in relationship to our spouse or to our children. Like our fathers before us, we often assume fatherhood and its responsibilities will be learned during the experience itself.

Most of our expectant fathers held such a belief. Almost none of them had considered the full range of responsibilities attached to being a father. These men had not thought about a child's effect on their feelings about commitment, marriage, family, sex, careers, changing roles or the division of labor in the family. Just like the social stereotype of fathers past, most said they considered only the financial impact before they made the decision to have a child.

> I never considered that planning for a baby entailed more than being financially stable. Debbie knows that she will take the first three months off from work, then we will find daycare. I guess that we'll sleep a little less and spend more time at home. What else will be different?
>
> - Bobby, twenty-five, salesman

> When you talked about changes in responsibility toward family, I always figured that having a child meant working longer hours to support three people instead of two. I didn't consider how my responsibilities to my wife and child would change. I remember that my mother's constant attention to us changed her relationship with my father. He always used to talk about mom putting us before him. He felt pretty bitter about that. But, I'm not gonna be like him.
>
> (Question from workshop leader: *I understand you saw your mother place her children before her husband. You can tell by the nodding heads of the other dads that you are not alone. Tell me, Drew, how do you expect your marriage to be different? And, what have you and Susan talked about?*)

I just know I'm gonna be different. We're gonna be different. We
don't have to talk about it because we both know we don't want to
be like our mom and dad. Why? What should we think about?
- Drew, twenty-seven, customer service rep.

Drew and Bobby are not alone in their lack of planning. But,
such haphazard approaches to future fatherhood will ultimately
serve you, your wife and your child poorly. If you don't know
where you're going, you'll probably end up somewhere else!

RESPONSIBILITY

Responsibility in fatherhood is an interesting concept. Responsibility means you are *accountable*; accountable to yourself, your
wife and your child. It suggests that you are *in charge* of something, have a *duty* to do certain things. Responsibility also implies
a *trust* you share with those with whom you live.

Another aspect of responsibility, the downside of responsibility, is that it is a *burden*. When we fail in our responsibilities,
we are assigned *blame* and *liability*.

Many fathers-to-be talked about how their awareness of some
kind of responsibility was crystallized and clarified as they moved
closer toward the birth of their child.

When Peggy and I first talked about having kids, the first thing I
thought about was whether my job was secure. Thinking about
having a kid made me realize that *they* will be depending on *me*.
Like real grown-up stuff. My idea about sharing the financial burden
was quickly changed from a "we" to a "me".
- Gene, twenty-eight, insurance underwriter

Awareness of financial security stopped some fathers from
having children earlier in life.

When Cheryl and I discussed having children, our first thought was
about job security. She had just started teaching and didn't have
tenure. I was completing graduate school and beginning my job
search. I knew I would find something in my field. But we didn't

know when. We waited another two years until Cheryl had tenure and I had some job security at the college.

- George, thirty-two, college teacher

Other fathers knew of their weak financial situation and decided to have a child anyway.

Both of us understood our jobs were not secure. The economy is really rocky and the plant was having layoffs every few months. But, we loved each other and figured we'd find a way to get by, even if it meant asking our folks for help.

- Paul, twenty-four, factory worker

Other fathers-to-be talked about how the decision to have a child forced them to grow up. These dads-to-be recognized that once the decision to have a child was made, they needed to turn more of their attention on their marriage and its health. Particularly among younger men, the decision to have a baby reshaped their roles in the family and forced them to make compromises between their friends and athletic/social activities in favor of their marriage.

Once the decision to have a child was made, almost all felt a sense of duty to be the best father they could be. Yet, when asked to describe what that father would do, what he would want to teach his children and how he would teach them these ideas, their screens went blank. These men had no idea what this "best father" should look like. Fatherhood was a responsibility and an opportunity, they said, which they looked forward to their entire lives. But, they were unclear about its purpose.

Our interview and workshop data revealed to us a group of men who were unprepared to discuss factors associated with the decision to have a baby. It was not that these men were unwilling to discuss relevant ideas about fatherhood. It was that these men didn't know *what* to discuss or *how* to discuss it.

Tomorrow's father needs to understand the meaning of responsibility and the role that it plays in establishing a healthy family. We need to be responsible (accountable) to the emotional needs of our current family rather than to the voices of *our fathers.* We need to define our responsibilities (duties and obligations) to serve our children's emerging needs for emotional involvement and physical presence. Our duty is to show them that fathers cry, laugh, love, succeed, fail and learn. Most of all, we need to take responsibility for teaching them that fathers, above all else, are involved with their children.

Our responsibility to our children is to give them role models who prepare them for tomorrow while anchoring them in the love, warmth and nurturance of today. We need to accept them and push them without unnecessary criticism. We need to know the difference between constructive feedback, which can help them grow, and destructive criticism, which can harm.

Tomorrow's world will demand flexible sex-role understandings and behaviors of our children, in contrast to our fathers' fixed sex-role patterns. Our daughters may be batting champions of their Little League team and carry that sense of competition and need to succeed into their work world. Our sons may want to learn to cook, experiment with dance class or freely show their emotions. We are responsible (accountable) for encouraging them to reach beyond the limits of yesterday to the promise of tomorrow. The greatest gift we can give to our children is to guide them to be better than their parents. Our responsibility (duty) is to cultivate a home life in which our children understand that their responsibility to themselves and to their family is to be the best that they can be.

We are responsible for teaching our children that they are limited only by their perception of the world. It is our responsibility (duty and obligation) to teach our children to reflect upon their beliefs, attitudes and values in their continuous efforts to reach a more fulfilling sense of who they are and who they want to be.

IDENTIFYING YOUR RESPONSIBILITIES

We have spoken about responsibility as defined in many ways. We have talked about responsibility as accountability, duty, obligation, trust, burden, blame and liability. Let us now consider some ways you can explore your ideas about responsibility and fatherhood.

As you complete the following statements, notice how our expectant fathers had difficulty in thinking through the various components of responsibility toward their families. Some were stuck fighting a battle with their fathers. Others found themselves preoccupied with doing things *for* their families rather than including themselves *within* their families.

My father's responsibility toward his family included:

My father saw his responsibility toward his family to be the nice guy. He never wanted an argument or any yelling. As a result, he taught us all never to show strong emotions. He was the consummate peacemaker and as a result he never taught me how to stand up for myself. Thank God, I met Kathy and she helped me through her strength.

- Edward, thirty-three, educator

That's simple. Dad put the food on the table. He taught us about the outdoors. Strong men, real men never show how they feel. It's a sign of weakness . . . wimps and such. He took the responsibility to show us how to have a good time. How to hunt, how to shoot and how to get a girl.

- Ricky, twenty-three, gardener

My responsibility toward my family includes:

I have listened to this lecture and realize I don't know what responsibilities I have. I know what responsibilities I am supposed to have, but I never questioned before what we want as a family. Maybe we have something to talk about tonight.

- Jack, thirty-one, physician

I am responsible for bringing emotion and warmth into their lives. But, I won't do it alone. I want my wife to be there with me, because she can show me how. I will be responsible with her to bring to them our understanding of equality and of communication.

- Jed, thirty-one, artist

I consider my duty to my wife to include:

My duty toward my wife is to love her. To provide for her. To protect her. I want her to know that she can talk with me when she needs to. My duty is to support her and care for her.

- Warren, thirty-three, accountant

I consider my duty toward my child to include:

My duty toward my child is to love her. I will protect her as I will protect my wife. My duty as a father is to teach her, to guide her. I am a teacher of morals, of rights and wrongs. I want to be the type of father whom she can point to and say, "My daddy knows the answer, let's ask him."

- Warren, thirty-three, accountant

What is my duty? First, to find a way to be around and participate more than my father did with me. I want to, it's gonna sound silly to you, but I wanna bake cookies with my kids, watch cartoons and read them books. I want to be there for their first movie, their first birthday party, and be the parent who goes to the PTA to be involved.

- Wes, thirty-four, real estate agent

In my family, I am accountable for the following:

I'm accountable for shopping. I want to help out by doing more chores around the house 'cause Kitty's gonna be busy with the kid. I'll vacuum and do the wash, sometimes.

- Don, thirty-three, house painter

I am accountable to my wife and my children. I want my kids to know who I am. I never knew my father . . . at least never knew how he felt about me or my sister. I want my kids to know I have feelings. I want my son to learn that men can express feelings and not feel ashamed of them. I will be accountable to myself for making sure I teach them that guys have feelings.

- Ben, twenty-eight, bank manager

The burden of having a family weighs heavily on me because:

My burden is about keeping money coming into the house. I know that my wife will get back to work soon, but still, I carry most of the weight. I've never had to carry this much responsibility before. It scares me. What if I fail?

- Bobby, twenty-five, salesman

I will take responsibility as well as blame for failure in:

I will blame myself if my kids always turn to their mother to talk about their lives. I want my kids to see me as open and available to them. I want them to know that they can talk to me about their feelings, their successes and defeats—they need to know that I want in on that part of their lives. If they don't include me in on that loop, I will have no on else to blame but me. I will make sure that doesn't happen.

- Marty, thirty-five, consultant

LEARNING ABOUT YOUR RESPONSIBILITIES

Use the following exercises to help you focus on ways to become more of a part of the emotional inner circle of your family. This is not the unique province of your wife. Your soon-to-be children will welcome you with smiles and requests for hugs, stories and guidance. Each step you take toward greater emotional involvement helps them to prepare better for their future. Your involvement in their emotional and physical development teaches them about fathering models, which will rattle around in their soon-to-be adult heads just as your father's rattles around in yours.

1. List five important ideas about responsibility in fatherhood that will bring you closer to the emotional center of your family:

2. Picture the ideal responsible father. In your mind's eye, observe how this imaginary new father behaves toward his child and his wife. What are the feelings and characteristics you see?

3. Describe this new father's responsibilities to his family and how he feels about those responsibilities.

4. Describe three beliefs and values about responsibility that will guide your actions as a father.

5. Describe three behaviors that represent responsible fatherhood.

6. Describe two steps that you will take responsibility for enacting during the next week that will move you closer to the emotional center of your family.

These exercises are only the beginning steps in moving away from the fatherhood model you inherited to a new, enlightened fatherhood. Revisit the first few exercises every few weeks and add new responses so that you are continually building and revising your fatherhood model. The clearer that you are about the beliefs, values and behaviors that bring you closer to the emotional center of your family, the easier it will be to guide yourself there.

[[15]]

CHAPTER

Commitment

She had met him while he was married to his first wife. He fell madly in love with Josie the first time they met. She kept her distance because he was married.

Bernie's marriage was failing. The possibility of Josie tipped the scales for Bernie and he ended his marriage.

Bernie and Josie dated for years before they decided to live together. Then, Bernie asked Josie out to The Garden, a lovely, romantic restaurant in Center City Philadelphia. The menu had been set in advance by Bernie. First the champagne, followed by crab and jumbo shrimp appetizers. Next, a dozen long-stemmed roses served on a silver platter. Wrapped around two of the stems was a sparkling 1.5 carat diamond engagement ring.

Josie never did find out what the main course was. She spent the rest of the night overwhelmed by its beauty and its symbolism. Her answer was yes. The date was set later that evening: July 15.

On July 14, Bernie called Josie, asked if she would have lunch with him and said that they had to talk. He came over to her office, picked her up and they drove to a fancy hotel. He had gotten a room just for the two of them. Kinda neat and a bit kinky, Josie thought, playing hide and seek the night before their wedding.

They made passionate love. Josie never did make it back to work. Around 5:00 P.M., just after they finished their white wine and oysters, Bernie turned to Josie and said he couldn't get married. He knew he loved her and only her, but the idea of marriage frightened him too much. He stood up, showered and drove Josie home.

They came into therapy about three months after this fiasco. After six months of exploration, discussion and couples therapy, they again decided to marry.

Same scenario. Josie and Bernie were forty-eight hours away from marriage and he called to talk with her. Again, he called off the marriage. This time, Josie walked away from Bernie vowing never to see him again.

This separation lasted about eight months. Then, Bernie called Josie and said that he had changed. Would she please reconsider seeing him?

She had never really gotten over her love for him. She melted at the thought of his changing, of a future together, of their happily-ever-after finally getting on track.

They dated for six months and then decided to marry. Bernie and Josie approached the fateful day with great confidence that this was their lucky time. They made it past the forty-eight-hour mark. They made it past the twenty-four-hour mark. Saturday, the day of the wedding, all involved parties held their breath as they awaited Bernie's car at the driveway of the church. It came. Bernie got out of the car and walked into the church area reserved for family members of the groom.

Josie sighed in relief. The organ played. The flower girl walked down the aisle. The bridesmaids and ushers followed slowly. Then the best man. Bernie's parents were next. They all gathered by the priest.

The crowd turned in anticipation to see Bernie walk down the aisle, but no Bernie. He was sitting in his car crying that he could not walk down the aisle. He couldn't get married. Josie, flushed with anger, ran toward his car. Bernie turned the key and disappeared down the tree-lined street.

THE DREADED "C" WORD

Much has been written in the popular press about men being "commitment phobic." This is the idea that men are unable to commit themselves to long-term, stable, monogamous relationships. Bernie is their poster child. He was unable to gather the strength he needed to commit to Josie within the institution of marriage. As wacky as their relationship was, I never had a doubt that both loved each other. But love was not enough.

Commitment is a complex word, poorly understood by most people. Look in a dictionary and you will find four general categories of meaning. Commitment refers to responsibility, duty and obligation. It also means dedication, devotion and faithfulness. Guarantee, pledge and promise are part of the idea of commitment. Finally, commitment involves taking a stand, making a decision and reaching a resolution.

When I asked our expectant fathers what commitment meant to them, most replied that commitment meant being committed to their wife and their future families.

> I know I love Jeanie and she loves me. We are committed to raising a family and committed to each other. I know I am committed to her because I am devoted to her.
>
> - Art, twenty-six, lawyer

> I am committed to my wife and my child. I am committed to making this marriage work, this family work. Commitment means giving to another person in a way that is reserved only for her.
>
> - Jay, thirty-three, chemist

Most people think about the idea of commitment as being committed to *someone*. Our expectant fathers talked much about their commitment to their wife, to their marriage, and to their family. In many ways, hearing their unambiguous support for and expectations about the longevity of their marriage was enchanting. However, I wanted to challenge them to reach beyond their current understanding to a new, different view of commitment.

Commitment to an Idea, Not a Person

Commitment should be to an idea about your life and its character. Commitment should be first to the idea of a healthy marriage. Commitment should be second to the idea of a healthy functioning family unit. Commitment to the particular persons who occupy the slots within the marriage and family is the next step in commitment.

Why is this important? Commitment to the idea of a healthy marriage keeps you focused on the purpose of your interactions with your partner. Each action, thought and gesture should be measured against your commitment to keeping a marriage healthy. There will be times in a marriage, or in a family, when you find yourself questioning your desire to be with someone within that relationship. For most of us, such questioning occurs only occasionally. If your idea of commitment is based upon your commitment to the person, and if your feelings about that person change, then your commitment to that person also changes. Changes in commitment provide the soil within which to cultivate the seeds of insecurity, inconsistency and unhappiness.

On the other hand, if your idea of commitment is based upon your resolve to maintain a healthy marriage, then when your feelings about your partner have those momentary variations, they do not impact your feeling of commitment. These variations may affect how you feel about your spouse, but they do not threaten the fundamental underpinnings of the marriage.

COMMITMENT TO FATHERHOOD

Commitment to fatherhood means that you have an idea about how to be a father. It suggests you have built a miniaturized model of a father and stuffed it into your brain.

Before you can build a model of fatherhood, you need to commit yourself to certain ideas about what it means to be a father, then build those ideas into the model.

Most of our daddies-to-be were committed to the general idea of being a father *but* in relation to their child. When we asked them to talk about how their ideas about commitment to their child would guide them, they looked puzzled.

> Nancy and I both are committed to being good parents. We will give our child everything that she wants. I don't understand why you are telling us not to be committed to our little baby. How can you

question my commitment to my baby? I love her even though she isn't born yet.

- Eric, twenty-two, mechanic

This is a tough idea to swallow. Are you saying that to be committed means to think less about our new kid and treat it like an object?

- George, twenty-seven, graduate student

Many responses were similar to those above. The idea of being committed, first to a way of life or an approach to family and then using that commitment to guide your actions and thoughts in your relationship with your children and wife, seemed alien. Most of us are accustomed to thinking about being committed to someone rather than to a set of beliefs and values that guide our behavior.

Yet, the art of successful family functioning is, in part, due to the clarity of the expectations defining and guiding that family. Similarly, the art of successful fathering, in part, depends upon the clarity of expectations defining and guiding a father in his role within the family. If the model to which you are committed is comprised only of expectations about fathering behaviors that guide you toward providing, protecting and making money, then your commitment is to those ideas. It doesn't matter that you feel a strong pull toward being more emotionally involved in your family. If the model in your head to which you are committed has not been changed, then the odds are that you will behave according to those guidelines, while feeling frustrated that you are not more emotionally involved in your family.

Changing your emotional involvement may not mean changing your relationship with your wife or your child. To change your emotional involvement requires that the ideas guiding your behavior change. It is the expectations about what a father does, how a father feels, what a father contributes and how a father participates that need to be reprogrammed.

Earlier we described four different aspects to the definition of commitment. Each has its place within commitment. Our view of commitment is concerned with dedication, devotion and faithfulness to an idea about participation. It asks you to define your duties, obligations and responsibilities linked to that idea. It asks for guarantees, pledges and promises about beliefs, values and behaviors that guide your actions regarding this idea. And, above all, commitment asks for a different type of decision making, providing a new resolution and the courage to take a different stand about what it means to be involved in your family.

Commitment Requires Effort

Tomorrow's father needs to make a commitment to a new vision of fatherhood. He needs to envision himself talking with his children about *his* feelings. He needs to see himself as contributing to healthy family functioning by giving of himself through his love, his energies, his stories and his help. This man can build a tree house, cook a dinner or shed a tear with a child's broken heart.

As you move toward this new man, you need to be involved with your daughter's ballet. Sure, it makes her happy but moreover, your involvement represents one aspect of how an involved father acts within this new model of fatherhood. Your commitment to help, to guide and to participate is based upon your belief that a family is healthier when father is involved in its emotional center. Of course, your wife will feel good about your participation, but it is not for her. Your children will love your stories, your tears and your vulnerabilities, but you do not share them because they make your kids feel good. You share them because the model guiding your behavior shows you that fatherhood is involvement at all levels of family functioning.

Building Toward Commitment

Commitment can be defined in many ways. This chapter has talked about being committed to an idea about fatherhood rather than being committed to a person. Let us look at ways for you to begin examining your notion of commitment and fatherhood.

1. My father's commitment to his family included:

2. My commitment to my family includes:

3. List five important ideas about commitment in fatherhood that will bring you closer to the emotional center of your family:

4. Picture the ideal committed father. Imagine how this father behaves toward his child and his wife. What are some feelings and characteristics you see?

5. Describe this new father's commitments to his family and some feelings he has about these commitments.

6. Describe three beliefs and values about commitment that will guide your actions as a father.

7. Describe three behaviors that represent a committed father:

8. Describe two steps you will enact during the next week that will move you closer to the emotional center of your family.

You'll want to review these steps periodically to build and refine your fatherhood model and to measure your journey toward it.

Who Does What
Around the House?

My three-year-old son came into the kitchen.

"Daddy, what you doing?"

"I'm washing the kitchen floor."

"Why?"

I wanted to say that daddy washes the floor because mommy has never met a mop with her karma, but I refrained. "Robbie, I am washing the floor to make it clean."

"I want to help!" he said. "Big boys do things together, right? I'm a big boy. I cleaning the floor just like a big boy, like daddy. Right?"

When my wife and I had our first child, we moved into a row home outside Philadelphia. The house had three floors with eight rooms and three bathrooms. The basement always had water in it.

Debra, coming from limited means as a child, had never lived in a big house before. She was a bit overwhelmed by the responsibility and effort it took to keep it clean. And, she dealt with this concern in a manner reflecting her style and wisdom.

"Jonny-B," she said, "I decided that I'll help you keep the house in order even though I just had a baby and I'm having difficulty walking around the house."

I was unaware there was a choice involved in this since we both lived in the house. I assumed we were going to clean it together, by splitting the chores and responsibilities.

"Yes," she said, "I will keep our bedroom straight and you will clean the rest. I can deal with that. How about it, Jon?"

I must have been stunned, or overcome by our new baby and the ecstacy it brought me.

"That sounds fair."

For the next two years, I cleaned seven rooms and she cleaned one. After two years, Debra extended herself to two other rooms, saying she was now prepared to do more work in the house.

This is how we decided who did what around the house.

THE WAY WE WERE

We are all brought up with some understanding of how a household is run. We understand that someone does the cleaning, the shopping, the cooking, the wash, the outside jobs, the inside projects and makes the beds. Most of us have been raised in a traditional, fixed sex-role home in which mom carried the lion's share of the housework. Recall that in earlier chapters, we cited information about the division of labor in a household according to time spent. When we were growing up in the sixties and seventies, our fathers' participation in family work was disproportionately less than the amount of housework done by our mothers.

Over the course of the past three decades, there have been changes in who contributes to work around the house. In the sixties, studies showed that a husband's contribution to family work averaged about 1 to 1.5 hours per day. This is compared to his wife's average family work load of 4 to 5.3 hours per day for a working woman and 7.6 to 8.0 hours per day for a full-time housewife.[1]

As more women entered the work force, a change occurred in the structure of many families. More recent evidence shows that husbands' and wives' average amount of family work load is converging. Husbands spend more time working around the home, averaging 3.3 hours per day when their wives stay at home and 3.9 hours when their wives work outside the home. Housewives spend a bit less time performing household jobs, averaging 6.8 hours per day, while working women were achieving almost parity with their husbands, averaging 4.0 hours per day.[2]

One way to look at these changes in time spent performing household jobs is that more men are involved in the day-to-day physical and emotional operations of their families. However, the role models we observed as children taught us that mothers and fathers contribute vastly disproportionate amounts of time to housework. We also learned that this imbalance is both okay and expected. Most of us have learned to expect that mom will do most of the housework.

Such expectations do not fare well in today's culture. Fifty-five percent of all women work outside the home, which translates into 53,987,000 working women.[3] Many of these women really do "bring home the bacon and fry it up in a pan." They have less time available, yet are often asked to do as many chores and assume as many functions as their soul mates from the seventies.

How can you teach your children to be less sex-role rigid, more open and enlightened? Many men are confused about this question. They understand that they are the new breed of teacher to their children, but they also understand they are poorly prepared to address this question.

> When we made the decision to have a child, I never considered that I would have to do more housework. I expected to work harder and to have less time alone with Gail, but vacuum, wash and iron. Never. This is like some bad dream.
>
> - Alan, twenty-four, carpenter

When you have a baby, the work load around the house seems to explode. You never expect that so much cleaning, dusting vacuuming, cooking and washing is needed for two adults and a child who wears disposable diapers and doesn't use utensils.

When you have a baby you learn to live by her schedule and timetable. This may be the first time in your life that you have had to put someone else's needs before your own. For some men, rearranging priorities by placing your baby first is a difficult transition requiring extensive personal and psychological changes. Among the most difficult are changes regarding sleep, free time and the sense of freedom to do what you want, when you want.

Your baby will need you when she needs you. Little babies don't "do" waiting. They want what they want now; not in a second, not in a minute, not in a moment. When babies want, they want it now.

> When we decided to have a child, no one ever told us how impatient they are. Before you have a child, you never stop to think about how your child's crying will affect you. That cry goes right through to your gut. It's a cry that demands attention.
>
> - Paul, thirty-seven, counselor

You live your life by your baby's biological clock. If your baby wants to feed at 3:00 A.M., there isn't a whole lot that you can do about it. When your baby needs to roll over on her stomach while you're in the throes of passion with your wife, guess who gets turned over? Just when your favorite television show is about to reveal the answer to the mystery you have been trying to solve for the past two years, you hear your baby cry from her crib. Guess who will be asking around at work about last night's ending? (I never did see the last ten minutes of the final *Newhart* show, though everyone I spoke with told me it was hysterically funny. I was upstairs sitting in a rocking chair, soothing away the demons in my daughter's bad dream).

Most fathers-to-be expected to change their timetable for their children. Few considered having to adjust to the new mother's schedule. She will have added responsibilities that must be shared with you. If she stays home with your baby, she probably will be physically and mentally exhausted by the time you get home from work. She may need time away, maybe to go to the mall, to the gym or to a friend's house. She may need time to sleep. She may need time to talk with you for it has been nine hours since she heard the voice of anyone over the age of six months.

Notice the first three words of the last few sentences: She may need. Your wife has gone through a major physical change over the past months. She has gone from slim, trim and career focused to pregnant and baby focused. She has grown a healthy baby inside her and then, miraculously, given birth.

PLANNING IS IMPORTANT

Couples who plan for the reorganization of housework have a greater tendency to want a second child. Interestingly, experienced fathers were found to be more concerned about planning with their wives for household reorganization than first time fathers.[4] It seems that experienced fathers understood the importance of planning for change. They had already been through at least one pregnancy and birth. The experience taught them that an important stress reduction technique is simply to talk about who will do what, when and how.

> My wife and I argue all the time about who does what around the house. I was raised in a family in which my mom did all the housework. When my dad came home from work, his dinner was on the table. I expect the same thing. My wife is a teacher. She gets home by four o'clock. She has the time to cook.
>
> Then I listen to how rigid I sound and laugh. I don't want to fit into my parents' roles anymore. I just have trouble turning off the tapes in my head. Once they are turned on, off we go, into another fight. I've got to learn how to turn them off, or at least buy another set of tapes to play.
>
> - Steve, twenty-nine, store manager

More than ever, there is a need for planning and reorganization. To avoid disappointments and battles, take the time to plan for the management and maintenance of your household. The folllowing exercise will help you to think through the different chores and responsibilities that need to be attended to during pregnancy and early child care.

1. Make a list of household chores and responsibilities and who currently does them.

2. Set priorities by dividing your list into three different lists. List one is for chores and responsibilities that need immediate attention. List two is for chores and responsibilities that need attention sometime during the week. List three is for those that don't need to be done more often than monthly.

3. Evaluate your lists. Cross off all items that can be eliminated until after the baby arrives. Which chores and responsibilities can be given less attention for the duration of the pregnancy?

4. Which of your wife's chores and responsibilities need to be assigned to you during pregnancy?

5. Which of your chores and responsibilities need to be assigned to your wife during pregnancy?

Sex and Intimacy

Sex and childbirth. While we know they are inextricably related, they seem about as compatible as the Hatfields and the McCoys. In some twisted justice, the fruits of this union forever change the future conjugal relations between husband and wife. If only because there is less time, if only because there is less space, if only because the passage of a large child through a narrow opening inevitably makes some short- or long-term changes. Then there are the hormones.

Somewhere nature screwed up. Hormones. Now after the birth, particularly if the mother is breastfeeding, she has these hormones pulsing through her body telling her "Be a mother," "Take care of your child," "Be nurturing." These same hormones often act like a cold shower whenever the topic of sex arises.

By itself that is not a problem, but there is no comparable release of hormones in the new father. His drives remain roughly what they were before the new addition to the family, discounting the effect of fear or worry about new responsibilities. So there is a sudden change in the mother and no corresponding change in the father. This can spell conflict.

So, you get into the trap of asking, what's normal? Should you be back into the swing of things by one month, three months, a year, in time to conceive the next child? You glean every scrap of information from every book about childbirth. The same books that reassure you that women's interest in sex often *increases* during certain stages of pregnancy, also will cite how it is possible to get back quickly to a normal sex life. However, possible is not probable!

You can't very well ask your friends about it. Can you imagine asking someone you work with how he manages to have sex with his wife when there are children in the house? Sam Keen's Group of Men met for ten years before they began to have candid discussions about sex. "The only subject we had more difficulty discussing was money."[1]

SEX AND FATHERHOOD

This puts you at a disadvantage, especially considering that your wife probably knows everything there is to know about the sexual habits of her close friends. Women talk about these things, at least some of them do. And of course whatever discussion you get into, she can find examples of people who have waited until their child is in college before resuming sexual relations after pregnancy.

There is no way to win a war of statistics or even get to the bottom of this "normal" question. But still, it is an interesting issue to roll over in your mind during the frustrating times when you feel like you have donned black robes and been enlisted into the monastic life.

The indisputable fact is that there is less sex after delivery. A study of 6,000 couples by *Parenting* magazine found that parents go into a sexual hiatus after birth that lasts for at least a year.[2] Twenty-two percent of the parents reported having sex once a month or less. The survey found that sex was not as much fun for most new mothers, but most fathers said it was just as enjoyable as ever.

The primary reasons women reported for having sex less often were fatigue and lack of desire. Not surprisingly, the primary reasons men reported were their partner's fatigue and partner's lack of desire. Lack of privacy and marital problems also contributed to the decline.

The silver lining to all this is that the study found that parents were more in love than ever. Forty percent of new mothers and fifty-five percent of new fathers reported they were more in love with their partners after the birth of their children.

You don't have to be Dr. Ruth to know that much of sex is in the mind, not just the body. For many men, intercourse is one of the few channels through which they feel secure enough to express their connection and caring for their wives. Or it can be one of the channels through which they feel their wives' concern for them.

After the baby, there are not only a lot of hormones in the house, there are also a lot of things going on in the minds of the various members of the family. The baby is thinking about how she is going to get all the cuddling, food, diaper changes and care that she needs. The mother is thinking about how to care for this cooing or crying little arrival and about how incredibly demanding this whole motherhood role has turned out to be. She might feel a bit like a ski jumper who has just gone airborne off the edge of the ramp and is now wondering how she is going to get back to earth without killing herself.

Then there's the new father. He tries to be the pillar. But he may catch himself thinking: Yo! Over here. What about me? Remember when I used to be the cute and cuddly one in the family? He might become a bit insecure, thinking that mother only wanted him for his ability to give her a child. He longs for the touch and comfort of his wife, but she is "touched out."

He feels something that is unspeakable: jealousy toward his own child! Fathers are not supposed to be jealous. They are strong men. They need no one. They are grown up. This creates an uncomfortable conflict between understanding his role in the family and his wife's role in nurturing the child and his . . . desires.

Connecting Emotionally

There is a difference between sex and intimacy. So often, intimacy means sex to men, while sex and intimacy may be different things to a woman. Intimacy is the emotional closeness that you and your wife share. Most often it is found in what you and your wife share. For example, one of the most intimate moments that my wife and

I shared occurred during a television show. We were laughing so hard at *Murphy Brown* that something magical happened between us for that instant. We experienced such a level of closeness, almost being one together, that we spent the next few minutes staring in each others eyes, blind to the passage of time.

So, guys, don't assume that when your wife talks about wanting to get close she is talking about your love machine. She may be asking to feel emotionally connected to you rather than physically connected. Ask your wife what she needs from you. Don't assume you know.

Practice the following mantras, three times a day:

Honey, what do you need?
Honey, what do you want?
Honey, how may I help?

Get Involved

Active involvement in caring for the family can provide some of the nonsexual contact the new father longs for. Caring for the child, actively holding and playing with the new baby and taking care of the new mother can provide the sense of connection that might be lacking. Even during the most distracting times, this kindness will often be repaid by both mother and child with strokes in return. This can be very rewarding.

And if fatigue is a major reason women don't feel like making love, the father's help in carrying that burden can make a difference in his wife's energy level. This can leave more enthusiasm for keeping your love alive.

Couples often do not discuss the purpose and meaning of sex in their relationship. They assume a healthy sex life will occur when the marriage is healthy. Yet, a healthy sex life takes work and discussion. Interests, desire and "staying-power" change over the course of your life. These changes need to be discussed and put into the general perspective of how your marriage is changing, developing and growing.

The following exercise will help you and your wife to look at the meaning and quality of your sexual relationship over the course of your marriage. Take turns responding to these questions:

1. What are your ideas about the purpose of sex in your marriage? How have they changed and how do you feel about these changes?
2. Describe two secrets about your sexual interests that have changed over the course of your marriage:

3. Have your wife describe two secrets of her sexual interests that have changed over the course of your marriage:

4. Describe how satisfied you feel about each other's sexual activity, interests and desires.

Talking about your sexual interests, activities and desires was probably a difficult exercise. Most people find that talking about sex is difficult. We can make jokes. We can talk about sex as an object of desire. But when it comes time to discuss our sexual behavior with our partners, we discover a giant obstacle. Talking objectively about our sex life is made all the more difficult because we have no language for it. We either have the clinical language of sex therapists or the street language of our youth.

Yet, it is important to find a way to talk about our sexual behavior and the changes that occur during our marriage. There are other ideas about sexual behavior you and your wife can discuss. We will provide some direction, but don't be too shy to add more ideas yourself.

I often hear couples talking about the difference between having sex and making love. Three distinctions are drawn. They are: (1) Sex is for me ("self indulgent" sex); (2) Sex is for you ("other indulgent" sex); and (3) Sex is for us (love making). Complete the following exercise with your wife and discuss the results.

1. Describe how each of you feels when you decide that you want self-indulgent sex.

2. Name four things you and your wife need to discuss before you participate in "self-indulgent" sex.

3. Describe how each of you feels when you and your wife decide to make love.

4. Name four things that you and your wife need to discuss before participating in love making.

LET'S TALK

While your new baby dominates your energy and time, you have many of the same needs and desires as before the pregnancy. The degree of your fatigue because of the new baby may reduce your libido a bit. But, not to the extent it will affect your wife's experience of being a woman. Remember, she is a few pounds heavier and that may influence how she feels about herself. Often, women feel less sexy, less desirable and less confident in who they are. The paradox is that your approach for "sex as usual" may be rejected even though she is asking for confirmation that she is still desireable. Don't be put off by her mixed messages. Ask your wife what she needs from you. Don't assume that you know.

There is nothing normal about sex after children. If it is a quiet symphony before children (B.C.), it is snatches of beautiful music after delivery (A.D.). It is like a lunar eclipse: the planets have to be aligned, the time has to be right. The mood has to be right. And, this is the important one, the kids have to be out of the house, preoccupied or asleep.

If you never had to talk much about sex with your spouse before children, you may be in for a rude awakening. You can no longer fling yourselves into each others arms with wild abandon on the living room floor if junior is playing there with his blocks. Even if that cute little bundle of joy is snoozing peacefully, he or she will inevitably wake up screaming the minute you and your wife have your clothes off.

With the decline of spontaneity, sex requires much more negotiation, discussion and planning. Seldom is there sex without discussion. Some couples make a date, planning when they will get together. This can help relieve anxiety about whether it will ever happen, but it also can turn out to be a time when neither of you are interested. Others just wait for the moment and seize it.

As urgent as your sexual deprivation may seem at some times, it is important to keep it in perspective. For most couples, even if sex is never quite the same as in their childless days, it returns to a more normal pattern as you settle into parenthood. If you have been able to talk about the issue, you will be able to discuss your hopes and fears. With consistent effort, you may be able to reach a deeper understanding of your relationship and a deeper level of intimacy.

After a reasonable amount of time, the scars of childbirth will heal, your wife's body will return to some sort of shape and the mothering hormones will be replaced with sexual hormones again. Enjoy these moments while they last. Unless you have decided to cap off your family's growth, all these renewed sexual feelings will ultimately lead to one thing . . . more children. And the great cycle begins again.

Sex After Baby

Life will slowly return to normal after you, your wife and new baby develop new routines around the house. Your sexual relationship with your wife will return to normal with some adjustments. Your responsibility (and your wife's) is to work together to find a level of sexual and intimate activity that fits your new home life.

You may find that your sexual behavior has been affected by the arrival of your baby. You may not have as much time as husband and wife. You may discover (or rediscover, depending upon your history) the "quickie."

If you are stuck in thinking about sexual activity in only one way, using only one method, then you might find yourself becoming bored with your sex life, whether you have children or not. Variety and flexibility are key in maintaining a healthy, satisfying and dynamic sex life.

Don't get me wrong here. Sex with your partner will not always be as exciting as the first few months you were together.

But, learning about each other and about different sexual behaviors can enhance sexual excitement and interest.

In the words of Lonnie Barbach, "Prolonging the love making,
making it a voluptuous meal rather than a quick snack can replace
humdrum sex with real excitement. Spending time enjoying the
scenery along the way rather than doggedly focusing on the
destination can result in a much more relaxing and sensuous
experience. And the longer and more enjoyable the whole
experience is, the more likely it is to include orgasm."[3]

Although sex is only one aspect of your relationship, it is an
important one. Both you and your wife must be committed to
being close and communicating about what you need and want
from each other. When you develop good communication skills
about sexual activity, it often brings a deeper, closer level of
communication and understanding to the entire relationship.
"Pleasing each other in bed can spread to pleasing each other in
additional areas."[4] Remember, when your sexual communication
is open and honest you reduce the level of frustration in your
relationship and often replace it with a high level of satisfaction.

Making the First Move

Sex after pregnancy does exist. However, many men find it
uncomfortable, even intimidating, to bring up the subject of sex
after pregnancy. Often the most difficult part of renewing sexual
activity after pregnancy involves making the first move. No, I don't
mean making the first move as in putting your hand on her thigh.
I mean making the first move as in bringing up the subject of
sexual activity in a safe, comfortable and trusting way.

Many men are convinced that their wife will reject their
advances toward renewed sexual activity, so they quit before they
start. Other men hesitate to talk with their wives about renewing
sexual activity because they are angry about having less attention
from her since the baby arrived.

It goes the other way, too. Women often reject their husbands'
advances because they are angry. Some women feel powerless in
their marriage. The only time they feel they can exert their power
is to say no in bed.

If your wife is angry at you for issues unrelated to sex, you may find that she is uncomfortable talking about her anger directly. Withholding sex is one way to communicate anger while not directly identifying the real issues that are of concern. Other women give in to their husbands request for sex but withhold full satisfaction from themselves and their husbands by not having orgasms."[5]

If you notice that the quality of your sexual contact is different from before pregnancy, talk with your wife about what you observe, what you feel and ask what needs to be done. Explore with her how she feels and what she needs to discuss with you, too.

Sexual intimacy and communication can enhance all marriages. When things are going well in the bedroom they tend to go well in other parts of your relationship, too. So, when you notice changes that may bother you, bring them up sooner rather than later. It's better for you. It's better for her. And it's healthier for the marriage. The following exercise will help you and your wife to identify options and ideas about sex and intimacy for future use. Take turns responding to these questions.

1. What does "intimacy" mean to each of you?

2. What does "sex" mean to each of you?

3. Do you believe that sex and intimacy can be separate? If so, how?

4. Describe four activities that you each enjoy that are physically intimate but not sexual in nature.

5. Describe four activities that you each enjoy that are emotionally intimate but not sexual in nature.

6. Describe four activities that you each enjoy that are nonsexual and touching in nature.

7. Describe four activities that you each enjoy that are touching and sexual in nature.

8. Describe your idea of the perfect scenario for emotionally meaningful and physically gratifying sexual contact.

These exercises should help to guide you toward discussing aspects of your sexual relationship with your wife. These discussions also help increase the emotional and physical satisfaction within your marriage.

[[18]]

CHAPTER

Work and Finances

A good provider. That was what it used to mean to be a good father—keeping food on the table and clothes on the backs of the family. That was all it took. And to some extent that is still a strong expectation for men in the family. Surprisingly, even the two-career family has not changed that. If finances work out, the woman often has the option of stopping work to care for the family, but the man rarely can.

We measure our value as a father by the size of the dinosaur we haul back to the cave. This leads to an irony in modern fatherhood. The time we devote to building a secure present and future for our families is subtracted from the time we can spend with them.

It has become too easy for men to run to their jobs to avoid the difficult emotional work of participating more fully at the emotional center of their families. Our culture has left us this door—this escape clause in each fatherhood manual—that says if things get too uncomfortable at home or if you feel too much responsibility is being placed on your shoulders, just exit the door and run away . . . to work. Since most work in our society is away from home, when men exit the home to run to a safe, secure place it is often far from the reach of their family.

Before the industrial age, fathers and children worked together on the land, planting crops and making homes. Work and family were intimately connected. But the factory took the father out of the home into a world completely foreign from the family.

Just as we now have to concentrate on getting exercise to remain in good health, we now have to concentrate on being involved fathers so we don't get left out of our family life completely. No farmer ever had to go to a health club. He worked from sunrise to sunset and beyond, bending his back to the earth. He also didn't have to give a second thought to fatherhood. It just happened. This is not to idealize agrarian society. There was a lack of consciousness in the process and an attachment to traditions that were often not conducive to the growth of the whole child.

But we have a much more challenging task than our fathers or our grandfathers. We have higher expectations for our relationships. Our children and spouses have higher expectations. To meet these expectations, we have to remake our images of fatherhood and remake ourselves. This is not a simple process. Often, these expectations are not met.

THE BREADWINNER SYNDROME

And as sure as there are dirty diapers, financial worries are an inescapable part of having a child. Two can live as cheaply as one, but not three. The average cost of raising a child is estimated to be about $180,000. Even the bargain-basement child will cost you a pretty penny. Of course, they're worth it. Who can put a price on those dance lessons that might be preparing the next Mikhail Baryshnikov or Suzanne Farrell?

But you can't pay bills with warm and fuzzy feelings. When the new mother is basking in the radiant glow of maternal bliss, the father is wracking his brains trying to figure out how to make ends meet. While the mother is waking up with ice-cream cravings, the father is waking in a cold sweat thinking about how to squeeze a little more income out of his talents and time.

But if the goal is to provide security to your family, that has to go way beyond financial security. Can a family without an active father provide a sense of security and self-esteem to the child? What good does it do if you pay your bills but don't pay attention?

Don't delude yourself into thinking that because your family looks like a family should (a house, a dog, a couple of kids), everything is hunky-dory.

My own family had a house and dog, a mother and a father, and a great bunch of kids. We went camping in the summer and to museums in the winter. We weren't rich, but we always had food on the table. But when the family unraveled emotionally, all that was lost. That is frightening as I try to obtain these things for my own family.

- Robert, thirty-one, writer

Most couples today are two-income families. Most companies provide the bare minimum time off from work to be with a new-born. The recently enacted *Family Leave* bill extends options for leave, but provides no assurance that the mother will be paid during her absence. The same is true for fathers wishing to take time off to be with their new arrival. The law now grants longer periods of leave, but provides no legal encouragement to pay the father while he is adjusting to his new family. The message from business is clear: take time to deal with your new arrival, but don't expect us to make it easy.

Consideration of the sometimes complex financial juggling act often brings stress, frustration and tension into the marriage.

When Nancy decided to leave work for two years to stay with the baby, all I could see looming was financial ruin. She brought in almost forty percent of our income. I didn't know if we could absorb that much of a hit.

- Eric, twenty-three, mechanic

Jen and I talked about having a big family. She knew that I was just starting out in my medical career. I never expected her to tell me that she didn't plan to go back to work for the first ten years of our child's life!

- Jack, thirty-six, physician

Experience will teach you that having a baby changes how some women look at themselves, their careers and their commit-ment to their new baby. Therefore, asking for commitment to a plan of action about how to structure the family is a sometimes risky proposition. Some women are able to honor the nature and spirit of their commitment to the family. Others find themselves so completely enthralled in the novelty and joy of motherhood that, despite their very honorable intentions before the birth of their child, once the baby is born they become committed to another course of action. At the same time, your responsibility is to talk with your wife about how the two of you plan to support the new family.

It is important to be aware of the tradeoffs between family and work. It is important to set priorities and goals and decide how to achieve those goals. It is important to set aside some time for your family and for yourself. This is vital to your peace of mind and well-being. In the following exercise, you can examine your attitudes toward money and also your family's financial needs.

FINANCIAL AWARENESS EXERCISE

The key to surviving the financial crunch that hits most of us during pregnancy and early family life is to be prepared for what is coming your way. The following questions, designed to be discussed between you and your spouse, will help you to adjust to financial challenges and changes.

1. What are your roles in providing support for the family?

2. How do you feel about your wife taking time off from work to be with your baby? How much time?

3. What financial/career tradeoffs are necessary to achieve the level of family involvement you seek? What are you willing to do to achieve them?

4. What are you each giving up for your wife to stay at home with the baby (psychological needs, emotional needs, financial needs, social needs)?

5. How much money does your family need to be comfortable? How can you achieve this goal? (Couples often find it valuable

to develop lists of necessary and unnecessary household expenses.)

6. What actions can you take to minimize the impact of your time at work on the family? (Can you rearrange your work schedule, take work home rather than staying late, work at home?)

7. Make a list and discuss four areas of household functioning that may need to be financially trimmed down.

If you or your wife is unsure about whether to stay home from work with the baby for a prolonged amount of time or to return to work quickly, complete the following exercise to help you to identify the advantages and disadvantages of staying home versus working. Then, discuss the results with each other.

If she stay home:

    your concerns   *her concerns*   *baby concerns*

If she goes to work:

    your concerns   *her concerns*   *baby concerns*

[[19]]

CHAPTER

Not Enough Hours in a Day

Earlier, we talked about the shrinking time theory. That is, hours are containing fewer and fewer minutes, or so it feels. Fatherhood teaches how time becomes a most precious commodity. Yet, we often don't know how to use time efficiently. You will need to establish priorities for your time. How much time do you *have* and *need* for sleep, work, socializing, to spend with your wife, yourself and your baby?

Use of time is a very big issue in all families. When your wife comes home from the hospital and provides around-the-clock service to your new baby yet has little or no energy left for you, how will you feel? Some men feel rejected. Some men feel angry. Some men feel hurt. A few understand and ask how they can contribute to the child's care. This is done, in part, to relieve the mother from continuous child care. It is also done because when you share responsibility for child care, together you are learning the ropes of parenthood.

A problem typical of many new families is illustrated by the case of Rob and Suzy. Lack of time with your wife may lead to feelings of rejection. Rob wants attention from Suzy. Suzy wants a pillow and no demands *from anyone*. If God came down to visit with her newborn, she would ask him to come back another time because she has finally found time to sleep.

Rob takes Suzy's request for a few minutes of restfulness as a sign that she is not interested in him. He walks away, hurt and feeling angry that her energies are all for her mothering.

Suzy feels his emotional distance, but often doesn't realize that he is reacting to his perception of her rejection. She often reacts to this increased emotional distance by, unconsciously, turning her attentions to her new baby. The new baby doesn't give her any signals of emotional distance. At least within that dimension, she doesn't have to put much effort into caretaking. Rob often returns to the room with an adolescent request (or macho-like demand) for attention. He senses that she has further retreated from him and turned toward the child. Disgusted, he turns away and goes downstairs. Infuriated, she yells something about his selfishness and insensitivity.

Of course all of this may be avoided with better communication skills and appropriate application of negotiating techniques. Rob needs some emotional cuddling from Suzy. If you were Rob, how you would let Suzy know that you needed more emotional cuddling than presently exists?

Compare your response to the following excellent example described in one of our interviews with an expectant father.

> Honey, I would love to find time to be close or to talk. I love the effort and care you are giving to our baby. I know how tired you have been with the new baby. You know I have been working pretty hard, too. I don't want to lose touch with what makes us special as husband and wife. May I sit with you for a while and talk?
>
> - Stan, thirty-four, statistician

Social Changes

Seldom do first-time parents anticipate the effects that a first child may have on their social life. Besides having less free time, there is another, more subtle yet powerful, change that also occurs.

Your single or married friends without children may not understand the new and dominant forces in your life. To them, your child is simply another mouth to feed and a minor change in your everyday life. To you, your child is a black hole searching to absorb more energy, more love, more time and more attention.

Changes that occur in your social circles may include your friends becoming increasingly frustrated over your inability to play when they want to play. Often, this causes tension within the friendship and needs to be discussed.

Your friends may experience your newly developed commitment toward your baby as rejection. In part, that is true. You are choosing to spend more time with your baby than with your friends. This is normal and appropriate. Yet, your friends may feel like you are not valuing your friendship as much as before because there is less time for them. I have found this to be true especially for friends who do not have children. The solution is to talk with your friends about the new demands placed on you by your newborn.

On the other hand, in their attempt to be respectful of your needs to spend more time at home with your baby, some friends may invite you out less often. Usually, friends understand that new parents need time with their new baby. They consciously decide to give the new parents time alone with the newborn. The parents, however, want to share their joy and expect that their friends will want to participate in the new baby's life. I have seen some new parents experience a sense of exclusion because of their friends' attempts to respect the *assumed* need to be alone with the newborn. As with all else talked about in this book, the best remedy is to sit down with your friends and explain to them the changes that have erupted in your life.

Once the new baby enters your home, many of life's priorities will immediately change. I recall that before we had children, Deb and I spoke of our dogs as our best friends. They were with us during our most difficult times. They always gave a wag, a jump of excitement and a paw of loyalty no matter how funky we felt. They were always eager to go for a jog, wrestle and give their love unconditionally. But, these wonderful animals who stuck by us through thick and thin became only dogs once we fell in love with our babies.

Many other priorities change. Some men find that their intensely narrow focus on career advancement and job commitment changes; not that it disappears, but, compared to the experience of fatherhood, being rewarded at work feels secondary.

Some men find having a child introduces them to their own mortality. There is something about having your own child that leads to the recognition that you are getting older. Kids don't have children, adults do.

Another change is the awareness that we are responsible for the fundamental well-being of our family unit. This doesn't mean that family well-being is the unique province of fathers. Nevertheless, many men find themselves concerned, often obsessed, with the need to provide for their families now and in the future.

A few months after the birth of my daughter, I was scheduled to fly to Palm Beach to conduct a workshop. I didn't take a step on that plane until I had arranged for enough life insurance to insure the economic well-being of my family if an accident were to happen. I know many fathers who have found themselves taking similar steps.

Priorities around the house also change. You may find that rather than vacuum the rug or wash the car, you prefer to play with your baby, walk with your wife or read. During the first two years of my children's lives, reading remained something that we talked about but seldom did. Either we were too preoccupied with being parents, too busy putting together loose ends from work, cooking meals for tomorrow's lunches and dinners, or just too tired. The same went for movies, plays, concerts, parties and other social gatherings. The only social climbing we did was from the living room to the bedroom.

Structured, lengthy physical workouts are often sacrificed. This is not to say that all fathers turn to flab. But, with time at a premium, it is very difficult to find two or three hours to work out every day or every other day. Each hour you spend at the gym, the track or the basketball court is an hour you take away from your family. Many men find themselves restructuring their physical workouts to fit their new lifestyle. Instead of running and lifting at the gym, some fathers have developed workouts at home using stationary bikes, rowing machines or other exercise equipement. And, of course, there is the ever-present aerobic video.

For some men, changing their workouts from the gym to the home means sacrificing some social interactions and camaraderie that defines male bonding. These changes may result in some fathers feeling outside their peer group. It is not unusual to hear about feelings of isolation, being controlled by the new circumstances of life, and anger at having lost a ritual that, for many, began as far back as elementary school. The key is to find a way to balance your need to spend more time with your family with your need to keep yourself feeling good about *you*.

IDENTIFYING THE STRESSORS

When life's satisfactions are reduced, there is a good chance that you will feel a higher level of personal stress and tension between you and your wife. Problem analysis is the first step in identifying the stressors causing dissatisfaction. A problem analysis entails identifying *what* is disturbing you and to what *degree*. Your main task is to describe precisely what it is about your current concern that feels dissatisfying. Begin by examining your present life. You may think of your work responsibilities, your free time and leisure, or your marriage and its obligations, changes and demands. Think about five areas in which you feel less satisfied now than before the pregnancy. Then, write a brief description for each area of dissatisfaction——what you did before pregnancy and what you do now. Finally, evaluate each area in terms of how much it bothers you and is a likely cause of stress.

For example, you may look at the relationship with your wife during the ninth month and decide that it is the constant fatigue that is distressing. This is too general. What is it about her constant fatigue that feels dissatisfying? Is it her lack of attention toward you? Her need to nap during the day leaving you to feel alone and abandoned? Do you feel rejected? Do you feel useless? These are the types of questions you need to answer in the problem analysis.

Once you have identified the problem factors causing your dissatisfaction, the next step is to develop a possible solution. Let us start with a fundamental idea in all behavior change programs: To change means you cannot stay the same. A change requires a change. Too many people define the problem and then sit with it and bitch and moan. This is *not* changing. A change means to develop something new that will relieve some stress.

There are two ways to approach problem solutions. The first way is to change the characteristics of the situation. The second way is to leave the characteristics of the situation alone and find a way to cope better with what exists.

If you opt for changing the situation, then you need to rearrange some of your behaviors, patterns or goals so that a different goal is sought. This is no different than the old vaudeville routine of the patient going to the doctor, lifting his arm in pain and saying, "Hey, doc, when I do this it hurts!" The doctor says, "Don't do this!" The same is true in behavior change. You won't feel better if you do more of the behaviors that bother you to begin with.

The second option is to find a way to adjust to situations you find displeasing. One way is to discuss with your wife how you feel about the situation of concern. Often, talking openly about what bothers you reduces stress.

You can also "reframe" an issue by placing a new and different interpretation upon the areas of concern. For example, rather than seeing your wife's fatigue as a sign of rejection or abandonment, you might remind yourself that you are providing her and your baby with opportunities to be healthier by allowing them time to rest.

Coping with Short-Term Frustrations

Pregnancy is filled with short-term frustrations, that is until your baby arrives. Short-term frustrations are the little pebbles that get in the way on our journey through life. Short-term frustrations may lead to a little annoyance, impatience or outright anger. Each of these produces some degree of stress. For example, you have just gotten into bed on a cold night and you hear your eight-month pregnant wife ask you to go downstairs and bring up something for her to drink. You hear the request as reasonable but also feel annoyed that she didn't ask you before you came upstairs. Often during pregnancy, a mountain of these short-term frustrations build and build until the mountain becomes a volcano. Too many volcanic eruptions produce distress and may cause serious problems for you, your wife and your marriage.

The first step in controlling short-term frustrations is to identify the culprit for what it is. In the example before, the stress factor is your wife asking you to go downstairs to get something to drink after you have gotten into bed. It is not that your wife asked you to go downstairs to get something to drink after you have gotten into bed and *this is another example of her selfishness, laziness or lack of responsibility*. Your wife made a simple request. You need to prevent your thoughts from turning that simple request into an indictment of her personality.

A second step is to talk with your wife when the short-term frustrations occur and about how they may be rearranged. For example, if your wife asked you to bring up something to drink before you went upstairs and got in bed, you probably would have a different reaction.

A third step is to remind yourself that many changes in routine and responsibilities are temporary, probably lasting just for the duration of the pregnancy. Many people feel better reminding themselves that these inconveniences are only temporary.

A fourth step is to remind yourself that as much as you dislike doing extra chores around the house, there is a part of your wife that feels disappointed that she isn't keeping to her prepregnancy part of the marriage bargain. She doesn't want to be continually tired, demanding or irritable. She having a rough time, too, don't forget.

A Word of Caution

As you discover that there are fewer hours in the day to complete what needs to be done, sleep often gets sacrificed. As we have mentioned, there will be few times during your life when you will feel as tired as when you have a new baby.

Our word of caution is: Be careful! Sleep deprivation is dangerous. According to recent research, millions of accidents a year are the result of trying to do too much while not getting enough sleep. In particular, many major accidents occur when people are not properly rested.

This has great significance for new fathers and mothers. First, you must accept the idea that rest is important to your well-being. When you are poorly rested you are not only crabby, grouchy and a general pain to live with, you are also more likely to injury yourself or get into an accident. Second, you and your wife must make time for each other to rest. Maybe you will need to take the baby out of the house for a few hours while your wife sleeps. Maybe, she will have to do the same for you. No matter how it is accomplished, each of you must help the other maintain a quality regimen of sleep and rest.

Often, it seems that we can sacrifice our sleep for obligations or commitments we believe are more important than sleep. When we were in our teens and early twenties, sleep was easily sacrificed and we bounced back quicker and livelier than we do now. But with a new baby, a job and responsibilities as a husband and a father, rest is essential. Sacrifice your rest and you will eventually sacrifice your health. So, take time to rest. And help your wife take time to rest.

Stress

When your new baby arrives, UPS delivers a daily surprise package of stressful events. If you and your wife have not planned for or negotiated a reorganization of household work, then the UPS man delivers two packages. One is labelled: High Stress—Family Edition. The other is labelled: High Stress—Individual and Marriage Edition. You really don't need that extra package. This chapter offers some tools for reducing and handling stress.

> Jenny and I talked about how we would handle our new baby. We are particularly concerned about nighttime. I have a stressful job. It is very labor-intensive. I need my sleep. We decided the baby would sleep with Jenny, and I would sleep in the guest room for the first three months.
> What a terrible idea! We discovered Patti couldn't settle down to sleep unless Jenny was in the room with her. Jenny felt trapped. I felt neglected. And we began to fight like never before.
> - Jack, thirty-six, physician

WHAT IS STRESS?

Stress is part of everyday life. It can be produced by anything that feels different to you. Technically, a stressor is anything that produces a physiological change. There are good stresses and bad stresses. When the amount of change or pressure is excessive, we experience "distress." Nonprofessionals refer to this "distress" as stress.

A stress reaction is a very primitive physical reaction. It is often called the "fight-or-flight" response. It works like this: When the body perceives a threat, it prepares itself to do battle to protect itself or to run away and protect itself, thus fight-or-flight.

When we were living with Fred, Barney, Wilma and Betty of *The Flintstones*, such reactions probably provided great advantages. It kept many alive because the stress reaction prepared them for threats, perceived or real. In today's society, we seldom have to fight off dinosaurs or other life-threatening challenges. However, we still have the same physiological response. We want to run or fight.

The physiological response results from certain glands in the body releasing their hormones, particularly adrenaline. Adrenaline is pumped into the body to provide us with an ample supply of strength and power to defend ourselves through fight or flight. At the same time, our blood circulation is detoured away from our digestive organs and to the muscles. Our breathing increases, providing more oxygen to be pumped into muscles being primed to fight. Our eyes dilate, internal body tension increases and readiness increases. We are, as they say, "ready to rumble."

Many people experience several stress reactions everyday. Perhaps your boss yells at you, you have a fight with your wife or a close call with a car while riding your bicycle on a lovely summers' day. Each time, your body gears up to fight or run.

When a person has multiple stress reactions every day for an extended period, there are physical reactions to the stress. Just imagine what happens to your body when four, five or six times a day you have high levels of adrenaline pumped into your body. First, you need to find some way to rid your body of the adrenaline, therefore you wind up expending energy. Second, there is a great strain on your body when it continually prepares for a fight that never comes or a flight that is impossible to take.

There are many different symptoms of stress reactions. Not everyone experiences the same symptoms and the same symptoms may not appear each time you feel stressed-out. Since stress is part of everyday life, the question is not if you have the following symptoms of stress. Rather, the question becomes what situations result in feeling certain symptoms. Once you are able to see how a particular situation causes a particular stress symptom, you are on your way to understanding and controlling your reactions.

The following is a list of general physiological responses associated with stress reactions. This list does not contain every possible reacton. For further information, pick up a book on stress and its management, attend a workshop on stress management or consult your physician or mental health professional.

- Backaches, e.g. lower back muscle tension
- Difficulty breathing
- Difficulty concentrating
- Digestive problems, e.g. indigestion, diarrhea
- Dizziness or lightheadedness
- Dry feeling in mouth
- Eating problems, e.g. loss of appetite or overeating
- Headaches
- Increased blood pressure
- Interpersonal difficulties, e.g. withdrawing from social situations
- Irritability
- Nausea
- Pounding heart
- Red blotches around the neck and chest
- Sleep difficulties
- Tingling of extremities

STRESS MANAGEMENT

Recent evidence suggests that there is a specific personality characteristic distinguishing individuals who seem able to transform stress into productive processes from those who transform stress into destructive processes. This personality characteristic is called "personality-based hardiness." Psychologically hardy people are open and can tolerate ambiguity or uncertainty. The concept of psychological hardiness, as summarized by Ann Starr and Janine Sagert, is distinguished by three factors: control, commitment, and challenge.1

CONTROL: Control is the tendency to believe and act as if one can influence the course of events rather than feel like a passive victim of circumstances. Those who possess a high degree of control want to know why something is happening. They not only consider how an event will affect the action or fate of others, but how they can influence its outcome.

COMMITMENT: Commitment is the ability to believe the truth, importance and value of oneself and what one is doing. It carries with it a tendency to involve oneself fully in the many situations of life, including work, family, interpersonal relationships and social institutions. There is an activeness rather than a passiveness about coping.

CHALLENGE: Challenge is the belief that change, not stability, is life's norm. Much of the disruption that accompanies a stressful event may be anticipated as an opportunity and incentive for personal growth—a challenge rather than a threat to security.

There is another related idea that contributes to the reduction of stress-related illnesses: *exercise*. Researchers have designed studies of the effects of training in psychological hardiness (by itself), exercise (by itself) and hardiness *plus* exercise. Individuals participating in the hardiness *plus* exercise group were found to remain healthier than those in the other groups. It is believed that hardiness buffers by transforming the meaning of events and decreasing their perceived stressfulness.

Feeling control is the result of being better able to monitor, identify and do something about your emotional reaction to a stressful situation *before* it becomes overwhelming. Specific exercises are recommended to build control. And these exercises must be practiced frequently. Failure to practice at least once per day results in a decreased ability to control stress.

Control may be achieved through a series of exercises such as deep breathing, relaxation and imagery. Increasing control behaviors has the following effects when the exercises are practiced frequently and applied consistently:

- Increased tolerance of minor irritations

- Increased tolerance in dealing with traffic, boring meetings, long plane rides and telephone calls at work

- Increased control over anxious thoughts, concentration, physiological states, interpersonal interactions

- Enhanced well-being

Beginning Stress Management: Deep Breathing

A stress reaction, as you recall, creates a change in our breathing pattern resulting from our body's preparation to protect itself. The increased oxygen is pumped into our muscles, turning us all into Arnold Schwarzenegger-types.

As you increase your breathing rate during a stress reaction, you contribute to the total readiness for fight or flight. A simple step in controlling a stress reaction is to monitor your breathing pattern. When you notice you are breathing faster than usual, begin an exercise called *systematic deep breathing*, which helps you to gain greater control over your increased breathing rate, resulting in greater control over your stress reaction. Here's how to do it:

Step One: Find a comfortable place to sit or lie down. The location should be as quiet and free of distractions as possible.

Step Two: Take slow, deep breaths that fill your lungs.

Step Three: Count silently to three. Then, exhale (breathe out) slowly until your lungs are empty.

Step Four: Repeat the process about five times.

To achieve the most from deep breathing exercises, you need to create an automatic rhythm. This allows you to focus on relaxing and reducing the tensions in your body. Most experts suggest practicing deep breathing exercises at least twice a day for about ten minutes. You will find deep breathing particularly helpful when you practice it immediately before or after a stressful experience. The following questions help you think about how to incorporate relaxation exercises into your daily life.

- Four situations in which I can use deep breathing exercises are:

- Two places (at home and work) where I can practice deep breathing that will be relaxing, quiet and comfortable are:

Systematic Relaxation

A common and effective stress reduction technique is systematic relaxation. Systematic relaxation techniques involve learning to relax your skeletal muscles by concentrating on efforts to reduce tension in each part of your body. It usually takes about fifteen-to-twenty minutes to complete. Often, when I have used systematic relaxation with clients, those who are highly stressed find themselves falling asleep the first few times they do the exercise. Apparently, even the beginning stages of systematic relaxation can reduce tension to the point of allowing highly stressed people to reach deep levels of relaxation. Here's how to do it:

Step One: Find a place where you won't be disturbed for about twenty-to-thirty minutes

Step Two: Remove or loosen any clothing that feels tight.

Step Three: Begin deep breathing exercises for about five minutes.

Step Four: Begin with your head. Tense your head muscles for about three seconds while you are inhaling. Take in air using deep breathing methods. Hold the air in your lungs and the tension in your head for about three-to-five seconds. Then exhale and release the muscle tension in your head.

Step Five: Repeat the exercise.

Step Six: Use the same technique of inhaling and tensing for each part of your body from your head down to your toes. Remember to inhale while you tense your muscles and exhale long and slow when you relax the muscle tension.

Step Seven: Once you have relaxed your body, stay still and enjoy the relaxation for at least five minutes.

My experience with systematic relaxation is that many people don't believe such a simple technique can reduce stress. However, with a few weeks' practice, people generally feel less tense. An important feature of a well-practiced systematic relaxation routine is that it teaches you how to identify which parts of your body are feeling more tension than others and how to reduce that tension through breathing and relaxation exercises.

• Two times when I will practice systematic relaxation are:

Using Imagery

Imagery has always been one of my favorite relaxation techniques because it is so easy to use. You can use in on a train, in a meeting, at your desk, in your bed, at the breakfast table and anywhere it is okay to close your eyes for a few seconds.

Imagery technique asks you to form a picture in your mind of a place in which you felt safe, comfortable, secure and happy. When you get that picture in your head, then "step into" the picture. Allow yourself to be in the picture, not just observing yourself in the picture. You need to allow yourself to feel the surroundings, hear the sounds in the image and see the sights.

My favorite image is of myself and my wife on a particular day of my honeymoon. I was just coming back from a jog along the beach when I saw this odd person sitting in shallow water, allowing herself to be toppled over by the waves. She looked like a giant beachball being knocked over by the waves, then righting herself for another wave. As I jogged closer, I realized that this odd person was the woman with whom I was going to spend the rest of my life and with whom I would raise children and attend formal affairs!

When I step into that image, I am right there beside her. I sit down beside her, holding her hand and let the waves do the rest. I feel the joy and playfulness we are sharing. I feel the warm Caribbean sun and sand and the force of the waves envelops us, our hands in each other's. I hear the crash of the waves, the songs of the birds and the whispering of the wind through the palm trees. Mostly, I hear us laughing. I smell the salt water, her perfume and the fresh Bahamian air.

When I feel tense, I take a few deep breaths using the deep breathing exercises. Then I close my eyes, still using deep breathing, and I place myself into that image. For as long as I close my eyes, I am there on Paradise Island feeling relaxed, in love and free of any worries except how much sand is in my shorts. When I open my eyes, I usually feel refreshed, connected to something that is nonstress producing and with a different attitude toward things around me. You should try it too, but not with my wife. Use your own image!

ADJUSTING TO THE CRAZINESS OF FATHERHOOD

A major cause of stress among pregnant couples results from the changes that occur from day-to-day. One day your wife may feel she is able to complete most of her household chores as you complete yours. Other days, she may feel too tired and ask that you contribute more for a few days or weeks. When these demands are different from what you usually expect, your stress level increases. There is more tension because you feel torn between accepting the responsibility to help your wife and feeling overloaded by the increased responsibilities and decreased time for you and your interests.

Usually, a good deal of stress couples experience during pregnancy results from unpredictable demands and changing responsibilities. There are two types of demands we will talk about: *cyclical activity* and *ambiguity*. Cyclical activity occurs when there are unpredictable and frequent changes in your daily activities with little flexibility. Ambiguity results when there are unknown expectations about what you are to do or when you are to do it. Not all task demands fit into these two categories, but most stressors do.

Specific irritants are another form of stress that interferes with your daily routine. These are interruptions like phone calls, having to go out the grocery store at three in the morning to get pickles, ice cream and peanut butter because your wife feels like a snack. There is not a whole lot to do about these interruptions except to remember that the craziness of pregnancy has a purpose: to have a healthy baby, and that you and your wife are working together toward that goal.

Cyclical Activity

As your wife moves further into her pregnancy, more responsibilities are placed on your shoulders. You are asked to do more housework and more shopping, and to change your sleep cycle, your work schedule and your opportunities to socialize, exercise or take time for yourself. As the pregnancy nears completion, you may be asked to hang around the house more so as to be close to her in the event of the big day. You may find that you go from feeling overloaded with work around the house to sheer boredom, because there is nothing to do. This represents cyclical activity. There are periods of high demands and periods of low demands and you are unable to predict when one or the other is required.

Estimating when you will be needed to do more around the house or for your wife will help you to gain greater control over cyclical activity-related stress. The better you can anticipate when you will be asked to do more, the better you can adjust your schedule to these demands.

The first step is to begin to record when you are asked to do more around the house. Recording allows you to learn if there is a pattern. For example, you might find that you are given greater responsibilities for housework or shopping once every three days.

The second step is to write down the responsibilities and demands being made on you during high- and low-demand periods. This will help you to anticipate what needs to be done and give you some control over when to do it.

The third step is to evaluate the importance of these responsibilities and demands by placing them in an *importance hierarchy*. Starting with the most important task to complete and working your way down to the least important task, rate each demand in its order of importance.

The fourth step is to talk with your wife about how you ordered these demands. Talk with her about how she would order them and find a way to compromise on those in which the two of you are out-of-sync.

Ambiguity

Ambiguity refers to situations in which you are unclear about what is expected from you. It is the enemy of good human relationships. We often live in a world of ambiguity, never knowing quite what is expected of us, taking stabs along the way, hoping we are correct in our guesses. Ambiguity is a big pain in the neck during pregnancy. As an expectant father, you know there are many things expected of you, yet couples seldom talk about these expectations. As a result, many feel disappointed, angry or frustrated over this lack of communication.

Ambiguity exists when you are uncertain which of several options is the one expected of you. "She said to get tea from the store. Did she mean regular tea or decaffeinated tea? Did she mean orange-pekoe or herbal? Did she want a 100-bag box or a smaller one? Will she want store brand or name brand?"

The confusion that arises from this kind of ambiguity often causes stress. You are unsure about your choices and unsure about her reaction to the choice you did make. Some men take the chance and choose what they think their wife wants. Others, when facing such a variety of choices, give up and go home without the tea, afraid their choice would be the wrong one.

The solution to ambiguity is to talk about what is really needed. Often, well-intentioned fathers-to-be complete a task or purchase a product that is light years away from what their wives had in mind. She politely thanks him for his effort and then directs him to return the item and buy the right thing. For example, the first time I bought diapers for my daughter, I had no idea that there were thick versus thin, white versus pink, high absorbency versus something else (I still don't know what this other option is), and that there is a difference between diaper brands. I also didn't think about different diaper sizes for different-aged babies, so I bought for my 6 1/2-pound little daughter a package of ninety-six blue diapers for babies weighing up to thirty-two pounds. To this day, my wife reminds me of my keen observational skills.

There are simple steps to resolve ambiguity in task demands. The first step is to ask yourself if you know what needs to be done. If the answer is that you are unclear, then the second step is to ask for clarification. The third step is to execute the task. If you discover your idea is clear but your execution of the task is not, then ask for further clarification. If there is no further clarification to be found, then slow down and think about the best way to approach the task. Talk with other people who have attempted the same task about how they accomplished the feat. This can come in very handy when it comes to assembling a crib, installing in a car seat or figuring how to get your nine-month pregnant wife out of the bathtub.

[[21]]

CHAPTER

Playing Favorites

Shhhh! No one ever talks about this next topic. It is taboo. We are all taught that we should love our children equally. Fathers shouldn't show favoritism. Indeed, we should never have a favorite child.

Baloney! I think that this folklore goes against human nature. I have favorites. Most people I know have favorites. Chocolate over vanilla. Baseball over hockey. Thrillers over dramas. Magazines over books. Assertive behavior over passive. Playful over boring. Talkative over withdrawn. Honest over cagey. We all have preferences. The trick is knowing what to do when you realize it is easier or more interesting to get along with one child than another.

I have talked with many fathers about how they experience their children. Uniformly, they talk about loving different children in different ways. Yet, there is still the underlying preference for the child who is most like us in terms of personality, personal strengths and weaknesses.

I find that my preferences change. When my daughter is going through a phase I love, my son may be driving me crazy during his current phase. When my son discovered Philadelphia Eagles football, I delighted in watching games with him. I felt less enjoyment in watching "Tom and Jerry" cartoons, my daughter's favorites at the time. When Maddi was turned on to books and drawings, while Robbie was slobbering over his GI Joe, Swamp Thing and X-man figurines, I gravitated toward Maddi's interests.

Part of the challenge of fatherhood is to stay aware of how your children's changing preferences and interests will reflect your own preferences and interests. When you recognize one child is touching you in a special way while your other child (children) may not, be careful not to overindulge your current favorite to the exclusion of your others.

RACES IN THE SAND

Recently, a client described to me a race he had at the beach with his children. Rob has two boys, ten-year-old David and seven-year-old Pete. David is very much like his father. He is competitive and athletic, crazy about sports. Pete, on the other hand, is not athletic, is not a sports nut nor does he share his older brother's natural athletic ability. The two brothers are just beginning to compete for everything in life, however Pete is at a disadvantage. Pete is an investigator. David is a doer.

Rob challenged David and Pete to a foot race. Each boy had a head start. David took off like a bolt of lightening. Pete wasn't far behind. Rob noticed that Pete was finally beginning to compete with David and doing a pretty good job of holding his own.

"Hey, dad!" yelled Pete, "look at me!"

Then, Rob took off after them. He began to realize that David was really "suckin' wind" and in high gear galloping down the beach. Rob became seduced into the race and his old competitive spirit kicked in. He raced by Pete and barely beat David by a few yards. But, there was no Pete.

Unnoticed by anyone but his wife, Pete had stopped racing as soon as his father swooped by him trying to challenge David. Pete stopped dead in his tracks and began to search the sandy beach for crabs. Whatever momentary excitement Pete felt from competing with his older brother and believing he was winning, were dashed when his father got caught up in his older son's zest for competition.

Rob didn't realize that he had missed a wonderful opportunity to encourage Pete to participate with him in an area of athletics that Rob enjoys. Instead, he let his competitive relationship with his older son interfere with his responsibility to respect his younger son's need to feel victorious.

If I were Rob, I would have held three races. Race one would have been Rob versus David. Race two would have been Rob versus Pete; I would have made sure that Pete beat me by a step or two. Race three would have been David, Pete and Rob. I would have made sure that David and Pete beat me, but I would have given them a race to remember!

Rob's favorite is David. They are alike in most every way. His unknowing favoritism enabled him to miss opportunities to encourage Pete to develop qualities that are endearing to Rob, thus increasing the chance that Rob and Pete will enjoy competition together in the future. Rob was sloppy in the direction of his energies. He needs to be better prepared to sacrifice his own need to connect with his favorite son in service of his obligation to encourage all his children equally.

EQUAL FATHERING DOESN'T MEAN
THE SAME FATHERING

I am not advocating that all fathering needs to be directed at all children in the same way. One child may need different qualities from you than another. But, you need to be aware that good fathering will provide more or less equal time and attention to each child.

In trying to feign fairness and equal treatment, some parents (and grandparents) will buy their little girls the same dresses, the same toys or the same school supplies. I recently heard of one mother with three children who keeps the receipts of everything she buys and places them on three different hooks. During the year, she keeps an ongoing tabulation of how much she spends on each child. She makes sure that each child receives the same monetary amount of goods, no exceptions!

I am not encouraging such attention to detail. But, I am asking you to be mindful of how you share your time, energy and resources. Whether you have a favorite or not, your responsibility is to all of your children, not just the one whom you like best.

PART FIVE

CHOOSING
NEW DIRECTIONS

Moral Directions

Recently, my three-year old son talked about "not liking black-skinned people because they don't have white skin like me." His teachers at day-care felt that he would "grow-out of this stage," as they put it, and did not talk with Robbie about his emerging belief. I, on the other hand, believe that emerging ideas expressed by our children must be explored and examined. Our children need to know that the family to which they belong stands clearly for certain ideas about life. One of those ideas is that black people are the same as white people who are the same as Asian people. Besides, I don't buy the old adage of "they will grow out of it." Emerging ideas like this provide the seeds for later bad habits. When I see something that doesn't fit with our family's values, it is never too early to discuss and modify it.

My wife and I called a family meeting after dinner during which we talked with our children about people who have different skin color. We asked Robbie and Maddi to talk about the differences they saw between black and white people. Remember now, that my kids are three and four years old, so our intervention is geared for their level of understanding.

Maddi liked black people. She knew several black children in her day-care and ballet classes and understood that skin color was an unimportant factor when it came to liking another person. She said: "I like Tammy because she likes to play with Barbies just like me. She likes to wear pretty clothes just like me. We play at being teachers. We're friends because we both want to be teachers." To

Maddi, friendship was defined by games that she was able to share with others, not by skin color.

Robbie felt afraid because he didn't understand why Warren's skin color was different than his. At three years old, he found it difficult to express much more than his fear, but in his awkward way he spoke about his belief that maybe something was wrong with Warren and that is why he has black skin.

We talked extensively about his concern. Relating it to his best friends, our three dogs, we explained that each dog had a different color coat, yet he loved them all. Bart and Oscar, our beagles, had black in their coats, as well as brown, tan and white. We asked Robbie if he thought that something was wrong with Bart or Oscar because they had black or brown or tan in their coats. He said no, that the dogs were his best friends and nothing was wrong with them. We also pointed out that daddy's friend Pam and her son Brian were black and Robbie had a really good time playing with them.

After thirty minutes of guided teaching, Robbie said he wouldn't be afraid anymore because black skin doesn't mean something is wrong with Warren. He said he really liked Warren now "because he was fun to play with and has a coat just like Bart and Oscar."

This example underscores a critically important aspect of my responsibility as a father. I hold a strong sense of duty to guide my children toward an enlightened, accepting view of people who share different values, different ideas and are of different color. I feel obliged to challenge, although gently, any misconceptions that may wrongly influence my child's view of other people. No, I don't tell my children that there is no Santa Claus, that Superman is really an actor or that the Klingon Warf is a make-believe character. But, I do question them on matters of humanity, for that is among the responsibilities I have assumed as their father. I am accountable for how my children learn beliefs, attitudes and values about their world. If they develop in childhood, and subsequently maintain as adults, moral ideas that run against those of our family, then I will blame myself for not being involved enough to have noticed their emergence during a time when I could have made a difference.

MORALITY

The study of moral thinking and moral behavior is a fascinating topic. Unfortunately, most of us don't begin to think about moral issues until we are in young adulthood, if we think of them at all. Moral issues involved in fathering are usually not considered until they fall into our lap with our children.

Morality involves understanding social rules. Social rules exist in families at many levels. There are rules between husband and wife. There are rules between parents and children. There are rules among children. Rules guide our behaviors in the real world. They point us in certain directions and direct our actions and activities. The clearer we are about our own morality, the easier it is to communicate these rules to our children.

Morality may be thought of as the guiding principles that channel energies toward yourself, your family and your social behavior. For example, most people believe that trust, fairness and family love are important guiding principles in their lives.

Describe four guiding principles that direct your energies. Include a statement about why they are important to you. These guiding principles reflect how you want to see yourself and have others see you. In effect, they define you. They give a purpose to your life and a direction to your energies. The clearer you are about your guiding principles, the easier it will be to develop them into a cohesive set of ideas, values and beliefs giving meaning to your life. I call this a personal mission statement.

Your Personal Mission Statement

A personal mission statement answers the questions: What do I stand for? What is my purpose in life? A mission statement helps you to define yourself and the roles that you play. It defines responsibilities, direction and general behavior. An example of a personal mission statement is the following:

> *I am committed to being honest, fair and hard working. I value education, family, personal growth and friendships. I believe that*

*good things come to people who work hard and sacrifice now for
reward later.*

Describe in a few sentences a statement about you and the
values and beliefs for which you stand, your own personal mission
statement.

A Father's Mission Statement

Fathering, too, needs a clear purpose. It needs a mission statement. You need to identify what it means to be a father. You
need to think about what you stand for as a father. You need to
consider what you will be responsible for as a father. You need to
ensure that when your children grow up they will understand and
appreciate the legacy that you, as their father, left them. Your
mission statement should be in accord with your personal mission
statement.

A father's mission statement is useful only to the extent that
you and the members of your family understand its purpose. The
key to a successful fathering mission statement is consistency. You
must live by the values, beliefs and assumptions that represent
your mission as a father. Therefore, coherent, clearly stated values
and beliefs are essential. They are the cement that holds the
family together through good times and bad.

An example of fathering mission statement is:

*I will be loving and available to each child as well as to my
wife. I will participate with them to the best that I can. I will
always choose to cooperate and understand rather than compete
and withdraw. I am committed to the idea that being emotionally close is better than being intellectually right.*

Now describe four guiding principles that direct your energies
as a father. Include a statement about why they are important to
you.

Next, describe in a few sentences a statement about you and
the values and beliefs for which you stand, your own fathering
mission statement.

Keep with you both the list of values and beliefs about fathering along with your personal mission statement. Read it occasionally as a reminder of the purpose of your fathering. Use it as a way of evaluating how your ideas about fathering may be changing over time. Finally, read it often so that you know it cold, so that when you are called on to make important fathering decisions they are consistent with what you have been preaching, consistent with what you say you believe.

Mission Statement and Commitment

In an earlier chapter, we discussed commitment to an idea rather than to a particular person. And, we cited a wonderful quotation from Sam Keen at the beginning of Chapter Four about needing to choose *where* you are going before you decide *with whom* you are going. A fathering mission statement is a commitment to where you want to go as a father. It is a map that guides you through the confusion and muddles of young parenthood. It is a survey of your rights and wrongs and how they will be carried out within your family.

Fathering is a tricky venture because no one method, no one direction, will always work. Your mission statement needs to be flexible enough to fit new and surprising events while at the same time maintaining a degree of consistency and clarity. This is no easy trick because it is often easier to abandon the highly intellectual moral principles that guide your goals for fathering in favor of following your gut reaction to do something expedient that will work *now*. Remember, though, each time you are tempted to abandon your heartfelt beliefs about what you stand for as a father and, instead, give in to convenience, emotion or social pressure, you are selling out your values and beliefs. You are teaching your children how to sell out their values and beliefs, too. And, you are showing that moral principles are an intellectual exercise to be considered only when there is time to reflect upon them, rather than a commitment to an idea and a way of living!

The new fatherhood asks you to consider the fundamental purpose of your role as father. It asks you to think through how you want to be with your children and what you want to teach them about being a man, being a father and being loyal to your values and beliefs. It is a tall order. Around every turn there are demons awaiting your slip, your hesitation, your indecision. When these demons appear, there are two sources to lean on. The first source is a reminder of who you want to be, a reminder of what you are committed to as a father.

A simple way to remind yourself about what you are committed to as a father is to step out of the present situation and pretend that it is six months from now. Look back over your actions when you abandoned your moral principles in favor of something easier or more convenient. Then, evaluate how you will feel about giving up your personal values and beliefs and embracing the demons of impulse. Think about how you will feel reflecting back on today and your decision to yield your fundamental moral purpose to some momentary whim.

The second source to lean on is the lovely woman with whom you share your life. Ask her to participate in developing a personal mission statement about herself as a mother and as a partner in this marriage. Join with her to develop a parental mission statement. Then, ask her to help you tame the beasts within you, the impulsiveness we all carry that shouts "Do it now! Worry about the consequences later." If you and your partner share a common purpose, see a common goal and agree to a common approach to parenting, then each of you can help the other in preserving the integrity of your legacy as parents.

MORALITY AND RESPONSIBILITY

Once you have determined an appropriate purpose and direction to your fathering, then you need to take responsibility for ensuring that you always follow your own path. As your children grow, you need to guide them toward the values and beliefs of your family and toward thinking about who they are and their place in their world. This means discussing with them their likes, dislikes, interests and passions (yes, you may need to watch MTV on occasion or, worse, listen to a couple of hours of heavy metal music).

Sometimes the purpose of your fathering will be challenged by your children. There will be times when they protest about a rule just because they want to protest—to assert themselves. Sometimes they will protest because they have outgrown the rule. Challenges like these focus us on the dynamic aspect of fathering, getting us to remember that as our children grow, we will need to change many ideas and values we hold about fathering.

Often, we forget to explore with our children how they think about ordinary ideas like winning, losing, loving, responsibility, pride, as well as many others. We forget that our children, *because they are children and not adults*, do not have an adult understanding of ordinary ideas. For example, my children are convinced that when I go to the office, I go there to make money. They don't have any idea about what *earning* a living means. They think that I have a money machine with which I make our money.

Forgetting that children don't think like adults, we don't always take the time to teach them fundamental ideas about life. In the end they learn for themselves, using the primitive thinking skills that are theirs. Our children develop partially developed ideas about life.

Pseudoconcepts

In the language of the Russian psychologist L. S. Vygotsky, this is a *pseudoconcept*.[1] A pseudoconcept is an idea taken in by a child from the adult world around him. It is not an idea that has been developed internally by the child. Therefore it is not a fully developed idea the child can use appropriately. Instead, a pseudoconcept reflects the child's half-baked understanding of how the adult world uses the concept. It is filled with misunderstandings, idiosyncratic meanings and errors. The result is a confusing, potentially inappropriate, understanding of its usage, meaning and application.

A father's responsibility is to know, to the best that he can, how his children think, learn and understand themselves and the world around them. In part, a father's responsibility is to identify pseudoconcepts and guide his child to a fuller understanding of the meaning of the concept.

When our children begin to outgrow the family rules set down during their early years, we need to recognize the need for us, as fathers and parents, to be open to a new vision of our family. As our children grow, they should be encouraged to participate in the direction and purpose of family growth.

The challenge for us is to be flexible. But fatherhood, just like parenting in general, entails a series of developments and changes that guide us toward change. Sometimes these changes are foreseen and can be planned and carried out in an organized and timely manner. Then again, the changes are thrust upon us unprepared, leaving us feeling vulnerable and torn between who we want to be as parents and what our children need from us. The following experience describes my family's most recent challenge.

Growing Up Too Soon

She had two big bags of ice on her eyes. When she raised her head, she was able to see under the icebags. She continued to talk with her head tilted in that weird manner. Then, she removed the ice. Streaks of dark black mascara drifted down her cheeks, cascading over her chin to the floor below. Tears galloping.

I queried. "Why are you crying?" You see, I had been working most of this evening; my last appointment left about two minutes ago. I hopped upstairs to say goodnight to our children but they had already sunk deeply into the rapture of little baby dreams.

"She didn't wave goodbye!" sobbed my wife.

"Who?"

"Our little baby. She didn't wave goodbye. When I left her at school today, she turned to me and said 'I'm almost five, Mommy. And little girls who are almost five years old don't need to wave goodbye to their mommies any more. Five-year-old girls only have to say goodbye once and have a big kiss. I'm growing up, aren't I?'"

Being a sensitive guy, I was tuned into her sense of loss. Right? Wrong! "That's wonderful. Maddi is really growing up and feeling comfortable experimenting with her freedom. I'm very proud of her."

"You just don't understand!" she said. "My little girl didn't wave when I walked to the car. I felt funny, but I felt I *had* to wave. I don't want her to grow up too fast. She's our little girl."

I wanted to break into a rendition of "Sunrise, Sunset" from *Fiddler On The Roof*. But, even *I* understood that would have been too insensitive.

"Put the icebags down so that we can talk," I said. She complied. "Now, what is this all about?" spoken, of course, like a real man, since I went straight for the information anticipating how to solve the problem rather than staying with the feelings.

"I needed to wave to her even though she wasn't there. I just don't want to let go, yet. She is growing up too fast. We are too busy in our lives to realize how precious these days are. We rush to drive them to school in the morning so that we are not late to work, ourselves. Then, we pick them up in the late afternoon. We spend three hours with them in the evening and then they go to bed. Our children are exploding with energy, love and curiosity yet I want them to stay little just a bit longer. I want to hug them on the couch. I want to teach them how to draw. I want to share their first circus, their first ballet class and their first hot fudge sundae. You have already taken Robbie to his first football game. I can never experience his joy at seeing a professional football game for the first time because that time has already gone by."

Deb was searching for the answer to a question that had her all tied up in knots. How can we, as responsible caring parents, savor the joy and rapture of our children's youth while also providing them with the avenues necessary to explore their independence?

The symbol of our daughter not needing to wave goodbye at the window of her school showed a new, bold initiative on her part to stride toward independence. It was appropriate and unprovoked. She took a giant step forward on her own accord, when she was ready.

It was the other symbol, Deb's need to wave at the empty window that underscored the paradox. We are impatient for our children to grow up and share with us in more adult ways. We anticipate with excitement their first date, first kiss and first job.

We dream about deep, heart-to-heart talks about life, school, boys, girls and grandchildren.

At the same time, we want our children to slow down. We want them to accept our parental concern and direction with the unabashed love and security that only comes from little children. We want them to jump up and down over a new pumpkin on the porch or the sight of a rainbow cascading across the sky. We don't want to let go of the crumpled leaf that they brought to us during breakfast announcing the coming of winter.

Parenthood is this mass of contradictions, challenges and sacrifices. It asks us to give all that we have so our children can move beyond what we can give to what they can achieve on their own. It's a dirty trick to fall so desperately in love with these little people who, as teenagers, will post a sign on their door that says "No parents allowed." We want to peek inside, yet we will respect their need for independence, all the while remembering the touch of their four-year-old hands in the grasp of ours.

Building Your Relationship with Your Child

Developing a strong, positive and open relationship with your child requires more than a passive understanding of what it takes to be a father. It requires action and new skills. It may take a conscious effort to listen to your child's stories and figure out their meaning. For example, I recall sitting on our porch with a friend when my son, who was two years old, came outside and asked for "dumb jews." It took my friend and me about twenty minutes to realize that Robbie really wanted "some juice."

Often you will need to translate your adult language into something that your child will understand. For example, when my wife and I painstakingly explained to our children that we were going to have another baby, our children raced outside to our car. They proceeded to take everything out of the car trying to find this new baby. When we explained that the baby was still "'growing' in mommy's tummy," they looked at her in horror thinking that soon, something will be growing in them. My daughter exclaimed that she didn't want to grow a baby inside her because she couldn't water it. So much for our lesson in reproduction, fertility and human biology.

Sometimes, despite your best efforts to understand your child's language, you will recall the prophetic words of the character in *Cool Hand Luke* who said that "what we have here is a failure to communicate." This will be a common experience for most fathers during the first year or so that baby begins to speak. My son, for example, was speaking paragraphs by the time he was twenty-two months. The problem was that it was all gibberish to us. No one understood him except his sister, who is a year older. Obviously they understood each other, but we couldn't make a dent in his meaning.

Body Language

Words are only a small part of the entire message we send and receive. We express ourselves through gestures, intonations, smiles, frowns, eye movements, body positions and a variety of other nonverbal messages. More than seventy percent of communication is nonverbal. When our words are misunderstood, it is often because the listener has been distracted by the louder messages of nonverbal language.

During the early seventies, many articles, books and lectures taught how to read body language. It was assumed that certain body language could indicate an openness to new information while other positions or movements suggested being closed off. As years passed, we have learned that there is no single dialect of body language. Each of us has some unique body language expression that means one thing to us but another thing to someone else. For example, when I am listening intently during a clinical therapy session, I send off body language signals that could suggest to some that I am closed down and threatened. I am most focused, most tuned in and most open to what is being said when my legs are crossed, my left arm is across my chest and my right arm, leaning on the arm of my chair, is supporting my chin. My eyes are fixed straight ahead, my head is tilted slightly to the right and my shoulders are square with the person who is talking. My openness, according to former body language lore, says in part "closed and threatened."

When it comes to fathering, one trick is to discover your child's body language dialect. The first step is to let her know that you are listening and paying attention. Thus, you need to learn about your own language. When talking with your child, there are four messages that are important to send with your body language: squaring, maintaining eye contact, leaning forward and opening your posture.[1]

Squaring: Your shoulders should be parallel to hers.

Eye Contact: You should be looking directly at her. Do not
                   stare, but use a direct, straight-ahead focus as
                   you scan her face for other nonverbal signals.

Leaning Forward: You should be leaning forward toward your
                   child. Most people view leaning forward as a
                   sign of attention and involvement.

Open Posture: You should maintain an open posture. Conven-
                   tional wisdom suggests that having your arms
                   and legs uncrossed communicates openness
                   and concern about what your child is saying.

If you are reading this book, you probably are planning to
have a child, have a child on the way or have just welcomed your
newborn into the world. Therefore, some of these exercises may
appear to you to be premature. We all know that an infant doesn't
care about her father's body language. Right? Wrong! You begin
to use your new fathering skills from day one. Don't wait for your
baby to grow up to start practicing these skills. If you think that
your child is too young for these exercises, then practice with your
wife and begin improving your communications within the
marriage.

Take three, ten-minute exercise periods during the week and
ask your wife to talk with you. The topic can be open, but you
must sit down with each other and talk for ten minutes. Your job
is to practice each body language skill described above. When you
are finished, answer the questions below.

1. How well did you maintain eye contact, a squared position, a
   slight forward leaning, and an open body position?

2. How comfortable were you with these positions?

3. How did your wife feel about them? How did she react?

ACTIVE LISTENING AND ACCURATE RESPONDING

Effective communication includes becoming aware of your true feelings and thoughts. It includes sharing your awareness of these feelings and thoughts openly and honestly. Effective communication does not blame. It includes discussing what you mean and what you intend. It also includes your listener's understanding of what you mean and intend. Such sharing helps to ensure that you and your child understand each other. It also involves exploring and discussing intentions.

Fathers who are effective communicators find that their families respond by giving them important feedback. Fathers who understand effective communication techniques let their families know they value what is shared with them without always needing to agree with the content of what is said. The message is, "I accept that you and I might differ and I respect that we can disagree and still value each other."

"I" messages are different from "you" messages. "You" messages are often blaming messages. They place all of the responsibility for the problem on your child. For example, common "you" messages are: You're a bad boy. You should have known better. Don't you ever do that again. You're not trustworthy.

"I" messages reflect how you react to your child's behavior. They focus on how you see her actions in terms of their effects on you. Examples of "I" messages are: I feel concerned when you are out that late. I want to help you when you feel upset, but I don't know how to reach you. I really care. I'm feeling angry about what has happened.

"I" Statements

An important first step is to use "I" statements. When you refer to yourself you show that you are sharing your experience and understanding of the message. When I say "I need to get some sleep," I clearly show that I am tired and need to sleep. If I say, "It's getting late. Anyone tired?" there is ambiguity about what I want.

When you use "I" statements, you are describing how you perceive the events and experiences around you. By sharing your experiences, you provide an opportunity to discuss differences and similarities between you and your child regarding the original message.

For the first two years of my marriage, my mother-in-law would turn to me during a television show and say, "Do you want some ice cream?" Now, to the untrained ear of a new son-in-law, I heard this as an invitation. I assumed that she was asking me if I would like some ice cream and that she would be happy to bring some to me if I did.

"No, thank you," I'd say thinking that the matter was closed.

"Are you sure?" she'd ask.

"Yes."

"Well, if you change your mind, please bring me some, too."

After two years of marriage I finally figured out that when my mother-in-law asks me if I want something, she is making a statement of something that she wants. After two years I finally caught on that her questions about other people's desires were her "I" statements.

When you talk about your inner feelings with your child, you are giving her a precious gift. You are sharing yourself and inviting your child to explore how daddy feels inside. Many people are unaccustomed to describing or sharing how they feel in clear, simple sentences. They often describe how they feel by asking questions. For example, one of our expectant fathers was angry at his wife for falling asleep during his acceptance speech at an awards banquet. He said: "I know that you're angry at me, so let's talk about it." She had no idea what he was talking about because she had been sleeping the entire time. What he really meant to say was that he was angry at her: "I feel angry at you for falling asleep during this important night." He felt too afraid to come right out and say how he felt, so he had to project his feelings onto her and pretend that it was her issue, not his. This is an example of poor communication.

In good communications, sharing your feelings means that you take responsibility for how you feel and express those feelings directly, simply and without blame.

Practice Time

Let's practice these skills. Change the following italicized statements into "I" statements reflecting your feelings:

- You are very tired and don't want to walk upstairs to kiss your child goodnight. Instead, you want your child to come down stairs to kiss you. You say, *You're getting big enough to put yourself to bed, sweetheart, so come and give me a kiss goodnight.*

- You have just had a bear of a day at your office. You come home and are told the wash has to be done. You say to your wife: *You look tired, why don't we worry about the wash tomorrow?*

- You are angry that your child has just put his GI Joe in your coffee. You say, *Why do you do stupid things like this to your daddy?*

Shared Meanings

When we talk, the meanings of our words pass through some filters. The first filter is from the brain in our head to the words in our mouth. Do the words accurately fit the internal experience that you are trying to express?

The second filter is from the words in our mouth to the ears on her head. Are the words that we speak clearly heard and understood by our child?

The third filter is from her ears to her brain. Do the words that she heard, which are now in her brain, find word-meanings that match the meaning we intended?

Accurate and clear communications is pretty complex. We speak so naturally that we don't stop to think about all the filters our words go through before we can understand each other. Added to all of this, we tend to interpret other people's meaning in light of our own experiences. Good communication requires that we continually clarify what we mean and share our interpretation of what our listener is saying.

When my son was two years old, Robbie and I spent a good thirty minutes having a disagreement over which crayon was yellow. He showed me his yellow crayon and said, "This green, daddy." I said, "Sweetheart, that is yellow." "No, daddy, green." For thirty minutes we went round and round until I finally said, "Robbie, show me a yellow crayon." He walked over to the bin and pulled out a green crayon and said, "Yellow, daddy." In his mind, yellow was green and green was yellow. Once I understood his meaning, we were able to communicate about his drawings.

Moral of the story: Clarify what is meant if your child's interpretation differs from yours.

Active Listening

Active listening contains four basic components. The first component is listening to the literal meaning of the spoken words, not the inferences you draw from the words. Words are the building blocks of communication. Inferences are interpretations of the meanings that you place on the words. Active listening requires you to focus on the words and their literal meaning, not your interpretation of them.

Examples of the literal meaning of words compared to the inferences you can draw from the words are:

Literal: "I love you."
Inference: *She cares for me more than she cares for him.*

Literal: "I need to sleep."
Inference: *He is lazy because he is always sleeping.*

Literal: "I don't want to go to work."
Inference: *He will never make anything of himself.*

Listening to the literal meaning in a communication helps to identify what is being said. There are several obstacles that get in the way of hearing words clearly. The most important obstacle is the implied meaning being communicated. However, it is important to teach your child that choosing to say words that do not match the intended meaning encourages misconception, confusion and mistrust. It also establishes a communications system that ultimately will hurt the foundation of all relationships. If you learn to listen only to intentions, rather than to words, then you learn to ignore what your partner is saying and you search for hints of what is implied. Many relationships have been destroyed because of such a communication style.

The second component of active listening is *learning to identify the important parts of the nonverbal message*. In the first part you have identified the important words. Now, you need to reflect upon the relevant nonverbal messages.

You need to ask yourself if the words match the nonverbal messages. If they do not, then you need to ask for clarification about their meaning. For example, if the words are "I'm not angry!" but the nonverbal message feels like anger, then you should describe the difference you hear and ask for help in decoding the real message: "I heard you say that you are not angry, but the tone in your voice and your clenched fist suggested to me that you might be. I'm unclear which message I should listen to. Would you help me?"

The third component in active listening involves *paraphrasing*. Paraphrasing is the ability to restate in your own words what was said. This technique provides three important features. Paraphrasing helps you to know if you have heard the message accurately, and it lets your child know that you have attended to her message.

Paraphrasing also allows feedback from your child about the accuracy of your perception. If you hear a "Yeah, that's right" then you know that your paraphrase was on target. If you hear, "Well, that's not quite what I meant to say, but . . . " then you must restate the message and put your listening ears back on.

Here are some practice exercises for active listening. Restate the following statements to incorporate the three components of active listening:

1. I know that I would like to take a trip tomorrow, but I'm afraid that I will leave my teddy bear at home. I want my bear to see all the pretty animals at the zoo, but he might be too tired to enjoy himself at the zoo. He also might get very hungry and I don't want to scare him with all the big animals.

2. My mommy and daddy will never leave me. I know that I will always be with them and they will always take care of me. I know that Joey's mommy and daddy do not live together. Joey is very sad. I feel sad for Joey. But, my mommy and daddy will never leave me, right?

3. I don't want to go to school if you and mommy are staying home, today.

Positive Ways to Explore with Questions

Wonderfully rich and meaningful conversations can develop when you ask the right questions. Too often, when the wrong questions are asked, we feel as if the principal is asking if we cheated on a test or pulled Sally's ponytail. Here, we offer several suggestions about how to explore areas of interest without sounding like you're blaming, accusing, trying to be right or knowing more than she does.

Open-ended questions invite openness and self-disclosure. These are questions that entice your child to answer on her own terms by directing the question in her own way. For example, a closed-ended question is: "Do you want McDonalds or tofu for dinner?" Compare that to this open-ended question: "What would you like for dinner?" The closed-ended question allows only one of two answers, burgers or tofu. The open-ended question allows unlimited options.

For example, if you are concerned about how your child is feeling, but don't want to put words in her mouth, you could say: "Honey, how are you feeling?" Too often we ask closed-ended questions that lead our child to give us the response they think that we want. For example, how often have you heard: "You don't feel very well, do you?"

Thought-provoking questions help you to elaborate and extend a conversation in which the answers you are getting feel too narrow, too focused or just plain off base. A thought-provoking question may ask your child to look at the situation from the opposite perspective. A technique that works well for me with my children is to ask how different people in their life may see the same incident. How do you think your father would respond? How do you think your best friend would react? How do you think our child would feel?

Thought-provoking questions also provide you and your partner with more opportunities to explore a variety of views and solutions that otherwise may not have been brought up.

Directed questions are the most difficult because they are so simple to think of but often convey the wrong message. Directed messages are intended to direct a series of questions and responses down a particular avenue. The dangerous part of directed questions involves being perceived as controlling or overpowering because they are your questions that are leading the discussion. The best way to pursue directed-questioning without also bringing on complaints of being too dominant or forceful is to agree up front to the use of a directed questioning technique. For example, "I know that the lamp is broken. I need to ask you a few questions about how it happened. Were you running in the living room at the time?"

Exploring Questions

Explore the following situations using each type of questioning technique discussed above.

1. Earlier today, your wife had an appointment with her Ob/Gyn for an ultrasound. You are unclear about the reasons for the ultrasound. Perhaps you are not sure what an ultrasound is, why it had to be administered to her, what the doctors were looking for or how she felt about the procedure.

2. Your child has come home from day-care crying. You cannot find why she is so upset. You want to discover the source of her distress.

DISCOVERING YOUR FEELINGS

Communication sustains relationships. Most people think about communications between people. This section talks about communication within people. That is, how you are able to be congruent with what you feel, what you think and what you say.

Congruence is an important idea in the psychology of relationships. It refers to a sense of continuity between how you feel and what you are experiencing. You are behaving congruently when your feelings match your experience of what is happening to you. For example, you are congruent when you feel happy and you are able to experience and express to others that you feel happiness. You are congruent when you feel confused and you are able to experience and express to others that you feel confused.

Incongruence exists when what you feel on the inside is twisted around or hidden so that you experience and express something else. In many relationships this happens with anger. You may feel angry about something that has happened or been said. Rather than being able to experience the anger and express it outwardly and constructively, you hide it from yourself or from others, directing the conversation to another topic.

To be congruent within yourself requires that you commit yourself to knowing and understanding your inner emotional experiences of what happens *to*, as well as *within*, you. Inner emotional congruence asks you to trust yourself and to believe that being aware of your inner emotional state and its effects on you is an important characteristic of all relationships. It demands that you take responsibility for knowing how you feel and for being courageous enough to allow those feelings into your awareness. Many psychologists and mental health professionals believe that the core of human suffering is the result of people being incongruent with themselves and with others. Congruence is healthy. Incongruence is unhealthy.

Congruence between people also is important. Once you have taken the important step to be congruent within yourself, then it is imperative that you express that awareness of your feelings to those around you. Congruence between people takes courage, too. You need to be committed to the idea that honesty and awareness of your feelings are important building blocks of all healthy relationships. Communicating to others how you feel inside requires determination. When parents are committed to the idea of a relationship in which each party is concerned about the other's feelings and experiences, then all will share their feelings and perceptions. Congruent communications involve displaying your feelings in a way that shows respect for the other person, without blaming.

Congruent communication with your children is especially important. Fathers need to be in touch with how they feel because children are very perceptive about what is being communicated. Very young children, in particular, are tuned in to the congruence between what and how you say something and its emotional meaning. When fathers say one thing but feel another, children often pick this up. When this happens frequently, children begin to learn two important and destructive things. First, they learn to mistrust what you say and to trust what you don't say through nonverbal messages. Second, they learn that acceptable communications involve saying what is false and inferring what is true. The opposite is what you should aim for: consistency between what you say and what you feel. Congruent communications between father and child leads to trust and mutual respect. When you are congruent, then your child learns that what you say is what you mean.

Being Congruent

1. Describe how you feel in the following situations. What would you feel? What would you say?

   • Your wife looks upset but tells you that nothing is wrong.

- Your toddler tells you that he didn't break the $200 vase in the living room, yet you see it in pieces all over the floor.

- Your three- and four-year-old children have put the cat in the washing machine. Fortunately, they didn't know how to turn it on. You hear the cat asking for help. You ask your kids if they put the cat in the washing machine and they say no.

- Your toddler wakes you up four times during the night with questions about her birthday party tomorrow afternoon. When you wake up the next morning, your wife tells you how rested she feels and asks how you feel.

- Your in-laws are invited for dinner. When they arrive, you discover that they have brought over their neighbors.

2. List three feelings you are most uncomfortable espressing.

3. Describe what you do when you feel when these feelings bubble up.

4. After your next conversation with your wife, write down your thoughts and feelings about what was just said. Ask your wife to complete the same exercise. Then list those feelings you were able to share with each other and those you felt you had to hold back. Discuss these results together and explore what made some feelings and thoughts easy to talk about while others were more difficult.

LEARNING TO CHOOSE, LEARNING TO ACCEPT

Life is full of choices: what to wear, what to eat, where to go, whom to spend time with at a party. A hallmark of maturity is the ability to make responsible choices. How you express your feelings is one of those responsible choices.

Congruent communication asks you to become aware of the correspondence between your inner emotional experience, your awareness of it and your ability to express it. Earlier we talked about expressing congruent emotional experiences in a trusting, respectful and appropriate manner. However, we did not talk about the role of choice.

Choosing the way in which you share feelings is a matter of skill. You first learn to become aware that you have choices about how you express your feelings. Then you learn how to identify when to exercise your choices to express these feelings. By learning to identify when a choice is appropriate, you can begin to become more aware of choices that are consistent with your goals.

You always have choices showing that you care for your child. You can choose to show love, anger, sadness or confusion. Properly done, each choice you make expressing how you feel tells others that you care. You may not always support your child's actions, but you can express your genuine desire to understand and discuss it openly, honestly and with caring intentions.

One way to keep focused on the choices you need to make is to be clear about the goals you want to reach. When your goal is to maintain closeness and open communications within the family, then your choices about how to express your feelings should be directed toward that ultimate goal. If your goal is to show your child that you are always right, then your choices should reflect that ultimate goal. If your goal is to show your child that you are always in control and more powerful than she, then your choices should reflect that ultimate goal.

I hope that you will choose to maintain close and open communications. They keep the family together, encourage trust and disclosure of feelings and create a safe family environment in which to talk about anything.

To be focused on being close and open does not mean giving up being concerned, expressing negative feelings or challenging issues of concern. It means that you are respectful of your child's right to express how she feels. It means you understand that different feelings are acceptable—even welcome—topics of conversation and exploration.

Being focused on close and open communications means you give up being aggressive and powerful, which says that only you are right, only you have the answers, only your feelings are acceptable. It means learning to accept feelings, experiences and ideas different from yours. It means rising to the challenge of examining how these differences have come about, what they mean and how a compromise can be reached. Accepting your child's view means you learn to cooperate in developing a common understanding.

When you face the choice of being critical of your child's perspective, think about your goal of maintaining closeness and openness. Then, find a way to cooperate and understand her point of view. Remember, understanding does not mean you will ultimately support your child's position. But it does mean you recognize her right to hold these feelings and thoughts without fear of being judged, devalued or unfairly criticized.

Understanding Your Belief Systems

Knowing how to talk with your child, like listening, is a critical fathering skill. In the last chapter, we outlined several ideas about how to be a better listener and speaker. This chapter will describe how we develop and modify our ideas about the world.

The way we think and perceive often governs how we feel and behave. When we believe that a situation is dangerous, we often prepare for danger and interpret the events around us as potentially threatening. When we believe that we are safe, secure and loved, we usually are open, vulnerable and trusting. As we discussed in the chapter about family history, our thoughts——whether verbalized to others or silently considered——evoke beliefs, attitudes and assumptions that are determined early in life. These are the cognitive building blocks of how we understand the world around us.

COMMUNICATIONS, COGNITIVE DISTORTIONS AND FATHERING

We all make decisions about ourselves and others based upon these cognitive building blocks. They develop into beliefs about the world around us and how we fit into to it. We make judgments, misjudgments, interpretations and misinterpretations about the world around us based upon our beliefs.

Belief systems form the rules and standards that guide us. They help us to structure our world by molding incoming information to fit the preconceived beliefs that we have about ourselves, others and the world. Thus, we all change the nature of the information we receive by shaping its form to fit our beliefs. These are called "cognitive distortions." They are not bad. Everyone has some cognitive distortions. It is important to understand how distortions operate when you receive information from outside and attempt to figure out a response.

Cognitive distortions are curious things when it comes to our children. When your baby arrives, you will develop many powerful cognitive distortions about her. Among the distortions many of us hold about our baby and our parenting are:

1. My baby is the most beautiful baby in the world.

There was no doubt in my mind that Maddi was the prettiest, cutest and most perfectly formed baby in the world. I was ready to sign the modeling contracts with the Ford Agency. Then, a year or so later, I looked at her early baby pictures. I had to admit that she looked about two steps away from a gorilla, with her wrinkled forehead, low hairline and chipmunk cheeks. But, at the time, I couldn't see anything but her beauty. It happens to all of us who have children.

2. No other child in the world is as bright, engaging or perfect.

People tell me this is a distortion, yet as my children make their way toward elementary school, I firmly believe they are the brightest, most engaging and most perfect. Although I will not give up my distortion, at least I have recognized that every parent feels the same way about his child.

3. As parents, we know what is best for our child.

Most of us go through a period when we believe we know what is best for our child. As a result, we do not listen to other people who offer their advice. For some parents, this belief never changes and, thinking they really do know all the answers, they refuse to seek advice from others.

4. My parents know nothing about parenting that I can't learn on my own.

   Many folks in our general age group hold a belief that they know more about parenting than their parents *who have already gone through it*! As a result, these parents cut off a valuable source of information and experience in raising their children.

5. The relationship between my wife and me will not change when we have children.

   Our workshop participants firmly held this belief about their ability to control and direct their newborn's influence on their marriage. It takes most couples about a week before they see, feel and hear the dramatic influence a baby has on a marriage.

   There are a few distortions about your baby that need to be changed. We all believe different ideas about the unique and special qualities of our baby. The only distortions that need to be identified, discussed and changed are those that may put the baby at risk. For example, believing your pediatrician should be consulted only for serious illnesses rather than colds, fevers or ear infections may lead to serious problems for your baby.

   Distortions that cause you to compete with other parents over whose baby is prettier, smarter, more advanced, brighter, stronger, walking earlier or more quickly toilet trained need to be examined. Competition and needing to win tell your child that the world is a place in which everything needs to be a contest. This may encourage rivalry where none really exists. It may promote races that never have to be run.

   The best distortions are those encouraging you to see your baby as special. You need to feel and believe that your baby is exceptional and extraordinary. You also have to recognize that most parents feel the same way about their children, too. The clearer your message is to your child about her unique qualities and distinctive energies, the more confident and positive she will be about herself and her abilities.

   Our belief systems affect our ability to perceive clearly what is being said to us. Beliefs mold the expectations we form about the nature and quality of the information being communicated. They direct our attention toward one thing instead of another. Positive beliefs about ourselves and our spouse mold expectations often leading to openness and exploration of the message being spoken. Negative beliefs about ourselves and our spouse mold expectations leading to feeling closed to the information and rejecting it before it has been examined.

If we are raised in a home environment in which we feel encouraged to be open and to share, positively challenged to explore other viewpoints, we have fewer negative distortions guiding the processing of information. By contrast, if we are raised in a home environment in which we are discouraged to be open and to share and encouraged to be competitive and narrow-minded, then we develop negative distortions. For example, if you believe you are right all the time, then each point of discussion may lead you to compete to show that your perspective is right. This conversation style requires that a discussion is over only when you have won and your child surrenders to defeat. Another example involves feelings of rejection. If you believe you are unable to cope with even the slightest rejection because you have to please everybody, you will strive to please your child at all costs. This style often leads to omitting important information about how you feel out of fear of being seen as a "bad person" by your child. Your needs will seldom get met because you are too afraid to voice them. These are the results of cognitive distortions that form our belief systems about the world.

Cognitive Distortions

There is a "top-seven" list of cognitive distortion that play havoc with many of us.[1] They include:

1. *Arbitrary Inference*. Conclusions are made without supporting evidence. For example, a man whose wife arrives home late from work concludes "She is having an affair."

2. *Selective Abstraction*. Information is taken out of context and certain details are highlighted while other information is

ignored. For example, a woman whose husband fails to answer her greeting the first thing in the morning concludes "He must be angry at me."

3. *Overgeneralization.* An isolated event is allowed to serve as a representation of similar situations everywhere, related or unrelated. For example, after a young man is jilted by his girlfriend he concludes "No girl will ever like me."

4. *Magnification or Minimization.* A case or circumstance is perceived in greater or lesser light than appropriate. For example, a father screaming at his baby when milk is spilled on the floor asserts, "The whole rug is ruined!"

5. *Personalization.* External events are attributed to oneself when there is no evidence to suggest we had anything to do with them. For example, a husband sees his wife remaking the bed and assumes "She doesn't like how I made the bed when I tried to help."

6. *Dichotomous Thinking.* Your experiences in life are seen as black or white, good or bad, a success or failure. There is no in-between, no grey area. For example, the wife asks her husband about the choice of color for the baby's room. He says to himself "She doesn't like anything that I do. I can't even choose a good paint."

7. *Labeling and Mislabeling.* One's identity is based upon mistakes and imperfections of past behaviors that together have resulted in "owning" a label about who we are as persons. For example, after accidentally falling down a flight of stairs, I acquire the nickname "goofy" and begin to measure my self-worth by the power of my own goofiness.

We all maintain some of these cognitive distortions. We all exaggerate. We all take some things too personally. We all label. We all overgeneralize. Cognitive distortion interferes with communications when we are unaware of its presence. When we embrace as true the exaggerated aspects of a cognitive distortion, we are unable to communicate clearly with our partner or children.

One way to dispel cognitive distortion is to discuss the expectations of behavior surrounding the distortions. Our distortions may be the result of unrealistically established, poorly evaluated or poorly understood expectations. For example, couples who hold unrealistic beliefs about the nature of intimate relationships have a higher level of distress than couples who set more realistic expectations. Therefore, the meaning and content of expectations is important when helping couples avoid marital conflict.

The first step in identifying cognitive distortions is to listen for them. When you hear a belief jump our of your mouth that is somewhere left of normal, then you must examine it. In a previous chapter, I described how my wife chided me for taking control of her life when I asked her to put less red peppers on the chicken. I responded by pointing out the cognitive distortion (arbitrary inference) and asking her to evaluate it rationally (explain to me how you got from red-pepper-on-the-chicken to controlling-your-life). The idea is to have the person examine the distortion critically, looking for evidence to support the belief. When no evidence is found to support the belief, then you need to find rational alternative explanations.

Reframing is another useful technique. Reframing involves reevaluating the distortion for a more positive aspect. The technique used to reframe is fairly simple. Write down examples of the distortion and its more positive opposite.

negative distortion	positive reframe
She's nasty and horrible to be with.	*She having a tough time with her postpartum reaction.*
He always gets on my case about being lazy.	*He really cares about the choices I make in my life.*

Few experiences are as frustrating in a relationship as labeling things as black or white. Being able to identify when this dichotomous thinking is occurring is key to changing polarized thinking. For example, during my wife's current pregnancy, she is more tired, withdrawn and less talkative than usual. I find myself, at times, feeling lonely, rejected and disappointed that she is unavailable. I occasionally fall into black/white thinking and I catch myself saying "She's angry that I'm working on this book, so she's letting me know it in this juvenile way by staying away from me." In fact, her behavior has nothing to do with my work, but with her pregnancy.

Once fathers learn to identify and label their distortions, they are able to take greater control of them and responsibly choose whether to continue to employ them.

Fathers need to follow the rules of active listening described in the previous chapter. Cognitive distortions need to be identified. It is easier to identify them when someone else can provide feedback. Therefore, active listening is critical in changing cognitive distortions.

The steps include:

Listen attentively: Keep good eye contact, body posture, squaring and forward leaning. Acknowledge that you are hearing what is being said.

Do not interrupt. It is difficult to hear when you are not listening.

Paraphrase. Rephrase what you are hearing in your own words. Ask for clarification if your paraphrase is incorrect or needs to be sharpened.

Reflect on what you hear. Consider both the words and the emotional message and play it back so your spouse can hear what you have heard. Then, ask for clarification.

Fathers need to be aware of the impact of their speaking on the listener. Ideally, it is the responsibility of both parties to describe their conversation clearly and succinctly, but without sounding like a textbook or Joe Friday ("Just the facts, ma'am"). But, you need to stay focused on your point. The more you wander away from your point, the greater the chances your listener will be confused.

However, most of you will be using this book when you have a young child who is unable to use active listening techniques. Therefore, you need to be doubly aware of the congruence between your words and your tone. You need to take greater care than usual in choosing simple, clear and meaningful words when talking with your child.

Another important component of good speaking technique is trying to understand what your listener expects from the conversation. When you are able to understand what the listener needs from a conversation, then you can phrase your concerns more clearly. A sacred commandment among expert communicators is: It is the responsibility of the speaker to express accurately the meaning and intention of the message. It is not the listener's responsibility to figure it out.

If you follow the above "commandment," then you will not blame your child for not understanding what you are saying. Rather, the responsibility for accurately conveying your message is yours. If a misunderstanding occurs because of your statement, then you should rephrase the message in a way that helps your child understand the meaning and intentions of your words. Here are some "speaker's rules" to follow:

1. **Speak Attentively**. You should maintain proper body language using squaring, forward leaning, eye contact and open posture. You need to look for appropriate eye contact and body position from you spouse or child, also. In particular, look for changes in facial expression or body position that appear tied to the ideas about which you are talking.

2. **Phrase Meaningful Questions**. In a previous section, we learned how different types of questions may be used to encourage exploration and elaboration of a statement. Such probing can illuminate a conversation and help open other

meaningful avenues for further discussion. When your child is older, it is better to ask open-ended questions that help her understand your meaning fully. (I began using open-ended questions when my children were three years old.) These questions also will help you to know how well she is following your meaning and intention.

3. **Do Not Overtalk**. Less is better when delivering a message. The simpler and clearer your statements, the easier it is to understand their meaning. A general rule is to share information in paragraph size chunks. Then, ask whether the meaning is clear using open-ended questions. When your children are below the age of three or four, use sentence-size chunks of information, instead.

4. **Accept Silence.** Sometimes the best way to make a point is to use silence so that the point can sink in. This allows both you and your child to absorb what has been said, consider it for a moment and identify questions that need to be asked. Again, this technique works well with children who are older than four years.

5. **Do Not Cross-Examine**. Avoid firing question after question at your child when she is attempting to learn something from the conversation. Especially do not use rapid-fire questions during consideration of a point. Your original message will be lost and you probably will redefine the message into an argument over who is in control of the discussion.

When you use effective speaking techniques, you will be able to follow your child's understanding of your message. There will be fewer misunderstandings as a result. Your message will be clearer and there will be fewer obstacles. Such communication skills result in more quickly establishing and maintaining a close, intimate and caring relationship.

When a misunderstanding does occur, there is a chance that the source is a cognitive distortion resulting from misinterpretation of your words. Therefore, potential cognitive distortions need to be identified. It is easier to identify these distortions when your child can provide feedback to you about how the words you used resulted in her misunderstanding. Therefore, using proper speaking techniques along with active listening is critical in identifying, understanding and changing cognitive distortions.

When your child is too young to provide feedback to you about her understanding of your meaning, stop and think about what you have said. Then, choose different words to convey the same idea. Too often, fathers repeat what their child was unable to understand the first time. This leads to frustration for everyone. If your child didn't understand your first message, then carefully choose another message to convey the same idea.

Healthy Couples

Fatherhood starts with a relationship with the woman you love. The relationship with your spouse precedes your children and is intended to continue long after they have grown and moved out of the house. Your love for your wife needs time, care and continuous attention. Here are ten ideas to keep your marriage healthy before, during and after your children enter your home.

1. *Healthy Couples Do Not Just Happen.* Healthy marriages take work. All healthy marriages involve attention. You must pay close attention to your wife and the same goes for her. This attention will lead you to a better understanding of what each other needs. The second part is that you must act upon that knowledge.

   Healthy marriages don't stand still. They are living, breathing organisms that need nurturing and room to grow. They go through good periods of growth and difficult periods of growth. The quality of the relationship depends upon the way you treat your spouse during both good and bad times. Responsibility for the health of the marriage is up to you and your wife.

2. *Healthy Couples Support a Healthy Family.* A healthy marriage lays the foundation for a healthy family. If the marriage is unhealthy, then the family will be unhealthy. A marriage under stress results in a family under stress with children who are

unhappy and parents who are impatient, irritable and in-
tolerant.

Another reason for keeping your marriage healthy is to be
positive role models for your children. As parents, we are
teaching our children about living. We teach them what it
means to be a mom, a dad, a sister, a brother, a married
couple and a family. Our children learn from direct observa-
tion when we show them how a husband and wife cooperate.
If you want your children to learn how to develop and
maintain a healthy marriage, show them by example. Let them
see the importance you place on taking time to be a husband
and a father.

3. *Healthy Couples Send Clear Messages*. A healthy marriage
sends clear messages about what is expected of each member
of the family. The roles of father, mother and children are
clearly defined. Healthy messages develop from clearly defined
expectations. An unhealthy marriage sends confusing messages
to all involved. It poorly defines who does what, when and
how. Most unhealthy marriages have unclear or confusing
expectations.

Your responsibility, along with your wife, is to work continually at being clear about expectations. With the changes
that often accompany pregnancy, some of these expectations
may become unclear or poorly defined. It is your responsibility
to talk with your spouse about the ambiguity of marital roles
and boundaries often found among couples who are pregnant.

4. *Healthy Couples Talk*. At the core of any healthy marriage is
a clearly defined set of expectations about behavior, attitudes,
values and beliefs that describes what it means to belong to
this relationship. Healthy couples talk about what it means to
be an individual within the marriage. They talk about what it
means to be a couple within a family. They talk about what it
means to be a father and what it means to be a mother. They
talk about the conflicts that pull them apart and the sharing
that brings them together.

Couples talk about how they are changing, what is compelling them to change and why they want to change. They talk about how this change will affect them, their marriage and their family. They talk about why they feel good, bad, hurt, lonely, sad, confused, baffled, fascinated, passionate and wide-eyed. Healthy couples talk about what is happening to them, around them, inside them and between them. Healthy couples talk!

Healthy couples create an expectation for openness that demands continuous dialogue. This continuous dialogue acts as a rudder that helps to navigate the strong and unpredictable currents that channel life's energies.

5. *Healthy Couples Understand Commitment.* Commitment is the soil that cultivates all growth in a relationship. It is an investment of time, energy, spirit and wisdom. Commitment means dedication to the idea that the family comes first. Sometimes commitment requires sacrifice of individual needs and passions for the greater good of the family unit.

In pregnancy, commitment requires two simultaneously existing beliefs. One belief is that you and your wife need to stay close and talk about the changes that are occurring within your marriage, your wife and you. The other belief is that you must allow your wife a new and exciting path toward exploring her relationship with the child within her.

Commitment during pregnancy is a bit unfair. You must continue to be open and caring while also maintaining continuous dialogue, continuous understanding and steadfast faith in the marriage. Your wife, on the other hand, is asked to do the same for you, unless she is involved with her new baby within. She has the opportunity and obligation to know your baby before you. She needs to be committed to you and the baby, yet you are often unable to feel a commitment to the baby until she is born. Commitment during pregnancy requires you to compromise your needs from your wife, while allowing her to reshuffle her commitments to you and the unknown black hole of love and energies that resides within her.

6. *Healthy Couples Take Time Together.* Healthy couples do things together. They walk, talk, play, explore and share quiet time with each other. Healthy couples take time to ask about each other's day, exploring interests and their concerns.

At different stages in a pregnancy, finding time to be together may be difficult. You have added responsibilities and demands. Your wife has responsibilities to care for herself better than before. She needs to rest more, eat more and sacrifice more during her pregnancy.

Last year, you went to fifteen movies; this year you'll be lucky to see three. During the second trimester, you were able to go out for dinner; now she is uncomfortable sitting in most chairs. Last month, you were able to take long walks along the beach; this month her feet swell and she can walk only a few hundred yards before the sand bothers her.

Your responsibility is to find new and cooperative ways to share time together that accommodate your pregnant wife's needs for different activities while allowing you, as a couple, to keep the importance of your marriage in clear view.

7. *Healthy Couples Plan for Intimacy.* The conventional view is that passion happens on its own, that it is spontaneous, not planned. During pregnancy, healthy couples find ways to make intimacy a habit.

Intimacy does not only mean intercourse. This is the arrogant presumption of the traditional male. Rather, intimacy means spending time revealing your emotional self to your partner. Stroke not only her physical body but her emotional being. Seduce her into the safety and power of your maleness. Allow her to embrace you into her femaleness. Together you will be able to share the joy and warmth as your emotional spirits interweave and spiral toward acceptance, security and oneness.

Men have such a poor reputation among women: all we want is sex. Yet, you and your wife need to make love without sex to recommit each other to the power and love that brought you together. If sex comes, then your union will be confirmed in another, important way. If the pregnancy makes sex undesirable, then discover the many various and exciting ways to embrace her with the emotional and physical experience that says: I love you.

8. *Healthy Couples Share Responsibility.* Making a marriage and a family work requires each member of the couple to take responsibility for the health and direction of the marriage. No one person is in charge of keeping the marriage healthy. No one person is in charge of keeping the family healthy.

Healthy couples share responsibility for what happens between them. They understand that their responsibility to themselves, to their partner, to their marriage and to their family lies in their ability to share, to negotiate and to problem solve.

No marriage, just like no family, will be problem-free. Healthy couples understand that marriage and family will face obstacles. Healthy marriages create problems that are of their own doing as well as imposed from the outside. Healthy couples do not place blame on their partner. They share responsibilities for the creation of these roadblocks and for their dismantling.

Healthy couples understand that a well-functioning unit distributes the workload and the obligations evenly, to adjust to new challenges. While not placing blame on either part of the unit, the healthy couple shares responsibility for finding new ways to improve or resolve current dilemmas.

During pregnancy, there is always the temptation to blame the one who is putting in less effort. You may have a tendency to blame your wife for a messy house or an increase in your household responsibilities. She may blame you for not being available to her for her emotional needs during the pregnancy. However, you need to remember that the pregnancy was a joint decision and a joint creation. This requires that you and your wife understand there will be times when one or the other will feel unfairly put upon. These will be the times when you and your wife need to remember the responsibility you both have to the relationship and talk with each other about the resentment, anger or disappointment beneath the surface of your marriage. You are jointly responsible for the ultimate fate of your marriage. Openly talking about your concerns, obligations and feelings of distress makes a couple stronger to face tomorrow's hurdles.

9. *Healthy Couples Respect Each Other*. We all know respect. We all talk about having respect for our partner. But, *showing respect* is the key to a healthy couple. Healthy couples show respect through their interest in each other. Healthy couples show respect through the safe and nonjudgmental acceptance of their partner's different views. Healthy couples show respect through their constructive comments. Healthy couples are honest about their needs, honest about their similarities and honest about their differences.

Too often, men are accused of being aggressive in their evaluation of their wives. "He's too critical," says one woman. "He always puts me down," says another. A third complains, "He always has to show me how I am wrong and how he is always right." These are all signs of disrespect.

Respect is accepting another's point of view as sincere and meaningful. It does not mean always agreeing, but it does mean recognizing that your spouse holds views just as much valid as yours.

In pregnancy, it is easy to show disrespect: disrespect for your wife's reduced responsibilities around the house, her moods, her physical ailments, nausea or fatigue. She may show you disrespect for your sincere but clumsy attempts to iron the clothes, do the shopping or cook dinner. Disrespect is the poison that destroys the love and safety of all relationships.

You and your spouse are responsible for maintaining the integrity of the consistent respect a healthy couple needs to flourish.

10. *Healthy Couples Know How to Fight Fair*. Disagreements and fights occur in every relationship. They create the dynamic tension between spouses necessary to confront issues needing change. You need not be afraid of fighting with your spouse if you both understand that the purpose of the fight is to take

a position that needs to be examined. A fight is not used to insult, show disrespect or threaten. A fight is a signal that something needs to be examined, probably during cooler times.

Healthy couples understand that fighting is a catalyst to change. Fighting about the issues allows the focus to be on how the issue needs to be changed. Fighting about the other's inadequacies, frailties, insecurities or vulnerabilities places blame on the person for being wrong, weak, stupid or bad. Such fighting creates great emotional distances to cross when tempers cool. Repeated fighting results in the creation of an unsafe, unwelcome and emotionally dangerous relationship.

Healthy couples know that fighting requires knowledge of compromise and negotiation. It requires both parties to enter an agreement stipulating that change is a necessary part of all healthy relationships. And, together you can change your relationship for the better.

In pregnancy, all couples will have fights. Fights may begin because you feel unappreciated. Or maybe your wife feels angry about your inattention to her. No matter what the cause, healthy couples create an atmosphere that encourages the open expression of both positive and negative emotions. Healthy couples stand firm in their need to share strong negative, as well as positive, emotions. They show their commitment, responsibility and belief in the underlying health of their relationship when they can take the risk of raising a problematic issue and reaching a positive resolution. Healthy couples don't hide from the demand to make their marriage better. Instead, together they rise to face the challenge of cooperative understanding and responsible change that creates a more satisfying, equal relationship.

CHAPTER

A Teacher to Your Child

> Nothing surprised me as much as the amount of arguing and disagreeing we did over how to raise our baby. I felt strongly that Jessie had to be disciplined when she did bad things. Sally wanted to reward Jessie when she was good and ignore the bad. The fights that we had!
>
> - Dick, thirty-two, computer salesman

There are three major theories about how a child develops. The first theory suggests that a child is naturally bad. It says that there are strong, animalistic impulses that surge through a child's mind and body. Left unrestrained, these impulses will lead a child toward hedonism, lack of discipline and a life of sin. In this view, the parent attempts to control and structure the impulses into socially acceptable behaviors.

The second theory is that the child is naturally good. The child is viewed as an unfolding flower who, with the proper nurturance and cultivation, will discover its own healthy, natural growth pattern. In this view, the parent attempts to gently guide, all the while believing that the natural tendencies of the child will lead to appropriate behaviors.

The third theory suggests that children are like a blank slate. The child is viewed as neither naturally good nor bad. The child is malleable and it is the responsibility of the parent to shape the child into a doctor, lawyer or Indian chief.

It is important that you give some thought to which philosophical idea fits your view of how your child develops. Different parenting behaviors are recommended for each philosophical perspective.

TAKE THE COMBINATION PLATE!

We recommend that you view your child as a combination of an unfolding flower and a blank slate. Children need direction and structure. However, they also need room to explore and develop in their own way. I have never met or observed a child who is fundamentally bad. Children are innocent, trusting and love-seeking creatures who depend upon us to show them how to grow, mature and develop.

The most important rule to follow in parenting is to reward your baby when she is behaving the way you consider appropriate. Too often we ignore good behavior and respond only to inappropriate behaviors. The result is we teach our children that inappropriate behaviors are rewarded. The lesson they learn is when children want to be noticed, they need to misbehave to get dad's attention.

For example, Mark and Janet recently came to me with a concern about their baby's crying. During the first two or three months of Maggie's life, they discovered that their baby went from sleeping soundly to crying loudly to sleeping soundly. They observed Maggie's behavior and determined that little babies cry when they want and sleep when they want. Parental behavior had little effect on such a little baby.

By the time Maggie was four months old, Mark and Janet noticed a change. Maggie would wake up and begin to look around her crib. Sometimes she would reach for a toy; other times she would lie quietly looking up at her mobiles. After a few minutes, she would cry. Then, Mark or Janet would come running into her room and pick her up.

As we discussed this behavior, it became clear they were teaching Maggie that when she cries mommy and daddy come running, pick her up and comfort her. I told them I probably would learn how to cry, too, if it resulted in people running into my room to meet my every wish.

I suggested they first allow Maggie to wake up and begin playing. Before she began to cry, but while she is playing in her crib, Mark or Janet should go into Maggie's room and reward her for playing by herself. The reward could be picking her up and talking to her. It could be hugging and kissing her. It also could be sitting quietly in the room with Maggie while she is playing.

The point was that Mark and Janet had some control over how often Maggie cried after she awoke. Mark and Janet needed to look at their behavior in *interaction* with Maggie and identify how they were inadvertently teaching Maggie to cry more often. The idea is to observe when your child is behaving in a way you want to encourage and then reward her for it. Each time you overlook a chance to reward your child for being good, you miss an opportunity to teach your child how you would like her to behave.

Let me give you a more adult example, simple and to-the-point. A few years ago I walked into the house after a long day at work. Deb asked me if I noticed anything different about the house. I looked around, saw nothing remarkable and said so.

Sorry! Wrong answer. She had vacuumed the living room and I hadn't noticed. She felt hurt. I felt awkward. And we had an uneasy dinner. But, up from the spaghetti sauce, came an intriguing conversation about how I needed to be more aware of the positive things she did around the house. Once said, I have been rehabilitated and now am quietly vigilant about noticing and commenting on her hard work. All she needed to do was point me in the right direction.

Rewarding your child for behaving as you want her to behave is no different. You need to point your child in the right direction and then reward her for all the wonderful things she does. Spend more time rewarding the stuff you like and you will find there will be less of the stuff you don't like to worry about. Remember that children learn by doing and then getting feedback about the appropriateness and quality of the things they have done.

TIPS FOR FATHERS: DO'S AND DON'TS

Let's begin with some basic ideas. Responsibility for your child's health and safety rests with you and your wife. Here are some fundamental do's and don'ts of fatherhood.

The Do's: Eight Rules to Guide You

1. Buy and install cabinet safety locks so that your baby cannot get into a potentially dangerous cabinet. When your baby begins to crawl around the house, she is likely to get into everything. The safety locks will make sure that she will be unable to get into unsafe cabinet areas.

2. When your baby begins to get into things you don't want her into, say no and gently pick up your baby and move her to something that is safe and okay for her to explore.

3. Spanking a baby before she knows the rules does nothing for the baby. When your baby continually gets into things she shouldn't, it may be a sign she needs more attention or novelty stimulation. Then, it becomes your job to provide more interesting, new, exciting, and safe objects for her to discover.

4. Have physical contact with your baby as often as possible. Your baby needs to know your touch and needs to feel safe, secure and protected. There is a fine line here between overprotecting your baby and providing contact that encourages appropriate bonding. You don't want to teach your baby to associate crying with picking her up. That will drive you nuts!

   On the other hand, you want to be responsive to her when she cries because she needs to be picked up. You also want her to know that you will pick her up without her having to cry for your attention. Teach her that her father enjoys having physical contact with her just because she is there.

5. Talk with your baby. Your baby will respond to your tone, your body movements and your mood with her own preverbal behaviors. Take your cues from her reactions to you and have a dialogue with her——your words and her movements.

6. Establish a structured routine for your baby. I don't mean for you to become boring and predictable. However, babies like structure and sameness. So, consider what you need to do for your baby and then try to do the steps in the same order.

   For example, when you are going to bottle-feed your baby, you may go into her room, pick her up, carry her to a comfortable chair, sit down with a towel over your shoulder and feed her. You will find that at first your baby will react with crying because the routine will be new to her. However, within a few days, you will find she stops crying and seems to be waiting for the proper sequence of behaviors leading up to her getting a bottle.

   Each of us develops a series of routines we provide to our babies. The key here is to become aware of the steps and to be intentional about their sequence. The sense of sameness provides a feeling of security to your baby. Some researchers have observed that babies with well-structured routines tend to fuss and cry less.

   We are not encouraging a rigid adherence to routines. Instead, we are suggesting that routines provide comfort. There will be a time, however, when your baby will need to learn variations on a routine or alternative routines, altogether. When that happens, your baby may react with surprise by crying or other alarm reactions. Simply reassure her that newness is not to be feared. The quicker a new routine becomes predictable, the sooner your baby will relax and enjoy.

7. Your baby needs to be interested in her surroundings and your job is to make them interesting. Babies who are challenged to explore their environment will learn more about their world than babies who are not.

8. Remember the *discrepancy-induced failure hypothesis*. These fancy words are very important to understand. Your baby will develop most fully when she is challenged. The discrepancy-induced failure hypothesis says when you play with your baby, you should continually set goals for her that are just beyond what you *know* she can do. You must introduce a controlled failure that motivates her to reach beyond her current behavior to search and develop a new behavior.

Allow your baby to feel frustrated about not reaching a goal *providing you are able to guide her to new behaviors that will help to attain the original goal*. This is not to teach you how to become the Marquis de Sade in father's clothes. The idea is not to frustrate your baby to the point of despair. The idea is to introduce goals she can reach if she develops a new set of behaviors to solve the problem.

When well executed, systematic failures that challenge your baby will interest her to solve new problems. It begins to lay the foundation for later problem-solving behavior through her continued early success at solving simple, sensory-manipulation problems in her environment. It teaches her that she can overcome obstacles in her world.

The Don'ts: Four Points to Remember

1. **Don't** place your baby near an electrical outlet. If you have not done so already, go to your local hardware store and buy plug covers for each outlet in your house.

2. **Don't** place your baby or her crib near a hot radiator or floor board.

3. **Don't** leave your baby alone with your pets. If you are unsure of how to handle your pet's adjustment to your baby, consult both your pediatrician and your vet.

4. **Don't** discipline your baby for crying. When your baby cries, it is usually because she wants or needs something. Explore

what your baby needs. Disciplining an infant does nothing for
the baby except teach it to be afraid of you.

[[27]]

CHAPTER

Connecting with Your Child

Last December, I had a wonderful experience with my three-year-old son, Robbie. Since my wife and daughter were at a birthday party, Robbie and I went to the mall. I told Robbie that for the next three hours *he* was in charge of where we went. Wide-eyed with excitement, Robbie began with every Ninja Turtle display available. We spent forty-five minutes looking at each Ninja Turtle figurine. We moved on to Superheros, next. Then, we traveled down the hall to a comic book store and he salivated over *Superman* comics, *Star Wars* books and *Swamp Thing* chronicles. Every second of those three hours was spent catering to his agenda. Before we left, we indulged in the obligatory cheeseburger, onion rings and hot fudge sundae. Mom only found out about the cheeseburger.

When I told this story to my close friend, he said he thought I was nuts. "I would never spend time like that," he said. "I love to have my kids with me, but I'm not going to waste my weekend time looking at Ninja Turtles and comic books. When I take the kids places, they come along and join me in my activities, not the other way around. Otherwise, you'll be spending all your free time doing what your kids want to do. I won't accept that for my life. They either come with me and help with my shopping or they stay home with their mother."

Two different ideas about how to spend time with your children. I believe children should be allowed, in part, to follow their own agenda. If they don't learn from us how to follow their own interests, from whom will they learn? Parenting is for the children, in my view. The most difficult emotional barrier for most fathers to bridge is to be available for their kids *in the way that their children need them.*

BEING A FATHER

Your children's experience of you as a father will be most influenced by your actions. It's not going to matter what you say, what you preach, or what you read to them. Your actions will teach them more about you and what it means to be their father than anything you can say. Little egos are fragile. They must be handled with care.

Most of us don't realize how much power we have over our children's development until we are right in the middle of it. We begin to recognize our immense influence when our babies become little people, that is when they begin to talk and socialize with us. But our influence begins years before we become aware of it. Our influence on our kids begins with the pregnancy.

During pregnancy we develop and express attitudes and values about fatherhood, motherhood and childhood that are reflected in our behaviors. Science has not yet determined whether paternal or maternal attitudes and values play any role in embryonic development, but I'd lay odds that eventually we will discover a direct association between positive attitudes and values and infant adjustment.

With certainty, we have influence over our children after they are born. Our first touch, our first smile, our first words make impressions on our newborns, if only to tell them in some primordial way that they are welcome, their world is safe, we are there as their guardians, their teachers, their providers.

With all the background work in discovering and reeducating the father and child within yourself, the father within will join with the child during every interaction with your children. This is why it is so very important to know how to show who you are as a father. Our children want to be loved, accepted and nurtured. They want to be challenged, embraced and directed. As someone once said, our children keep teaching us lessons until we get them right. It is in our interactions with our children that we learn how we want to be as fathers. We learn what works and what doesn't work.

If we don't share ourselves with our children, our children will have the same questions about us that we have about our fathers. We can talk all we want about wanting to be closer to our children, but unless we are willing to give not only of our time but also of ourselves, we can't expect to be more than a shadow in their lives. We need to share our stories and our lives. This chapter provides suggestions about how to share yourself with your young child.

Time Away from Mom

For most of us, mom is the primary emotional caretaker in the family. She will spend more time with our children than we will. She will bath them more often, feed them more often, take them to the doctor more often and probably talk with them more often. She will always be a factor in our relationship with our children. She might tell us not to play so rough or to stop spoiling them so often. In her desire to help us understand our children as well as she does, she may inadvertently get in the way of our relationship with them. She may save us from embarrassment rather than let us stumble until we succeed. She may remind us about a forgotten promise rather than allow our kids' cries of disappointment and anger to remind us.

To grow as fathers we need to experience our own failures. We need to stub our toes as we walk along the often-confusing sidewalk of promises, obligations and wishes we hold for our children. In short, we need our wives to let us take responsibility for being fathers. When we forget or stumble, we need our wives to allow our children to tell us of our mistake. We need to see the disappointment in their eyes, the anger in their tears and the guilt in our soul when our children remind us in their innocent ways about our mistakes and broken promises.

Fathers are sometimes reluctant to go off on their own. It is frightening having responsibility for a small child. It is much more comfortable to have a family relationship rather than a personal relationship with your children, but it is important to take the time. It is in the stillness of those times that you get to know your children and they get to know you.

Father Options

Fathers need to have physical contact with their children. We need to pick them up and play with them. We need to introduce them to our world, a world which feels different than the world of their mother.

Fathers smell different than mothers. Their hands, arms, chest and shoulders feel different than moms, too. Our babies need to experience these differences. They need to have experiences that invite them to explore and trust our world of maleness. Maleness can be introduced to our babies at the same time as mommy's femaleness is introduced.

I remember I began to dance with my daughter only four hours after she was delivered. She was no more than seven pounds, yet I picked her up and began to dance with her, twirling her gently in the air, on to my chest, from my forehead to my waist.

My wife, of course, was going into cardiac arrest as she watched me become so physical with my daughter so soon after birth. But, Madeline wasn't making a peep and I was having the time of my life beginning my relationship with my daughter.

My first days with my son were different. He spent his first few days in neonatal intensive care, so dancing was out of the question. But, I was able to visit him and place my finger into his tiny, fragile hand. He grasped my hand and I swung it back and forth, up and down. Robbie and I touched like that for the first four days of his life. Then, once he was out of ICU, he, too, became a dance partner.

Introduce your child to your touch, your smell and your love in a way that says, simply and safely, that you are there for her to trust, to love and to discover.

Early Infancy

When your baby is little it is difficult to take her to the movies or a ball game. She probably won't be much fun at a Broadway show and will provide little competition during a tennis game. When your baby is still an infant, there appear to be few options for original, dynamic bonding experiences.

However, there are ways for you to bond with your baby during her first few months. The first thing to do is to buy a baby carrier, or papoose, which allows your baby to look at you. In a baby carrier mounted on your back, your baby is able to see the back of your head, the color of your hair and the world around her. She does not have an opportunity to look at you.

A papoose allows your baby to ride with you, close to your chest. She can feel your breathing. She can see your eyes and hear your words. She can experience your movements because she is tucked tightly, safely into your chest area. The papoose allows for frequent, direct contact between you and your baby. You are able to talk with her and acknowledge her beginning responses to you and the world around her. You are able to have direct, unobstructed eye contact with your child. She can look at you, too. She can scan your face, study your behaviors and begin the process of understanding the man she will call Dad.

> When Taylor was three months old, I had a very important paper to complete. I wanted to spend time with my new baby but also had this heavy deadline hanging over me. I took Taylor into the office with me. I wore our papoose the whole day and she slept. I worked on the computer for about three hours before she woke up. Then, after I fed her, she snuggled down into the papoose and began to coo for another thirty minutes or so. All the while, I got my work done. It was a wonderful way to share my time with her.
> - Alan, thirty-eight, lawyer

> I took Jack on bike rides with me at the shore. I bundled him up and put him in our baby-knapsack. I had my workout each morning while he rode on my back. I don't know how much of the shore he saw

because each time I'd finish the ride, Jack was asleep in the knapsack.

- Bobby, twenty-five, salesman

Fatherhood Group at the Y

As babies grow toward infancy, some fathers began more novel and interactive experiences with their children. A wonderful idea about how to spend time with your children was suggested by friend and fellow psychologist Eric Kramer.[1] Eric talked about a father's group in which he is involved. It meets every Saturday morning and includes three fathers and their children.

The group began in 1987 when Eric decided to take his newborn daughter out Saturday mornings to give his wife a break from childcare responsibilities. He also felt a need to spend more time with his daughter, just the two of them. He took her to the local YMCA to go swimming. They enjoyed it so much that Eric decided to commit himself to a weekly Saturday swim at the Y.

At the same time, Eric found that the responsibilities of fatherhood had robbed him of opportunities to share time with his friends. He invited two of them who also had young infants to join in their Saturday swim. Four and a half years later, the same three fathers spend every Saturday with their children. However, the ranks of the children have grown from three to seven.

Eric describes two important elements that feed the group's energies. First, each father has an opportunity to spend continuous, uninterrupted time with his children. Second, each father has an opportunity to bond with other men who are experiencing early fatherhood. Eric sees the male bonding experiences with as much endearment as the time spent with his children.

A fatherhood play group like Eric's is a wonderful idea for both you and your children. The group works best when there are about three fathers per group. The rules are simple. Every father shows up every Saturday morning he is in town; no excuses for not showing up unless father is out of town. The commitment is unbreakable and the time is dedicated to the growth of the father-child relationship.

YOU CAN TAKE THEM ANYWHERE

I discovered I could take my babies anywhere. When my children were still crawling, I found I could take them shopping with me, browsing in malls or on some (I repeat, some) business appointments. There were even times when I had my infant stretched out on the floor of my office during therapy sessions. Maddi would be snuggled under a cover, sleeping away her little baby sniffles, while I worked with clients.

The point is that you can take your baby almost anywhere. All you need is a diaper bag, something to carry her in, something to feed her with, somewhere to go and a little——no, maybe a lot of——patience. You and your baby can learn about each other during everyday activities. Occasionally you can find ways to take her along to the office. You can find ways to share your interests with her, too. You can find ways to introduce her to her father and his way of traveling through his world. All you need is a little imagination and the willingness to spend time with your children.

The most important idea to grasp is that bonding with your children is a two-way street. As a father, you need to invite your child into your world. Teach your child about your life, your loves, your work and yourself. You also need to allow your child to invite you into her world. You need to allow your child to teach you about her life, her loves, her interests and herself. No matter what the age, part of your responsibility is to know your child and her world.

In the following section, my co-author describes a moving experience he had with his son, Anders, who at the time was four years old. Robert describes the joy and wonder of inviting his son into his world of work. During Anders' trip to the city with his father, notice how Robert talks about stepping into his son's world of cowboy and Indian fantasies while also having Anders step into his world of computers, staples and commuter trains. Such are the experiences we encourage you to share with your child and your child to share with you.

A Visit to the Office

I guess it was the morning that my four-year-old son walked six
blocks to the Wayne train station that I finally understood the
depth of his fascination with my work. I was racing out in the car
to run an errand before heading to the station when Anders ran
out the front door to see me off. I saw him waving in the rearview
mirror. And that was the last I saw of him.

My wife looked all around the house before she thought of
the train. In a panic, Cindie dashed up the station steps and
stared across the tracks. There was Anders standing serenely on
the platform in a sea of grey-coated businessmen. Clutching a red
plastic lunchbox as a briefcase, he was staring straight ahead as if
he were one of them. He was so self-assured that no one even
stopped to question this elfin commuter.

Anders himself had completely forgotten that he was a
preschooler. When my wife stepped up next to him on the
platform, he was annoyed. "What are you doing here?" he asked
her. What, indeed!

I suppose I should have gotten the hint before that. Many
mornings, as I headed out the door, he would set traps with chairs
and belts so I couldn't escape. He would send surrogates in the
form of tiny plastic people or animals stuffed into my briefcase.
And I would have to give him reports in the evening of how the
little cowboy and Indian started a war in the middle of my desk.

Anders and I had stopped in at my office a few times on
weekends, to write stories on the computers and check out the
office supplies. But it wasn't the same as putting on a suit and
being a part of the stream of commuters headed into town during
the week. So I took the day off from work, and made plans to
take him in.

If I had any doubts about his interest in the expedition, they
vanished when I told him about it the night before. He couldn't sit
still. He rummaged through his drawers and set out a red suit,
underwear, socks and shoes by his bed for the next day. Then he
went into my drawers and closets to gather up my suit, shirt,
underwear, socks and shoes. These two piles of clothes waited for
the big day.

That morning, Anders bubbled with enthusiasm and pride. As we finished getting ready, Anders said "Every night when I go to bed, I dream about going to work with you." In just a few short years, he had mastered the art of making his parents melt.

Usually I'm so preoccupied with reading that I don't look out the window on the way into Philadelphia. I was surprised at what we saw. There were cowboys and Indians battling beside the tracks and huge dinosaurs digging in the dirt. We were glad when we reached the safety of the office.

We came, we saw, we stapled. We wrote on the computer. We photocopied. We sent electronic mail. As I talked to a printer's representative, Anders grabbed the camera and roamed around the office taking snapshots of co-workers. He even got a shot of the office fire extinguisher. Then he took the tractor-feed holes off some old computer paper and pretended they were explosive caps that he placed, with a devilish grin, in strategic locations around the office. Exhausted from this strenuous activity, we went to lunch.

The trip home on the train that evening was like any other, but something had changed. The home and the office had been two different worlds, intersected by an occasional phone call from one to the other, a one-minute visit or an office party. There is a different uniform for each place, different roles to play, a different set of rules and a different tone of voice. It was a little uncomfortable to have these two worlds come together, but it was exciting to be able to share my world with my son.

Since that day, Anders hasn't made any more solo trips to the train station. He hasn't set traps or begged to follow me to work, although he does talk about going to work "every time it is that day again."

Maybe he is growing up, maybe some of the mystery has faded. Or perhaps he is content just knowing where the tracks lead each day and knowing they always bring me back home again.

More Stories from the Front

The day my wife gave birth to my son, Robbie, I took my thirteen-month-old daughter out for lunch to talk with her about her new brother and the changes we expected. I dressed her in her favorite dress, bought her a big, red balloon and drove to *TGI Friday's* on City Line Avenue in Philadelphia.

Maddi and I were ushered to a table by the window. We sat down and she immediately spilled the water. None got on her dress. She had the wisdom (maybe it was just luck) to knock the glass toward me. I got wet. She just looked surprised and laughed at how daddy jumped up from the table using words that she had seldom heard before.

We ordered lunch. She pointed to a picture of a grilled cheese and potato chips. I asked for soup and salad. The lunch was promptly served and just as promptly rejected by my daughter.

"No!" she said pointing to her grilled cheese.

"What do you want, sweetheart?" I asked.

"Dat," she said pointing to a bowl of chicken soup at the next table.

"Have some of mine," I said, moving the soup bowl toward her.

"No! Dat!"

"It is yours, Maddi. Daddy gave you his soup. Try the yummy soup."

"No! Dat!"

Rather than enter a fight I knew I was going to lose anyway, I ordered Maddi a bowl of chicken noodle soup. I finished my salad and noticed that Maddi was putting her noodles on the chair. I asked her to eat her soup and to stop playing with the noodles.

She told me where to go, in her own toddler way. Then, she asked for some of her grilled cheese. This, too, had to be placed on the chair next to the noodles.

This lunch-from-hell lasted forty-five minutes. I had taken her to the restaurant to celebrate with her the birth of her new baby brother. I was determined that nothing was going to distract us from the celebration. So, I accepted her toddler explorations with noodles and grilled cheese.

In fact, much to the surprise of the people sitting around us, I walked over to her side of the table, sat down next to her and talked with her about her noodle design. I didn't understand a word she said to me, but I listened. I asked more questions and she continued to babble, I assume about the design.

I have no idea if I was able to communicate to her that I wanted to enter her world of pasta art, but I know that for those fifteen minutes playing with her noodles and grilled cheese, my daughter and I connected within her world, with her rules and her objects of desire.

When lunch was over, I took her to her favorite ice cream store for a chocolate ice cream cone with rainbow sprinkles. She ate most and placed the rest strategically on the front of her red dress.

We spent those two hours involved in our father-daughter dance around food. And, we also talked——well, I talked. I told her about her baby brother. I told her how the baby inside mommy's tummy was now in a crib and wearing diapers, just like her. I told her about how much fun she was going to have with her new brother. I told her how much we loved her. Finally, I spoke with her about how very proud I was that she was my little girl. I explained that nothing would ever replace her being my first and oldest little girl. I told her about how very important it was for daddies and daughters always to talk with each other, just like Maddi and I were doing then.

As the day wore down (or was it I who wore down?), I drove Maddi to the hospital for her first visit with her new baby brother. The light in her eyes, the excitement in her face told me she understood there would be a new baby in our family. And she was going to welcome him with love and sweet dreams.

[[28]]

CHAPTER

The Road Ahead

"How many more miles?" You're driving along the expressway, drifting off into your own world, thinking about your job, your life, maybe fantasizing about a romantic weekend on a tropical island. The waves are lapping over your feet as the sun beats down on you, and you are melting into the relaxation of the warm rays. And she is by your side, holding your hand. All is quiet except the rushing surf . . . But there's that voice again, drawing you back. It comes from the back seat. "Dad, how many more miles?"

You turn around and you see that not-so-little, no-longer-cute, questioning child staring up at you. You start to answer with annoyance, then something nudges you——maybe it's your wife's elbow or maybe it's your mind.

You remember what it was like to ride in the back seat, helpless and dependent on that huge man holding the steering wheel in his rough hands. And you realize your child's life depends so much on your life——from the care you take in driving from place to place to the way you respond to questions along the way. And a little voice inside says, "God, I want this kid to have a good life." And so, you answer lovingly, "It's not far now. Just a few more miles." And you start a game of counting trucks to pass the time.

When you cradle a tiny baby, who stretches only from your elbow to your palm, it is hard to believe that this infant will someday stand as tall as you. Our sons will soon grow to be fathers themselves. Our daughters will grow to be mothers. They will set out on their own journeys. We cannot decide where they will go, but we can give them a good place to start from.

COMMITMENT TO THE FUTURE

Starting a family is a commitment to the future. That future can be a repeat of your own past, or it can be an attempt to build a better life for your children. Change requires exploration. You must be prepared to take a journey.

Our own forefathers made a perilous journey. They left the warm familiarity of the cities and villages of their homelands to seek opportunities in the new world. They sailed past the Statue of Liberty and had their family names rewritten on Ellis Island. They took a stab into the unknown to find a new world for themselves and for their children. We would not be where we are today if it were not for the courage——or desperation——that drove them across the ocean.

The way was not always easy. Often they found poverty instead of streets paved with gold. They struggled with scarcity and hardships as they made their way West. They continued to seek that promise, and continued to look for home.

YOUR FAMILY IS YOUR HOME

My co-author likes to tell how——a few years after the birth of his first child——he packed up the family and traveled across the United States. Like many others, they drove away from the Atlantic shore, passed the Gateway to the West, camped in the dust of New Mexico and dipped their feet in the Pacific. They arrived back home, having crossed thousands of miles, with a new appreciation for where they lived. It also gave them the knowledge that their family was their true home——whether it was camped on the edge of the Grand Canyon or curled in bed in New Jersey.

The end of any journey is not to reach some promised land. The end of the journey is to arrive at self-knowledge. It is to gain a better understanding of what is important to you. As the poet T.S. Eliot once wrote, "We shall not cease from exploration, and the end of all our exploring will be to arrive where we started and know the place for the first time."

A QUICK GLANCE BACK

If you have been vigilant and completed the family history exercises in the beginning of this book, then you have discovered similarities, trends and patterns in your legacy. You have been asked to evaluate your understanding of fatherhood and to make changes where changes need to be made.

Until you know and understand the family from which you come and understand the ideas about fatherhood that have been planted in your head, you will father your own children in the ways of your father. In the words of John Bradshaw: "If we do not know our familial history, we are most likely to repeat it."[1]

TAKING OFF YOUR MASK

All of us live behind masks representing who we are supposed to be. We rarely examine these masks. Most of us do not look at who we are behind the mask until we are in our thirties and forties. When we begin to scrutinize and evaluate the person behind the mask, we often see ourselves driven by the expectations and life directions of others, usually our parents. We act out much of our lives based upon scripts we never wrote and, until recently, have taken great effort to avoid reading.

This is harmful to us and potentially destructive to our children. As a clinical psychologist, I have seen many men come into therapy during their thirties and forties carrying huge, heavy bags of guilt and anger. They feel excited because they realize how important it is to free themselves from the bonds of their familial script. Although they do not know how, they understand that psychology, spirituality and reflection may show them the way.

They also feel guilty; guilty that their insight into how they need to change as men, as fathers, as husbands often comes too late for the ones they love. Their grown children have left and seldom call or visit. Their young children have hidden their emotional life, fearing rejection or emotional abandonment. Or, their children have rejected them outright, rebelling into the never-never land of substance abuse. The horror is that fathers (and mothers, too) who do not examine their life scripts, who do not understand how the familial influence is directing their lives, are teaching their children how *not* to examine and understand their lives.

As Bradshaw writes, "Parenting forms children's core beliefs about themselves. Nothing could be more important. Children are any culture's greatest natural resource. The future of the world depends on our children's conceptions of themselves. All their choices depend on their view of themselves."[2] And their choices depend upon how we have been taught to figure out who we are, how we should be as a father, as a man, as a human being. For so many men, this recognition comes after the opportunity to father has passed. Be different. Don't let opportunity pass you by.

A FINAL WORD

My journey toward fatherhood has given me a deeper appreciation of where I have come from, where I would like to go, and who I would like to have go along with me. I will not always play this role. My children will grow up and move away someday, but this experience will never leave me. And I will always treasure it.

I hope you will be fearless in your journey. I hope you will find the strength to acknowledge and change your past. I hope you will use this opportunity to work and build a strong future for yourself and your family. I hope you will be able to see the adventure even when you are weary of the road. I hope you will continue to see the joy and humor in the struggle. I hope you will find great satisfaction and fulfillment, as I have, in being a man, a husband and a father. Good luck and Godspeed.

Notes

Chapter 1: Rude Awakenings

1. Keen, *Fire*, 227.
2. Siegel, "Bringing Up Baby," 18-26.
3. Pleck, "Husbands' paid work," 251-333.
4. Napier, "Heroism, Men, and Marriage," 9-16.

Chapter 2: I Don't Want To Be Like Dad

1. Price-Bonham, "Comparison of Black and White Fathers," 53-59.
2. Levant, "Education for Fatherhood," 253-76.

Chapter 3: Looking Back to Your Future

1. Bradshaw, *The Family*, ix.

Chapter 4: Who Are We Suppose To Be?

1. Keen, *Fire*, 12.
2. Bly, "What Men Really Want,"
3. Streiker, *Fathering*, 48.
4. Ibid., 48-49.
5. Bly, "What Men Really Want"
6. Keen, *Fire*, 3-24.
7. Streiker, *Fathering*, 117-131.
8. Fields, *Like Father*, 270-274.
9. Keen, *Fire*, 212-232.

Chapter 5: The Many Faces of Father

1. Anderson, *Father*, 4.
2. Bly, *Iron John*, 118.

Chapter 6: Discovering the Child Within

1. Bradshaw, *The Family*, 10.

Chapter 9: The Second Trimester

1. Shapiro, *Men are Pregnant*, 106-112.
2. Ibid., 115-119.
3. Streiker, *Fathering*, 58.
4. Shapiro, *Men are Pregnant*, 107.

Chapter 10: The Third Trimester

1. Shapiro, *Men are Pregnant*, 128-129.
2. Ibid., 130.

Chapter 11: Honey, Get the Suitcase!

1. Parke, *Fathers*, 14-15.
2. Samuels, *Well Pregnancy*, 321.
3. Ibid., 23.
4. Ibid, 19.
5. Ibid., 25.
6. Ibid., 24.
7. Samuels, *Well Pregnancy*, 284.
8. Ibid., 285 - 289.
9. Ibid., 325.
10. Ibid., 350 - 351.
11. Keen, *Fire*, 30.

Chapter 14: Responsibility

1. Shapiro, *Men are Pregnant*, 30.

Chapter 16: Who Does What Around the House?

1. Levant, 253-55.
2. Pleck, "Husbands' Paid Work," 251-333.

3. Hoffman, *World Almanac*, 137.
4. Ibid., 56-57.

Chapter 17: Sex and Intimacy

1. Keen, *Fire*, 71.
2. Rubinstein, "Sex After Baby," 76.
3. Barbach, *Yourself*, 121.
4. Ibid., 122.
5. Ibid., 122.

Chapter 21: Playing Favorites

1. Starr, "Developing Hardiness," 38-43.

Chapter 22: Moral Direction

1. Vygotsky, *Thought*, 66-71.

Chapter 23: Building Your Relationship with Your Child

1. Levant, *Education for Father*, 5-8.

Chapter 24: Understanding Your Belief Systems

1. Dattillo, "Cognitive Marital Therapy," 27-42.

Chapter 27: Connecting with Your Child

1. Kramer, Personal Communication, January 16, 1992.

Chapter 28: The Road Ahead

1. Bradshaw, *The Family*, ix.
2. Ibid., 1.

Bibliography

Anderson, C. *Father: The Figure and the Force*. New York: Warner Books, 1983.

Barbach, L.G. *For Yourself: The Fulfillment of Female Sexuality*. New York: Doubleday and Company, 1975.

Bly, R. *Iron John: A Book About Men*. Reading, Mass.: Addison-Wesley, 1990.

Bly, R. "What Men Really Want." *To Be a Man: In Search of the Deep Masculine*, edited by K. Thompson. Los Angeles: Jeremy Tarcher, 1991.

Bradshaw, J. *Bradshaw On: The Family*. Deerfield Beach, Fla.: Health Communications, 1988.

Brenton, M. *The American Male*. New York: Coward-McCann, 1966.

Briggs, D.C. *Your Child's Self-Esteem*. New York: Dolphin Books, 1975.

Bronstein, P. and C. Cowans, eds. *Fatherhood Today: Men's Changing Roles in Society*. New York: Wiley, 1988.

Christophersen, E.R. *Little People: Guidelines for Common Sense Child Rearing*. Austin, Tex.: Pro-Ed, 1982.

Cowan, C., & M. Kinder, *Women Men Love/Women Men Leave*. New York: Clarkson N. Potter, 1987.

Dattillo, F.M. "A Guide to Cognitive Marital Therapy." *Innovations in Clinical Practice: A Sourcebook*. edited by P.A. Keller and S.R. Hegmen. Sarasota, Fla.: Professional Resource Exchange, 1989.

Dinkmeyer, D. and J. Carlson, *Time for a Better Marriage*. Circle Pines, Minn.: AGS, 1984.

Eversoll, D. "The Changing Father Role: Implications for Parent Education Programs for Today's Youth." *Adolescence* 14 (1979): 535-44.

Fields, S. *Like Father, Like Daughter*. Boston, Mass.: Little Brown and Company, 1983.

Gould, J., and R.E. Gunther, *Drug-Free Families*. Manuscript, 1992.

Green, M. *Fathering*. New York: McGraw-Hill, 1976.

Hoffman, M.S. ed. *The World Almanac*. New York: Phanos Books, 1991.

Josselyn, I.M. "Cultural Forces, Motherliness and Fatherliness," *American Journal of Orthopsychiatry* 26 (1956): 264-71.

Kramer, E. Personal communication with author. 16 January 1992.

Keen, S. *Fire in the Belly*. New York: Bantam Books, 1991.

Keller, P.A. and S.R. Hegmen, eds. *Innovations in Clinical Practice: A Sourcebook*. Sarasota, Fla.: Professional Resource Exchange, 1989.

Kulhavy, R.N., & S.E. Krug. *Individualized Stress Management*. Champaign, Ill: Institute for Personality and Ability Testing, 1984.

Levant, R.F. "Education for Fatherhood." In *Fatherhood Today: Men's Changing Roles in Society*. edited by P. Bronstein and C. Cowans New York: Wiley, 1988.

Levant, R.F. and G.F. Doyle. *Boston University Parent Education for Fathers: A Personal Developmental Program*. Boston: Boston University Press, 1981.

Levant, R.F., & J. Kelly. *Between Father and Child*. New York: Penguin Books, 1989.

Lopata, H.Z. *Research on the Interweave of Social Roles of Men and Women*. Vol. 3. New York: JAI Press, 1981.

Napier, A. "Heroism, Men and Marriage." *Journal of Marriage and Family Therapy*. 17 (1991): 9-16.

Nichelson, J. (1986). "Men and Women: How Different Are They?" In A. Towle, ed. *Fathers*. New York: Simon & Schuster, 1986.

Norwood, R. *Women Who Love Too Much*. New York: Simon & Schuster, 1985.

Parke, R.D. *Fathers*. Cambridge: Harvard University Press, 1981.

Pleck, J.H. "Husbands' Paid Work and Family Roles: Current Research Issues." In *Research on the Interweave of Social Roles of Men and Women*. Vol. 3. New York: JAI Press, 1981.

Price-Bonham, S., and P.A. Skeen. "A Comparison of Black and White Fathers with Implications for Parent Education." *The Family Coordinator* 28 (1975): 53-59.

Rosemond, J. *Six-point Plan for Raising a Happy, Healthy Family*. St. Paul, Minn.: Marriage Encounter, 1988.

Rubinstein, C. "Sex After Baby." *Parenting* (March 1988): 76.

Samuels, M., and N. Samuels. *The Well Baby Book*. New York: Summit Books, 1986.

--- *The Well Pregnancy Book*. New York: Summit Books, 1988.

Sears, W. *Becoming a Father: How to Nurture and Enjoy Your Family*. Franklin Park, Ill.: La Leache League International, 1988.

Shapiro, J.L. *When Men are Pregnant: Needs and Concerns of Expectant Fathers*. San Luis Obispo, Calif.: Impact Publishers, 1989.

Siegel, E. "Bringing Up Baby." *Publisher's Weekly* (June 14, 1991): 18-26.

Starr, A., and J. Sagert. "Developing Hardiness Through Stress Management," *EAP Digest* (September/October 1990): 38-43.

Streiker, L.D. *Fathering: Old Game, New Rules*. Nashville, Tenn.: Abingdon Press, 1989.

Thompson, K., ed. *To Be a Man: In Search of the Deep Masculine*. Los Angeles, Calif.: Jeremy Tarcher, 1991.

Towle, A. ed. *Fathers*. New York: Simon & Schuster, 1986.

Vygotsky, L.S. *Thought and Language*, Cambridge: MIT Press, 1962.